A Drizzle of Honey

Also by David M. Gitlitz

La estructura lírica de la comedia de Lope de Vega

Francisco de Quevedo: Songs of Love, Death and In Between

Critical Perspectives on Calderón de la Barca,
ed., with Frederick A. de Armas and José A. Madrigal

Beware of Still Waters (Guárdate del agua mansa)

Fenisa's Hook, or Fenisa the Hooker (El anzuelo de Fenisa)

Secrecy and Deceit: The Religion of the Crypto-Jews

Los Arias Dávila de Segovia: entre la iglesia y la sinagoga

Also by Linda Kay Davidson (with Maryjane Dunn)

Pilgrimage in the Middle Ages: A Research Guide

The Pilgrimage to Santiago de Compostela: A Comprehensive, Annotated
Bibliography

The Pilgrimage to Compostela in the Middle Ages: A Book of Essays

The Miracles of Saint James: Translations from the Liber Sancti Jacobi (also with
Thomas Coffey)

Lindo sentido que me he consolado mucho quiera aquel
hombre q~te sucda ansii. Y Botello le dixo en tu mano
esta el librarte o no. Tu veras lo que te conuiene, O
quedar libre O asentado por toda La vida. Yo muy
bien se que me he de librar que ya estoi deseando
que llegue La ora para verme libre. Y Ju~ de Leon Le
dixo, yo tanbien, y si quieres por el te mal sueño, y q~ tenga
buen suceso, y le hagamos a aquel hom~ para q~ nos enuie algun con-
suelo en la semana tres Subtiles, que yo te ayudare cuando tu
quisieres. Y Fran~ Botello respon, que si, y se concertaron, y dixo
Ju~ de Leon pues sea desde mañana Lunes, y miercoles, y Viernes,
porque seguidos no puedo, y botello dixo sea en ora buena q~
que yo te ayudare de mui buena gana, que aora es buen t~po y q~
nadie ade... gane nada. Y para disuadir los de si acaso
nos hubieren oydo, Lo que no he bebido en Carnal, hago en
quaresma, y pido carne p~ probar, y atestiguar con ellos mes mos,
como comer carne en quaresma, y desmentir si huuie algunas
personas que aya entendido que signifca Subtiles. Y des-
de... Noche pido miel, y otras cosas, Las quales guardo para en acauando,
y la carne La bebo donde no se Vea. Y Ju~ de Leon le dixo
me parece bien, porque yo hago lo mesmo, y pido carne y no
me contento con lo que me dan, y me traen mas carne, y les dy
a entender que no me sattisface, porque es poco, y de noche
pido dos platos de miel, y que me den dos Ollas de atole o tras
noches ensalada, y otras cosas p~ guardarlo para en acauando
tener q~ comer, y Botello dixo pues estas en que hemos comido carne la quaresma, y desde el Lunes empecar Los
Subtiles como se deue, con sus Vitos y ceremonias, Lauandonos
y encendiendo Las candilexas, y haciendo alg~ oracion a aquel
hombre.

(Notas al margen izquierdo:)

Botello dize la
Goca de la costumbre
p~ q~ ... ngan.

se convienen en ha~ buen suceso, y
le hagamos a aquel hom~
su ayuda q~
no ... buen
suceso de dho ...

Botello dize Sa de
pedir carne en tiem~
quaresma, y q~ sus
ayunos.

dicha la carne de
noche se pide miel, y de
noche pide miel y
otras cosas q~ p~ ayu-
nos.

Todo esto Saca muy
bien sus ...

Ceremonias que hazen
Saca con otras cosas ...

A Drizzle of Honey

The Lives
and
Recipes of
Spain's
Secret Jews

David M. Gitlitz &
Linda Kay Davidson

ST. MARTIN'S PRESS ☙ NEW YORK

Illustrations © 1999 by Joanna Roy

DESIGN BY RALPH FOWLER

The trial testimony and poetry translations from Spanish, Portuguese, and Catalán, and
the translation of a passage from *Don Quijote* by Cervantes are by David M. Gitlitz. The
medieval cookbook translations are by Linda Kay Davidson, unless otherwise indicated.

The document reproduced on the frontispiece and on the back cover of the jacket is from a
1646 manuscript in which Juan de Leon, in prison in Mexico, asked his jailers to bring him
"two dishes of honey," with which he intended to break his fast. Sección Inquisición,
volume 1531, folio 222r, Archivo General de la Nación, Mexico City. Used by permission.

Library of Congress Cataloging-in-Publication Data

Gitlitz, David M. (David Martin)
    A drizzle of honey : the lives and recipes of Spain's secret Jews / David M. Gitlitz,
Linda Kay Davidson.
      p.   cm.
    Includes bibliographical references and index.
    ISBN 0-312-19860-4
    1. Cookery, Jewish. 2. Jews—Spain—History. 3. Marranos—History.
I. Davidson, Linda Kay. II. Title.
TX724.G58   1999
641.5'676—dc21   98-47430
                                                     CIP

First Edition: February 1999

10 9 8 7 6 5 4 3 2 1

To Ruth Kaletsky Gitlitz
and
Helen Scott Davidson,
in whose kitchens
we learned so much

CONTENTS

Recipes, Stories & Commentary

ACKNOWLEDGMENTS

While we take full responsibility for errors, omissions, and culinary oddities, we thank several people who contributed to the book's completion: Andrée Brooks, for her encouragement; Jeanne Fredericks, for believing in the project; Constance Hieatt, for taking time to read a portion of the manuscript and giving important historical data; Susan Offer, for critically reading portions of the manuscript and adding valuable suggestions; Charles Perry, for sharing his knowledge about Arabic medieval cooking; and the librarians of the University of Rhode Island, who helped us track down rare material. Our thanks to Elma Dassbach, Julie A. Evans, Michelle LaRoche, and David Riceman, for data that they shared with us; and Abby and Deborah Gitlitz, whose helping hands and good ideas lightened our work in the kitchen. We especially want to thank Jennifer Weis and Kristen Macnamara at St. Martin's Press, for shepherding the manuscript through the publication process, and our copy editor, Estelle Laurence, for her meticulous attention to detail. Lastly, we appreciate family, friends, and students who have braved the experiments of our kitchen and whose critical palates have helped us refine these dishes.

PREFACE

Beatriz Núñez was arrested by the Spanish Inquisition in the spring of 1485. She and her husband, Fernán González Escribano, had converted from Judaism to Christianity a few years earlier, but Beatriz still kept a kosher home. One of their maids, Catalina Sánchez, was a witness for the prosecution. Among the particulars of the family's Jewish practices that she denounced to the Tribunal was a recipe for a Sabbath stew made of lamb and chickpeas and hard-boiled eggs. The Guadalupe Inquisition found Beatriz guilty of being an unrepentant heretic and burned her alive in 1485.

Beatriz Núñez's Sabbath stew is one of approximately ninety detailed references to Jewish cooking in Iberia and the Iberian colonies that David Gitlitz found during two decades of reading Inquisition testimony. These "recipes" bring to life an important part of the daily routine of the *converso* residents in the Iberian Peninsula and its colonies some five hundred years ago. They also vividly demonstrate how the Inquisition used cultural information to help build a case against those it was investigating for heresy.

The documentary references to foods, rarely more than a list of main ingredients, point to a varied cuisine enriched by many flavorings, sometimes named and sometimes only alluded to. The ninety recipes include dishes in traditional food categories such as snacks, salads, stews, vegetables, fish, and desserts. Several recipes describe special holiday foods for Passover and for breaking the Yom Kippur and Purim fasts. Most are from Spain in the late fifteenth and early sixteenth centuries. A few are from Portugal and a few come from the American colonies of Mexico and Brazil in the seventeenth century.

For two years we have experimented with these embryonic recipes in our kitchen to make them accessible to modern cooks. Remembering that most of the historical references come from the time just before Christopher Columbus and the *conquistadores* brought New World products back to Europe, we put away the American staples such as tomatoes, corn, bananas, potatoes, and chile peppers. In return, we renewed our acquaintance with some of the tasty Old World standards like turnips, parsnips, and quince. We went through the pantry and excluded those spices that were available only after the sixteenth century (such as allspice and paprika); in their place we could experiment with now-ignored spices that were highly prized in medieval Europe (galingale and grains of paradise, for example). To contextualize our work, we pored over medieval cookbooks and modern studies of medieval cuisine.

What surprises anyone in his or her first contact with medieval cooking is the rich variety of edible materials. The main foods mentioned in these recipes are almost all still used today worldwide. But during the fifteenth and sixteenth centuries, some were specific to the Iberian Peninsula, others limited to certain areas of the Peninsula. The now-ubiquitous eggplant, for example, was brought to Europe through the Peninsula, and was hardly known outside of Iberia until perhaps as late as the seventeenth century. In thirteenth- and fourteenth-century Iberian cookbooks, it is often associated with the Muslims and Jews living on the Peninsula. The chickpea is a very common ingredient in the *converso* Sabbath stews; but contemporary Peninsula cookbooks of the well-to-do households rarely call for it, and a thirteenth-century Arabic cookbook states that it is eaten only by the poor. Salad was not limited to just lettuce, but embraced a dozen or more garden crops, including lavender, rue, and portulaca, which were topped off with anything else at hand.

The same abundance holds true for herbs and spices. Where a twentieth-century cook might prefer to emphasize one specific taste in a dish, using a limited number of aromatic ingredients, medieval cooks believed in the dictum "more is more." It is not unusual to have eight to ten seasonings in a single dish. Popular legend would have it that spices were too expensive to be much in evidence in the cooking pot. Not so. Many spices may have been costly, but they were highly sought after and recipe books call for their use continuously. Some standards, like pepper, continue to be standard in the modern kitchen. Other often-used spices, such as cassia and cardamom, are used more reservedly now.

Also noteworthy is the sweet tooth in Europe at that time. Both sugar and honey were popular sweeteners, added to dishes or even eaten alone. The document reproduced on the frontispiece records how Juan de León, in prison in Mexico in 1646, asked his jailers to bring him "two dishes of honey," with which he intended to break his fast.[1] A drizzle of honey or a sprinkling of sugar over a dish often added a finishing touch. In some parts of the Iberian Peninsula, a cinnamon-sugar topping was not limited to bread. It was sprinkled, liberally, over vegetable, egg, and meat dishes, even the dish with ten other seasonings. And then it was likely to be followed by a drizzle of rose or orange water over everything.

We want to make clear that the recipes offered in this book lay no claim to being precisely those dishes that the informants set on their tables in Castile or Portugal during Inquisition times. At best the historical documents have hinted—by recipe name, by list of principal ingredients, or by context—at the nature of the dish enjoyed by a particular Jewish or crypto-Jewish family at a particular time. We have taken these clues and carefully contextualized them in the world of late medieval Iberian cooking, a world which has proved notoriously imprecise with respect to measurements, methods of preparation, or even the nature of specific sauces or combinations of spices. Within the constraints of the medieval Iberian kitchen, we have experimented quite freely along all of these dimensions, and as a result we have often produced two or three versions of a given dish. Frequently we suggest—in the "Variations" section of the recipes—lines of experimentation which you, too, might follow. If you are new to medieval cooking, see the chapter titled Cooking Medieval in a Modern Kitchen (page 13) for some basic information about approximating medieval ingredients in the modern kitchen.

Each of the recipes that follows, then, is our modern re-creation of an Iberian Jewish recipe from around the time of the expulsions, with the addition of a few curious crypto-Jewish recipes from trials in the American colonies of Spain and Portugal. Each recipe has been developed based on our knowledge of Iberian cuisine of that time taken from relevant fourteenth- through seventeenth-century sources.[2] Each has been field-tested a number of times, with ingredients readily obtainable in American supermarkets. And each is placed into its historical milieu, insofar as possible, with information from the trial testimony about the cook or about the person who turned him or her in to the Inquisition.[3]

Our research has a somber side as well. Through these recipes we also can see how societal pressures related to eating were especially intense for the *conversos* on the Iberian Peninsula. Preparing a stew on Friday night for its consumption on Saturday put that family at risk because it was an open announcement that the family had not completely abandoned its Jewish practices. For that reason the Inquisition consistently asked questions of the accused's neighbors and house staff about the foods that were or were not consumed and how they were prepared. For the *converso* family struggling both to maintain its traditions and to evade the Inquisition, the preparation of each Sabbath stew or plate of matza for Passover was at once an act of defiance against the pressures of assimilation and the risks of disclosure and an affirmation of pride in the preservation of family and religious heritage. In this spirit, we dedicate this book to the memory of those courageous cooks. We hope that from the fragmented vignettes of their lives will emerge a mosaic of Iberian crypto-Jewish culture.

A Drizzle of Honey

INTRODUCTION

Jews and Conversos in Late Medieval Iberia

Substantial numbers of Jews lived in the Iberian Peninsula for a millennium and a half prior to their expulsion from Spain (in 1492) and Portugal (in 1497). They were termed Sephardic Jews in accord with the medieval tradition of identifying biblical Sepharad (Obadiah 1:20) with the Iberian Peninsula. From the early tenth century and for three hundred years or so in Muslim-controlled Iberia, they flourished to such an extent that we recognize that period as the Jewish Golden Age. Hasdai ibn Shaprut, Judah Halevi, Moses and Abraham ibn Ezra, and the great Maimonides are but a few of the extraordinary Iberian Jews whose philosophy and poetry are meaningful even into our own times.

As the northern Iberian Christian kingdoms of Navarre, Aragon, Castile, and Portugal gradually reconquered the Peninsula from the Muslims, pushing the frontier farther south each year, more and more of Iberia's Jews found themselves living under Christian control. From the twelfth to the fourteenth centuries, while the issue of the eventual dominance of the Peninsula remained in doubt, in most Iberian cities Jews and Christians and Muslims lived side by side in a tenuous and complex coexistence that historians generally refer to as *convivencia*. The three religious communities prayed in their respective liturgical languages, of course, but in the street they all spoke in a common tongue which liberally mixed words of Semitic origin into Latin-based Spanish. "We will live together, Allah willing—*Ojalá*—," all three would cry, "for if not we are truly unfortunate—*desmazalados*." They sang each other's songs, imitated each other's poetry, and played each other's games, especially the Muslim-introduced board game of chess (*ajedrez*). And they grew fond of each other's cuisine.

Toward the end of the fourteenth century in Spain, and to a lesser extent in Portugal, this tradition of *convivencia* began to come apart. As cities prospered and capitalism took root, popular resentment grew against some Jews' roles as administrators, tax collectors, and money lenders, this last activity expressly forbidden to Christians. Legislation restricted the rights of Iberian Jews, required them to wear an identifying badge, and forced them to relocate their homes into crowded *aljamas* or *juderías* (Jewish neighborhoods). In the streets, Dominican and Franciscan friars ranted about Jewish responsibility for the crucifixion, preached the compulsory conversion of the Jews, and incited mobs to despoil the Jewish neighborhoods.

Matters erupted in the summer of 1391 in Seville, where clergy-led mobs burned the Jewish neighborhood, slaughtered hundreds of its residents, and forcibly baptized the rest. Over the next few months the thousands of Aragonese and Castilian Jews who were caught by the conversionist mobs were compelled to accept baptism. In the years that followed, an even greater number willingly changed their faith, dispirited at what they saw as clear historical evidence that God had changed his allegiance to the Christians and attracted by the increased social and financial opportunities offered by conversion. Most of the forced converts (*anusim*) and their children, and some portion of the willing converts (*meshumadim*), continued to identify with Judaism. They lived next door to Jews and they had Jewish relatives. They could hear melodies of the chants emerging from the synagogues and on Friday evenings could smell Sabbath cooking in the air. Many of the men continued to pray with their Jewish colleagues, to fast on Yom Kippur, and to refrain from work on the Sabbath. Their wives kept a kosher home, continued their monthly visits to the *mikvah* ritual bath, and educated their daughters in the ways of Judaism. While it is likely that the majority of the converts were successfully blending into the Catholic mainstream, abandoning as many of their former Jewish customs as they were able, in the eyes of the so-called "old-Christian" leadership, all of the converts were suspected of being Judaizers, or backsliders into Jewish customs.

The old-Christian establishment increasingly called for drastic measures to speed up the assimilation of the converts: prohibit by law any association between new-Christians and their Jewish former co-religionists, police their adherence to their new faith, maybe even expel the Jews altogether. The forced separation of Jews and converts, legislated repeatedly from 1411 onward, seemed to have little effect on the customs of the converts. The second approach, policing, began around 1480 with the founding of the Spanish Inquisition. After a decade of investigations, trials, and public burnings of Judaizing converts, that, too, was perceived to have failed to achieve the desired results. The Christian authorities concluded that as long as Jews were permitted to live openly on the Peninsula, the converts would never fully assimilate. The Spanish expulsion order was signed in March of 1492. Five years later, in response to intense Spanish pressure on the Portuguese monarchy, the Jews were expelled from Portugal as well, and in 1498 from Navarre. From that time on, anyone living on the Iberian Peninsula was perforce a Christian, subject to the laws and practices of Catholicism.

And the converts? Those first- and second-generation *conversos* who continued to self-identify as Jews tended to try to preserve as many of their former Jewish customs as they could, living as secret, or crypto-Jews. They had firsthand knowledge of Jewish practice prior to 1492, and they replicated as much of it as they were able. The much smaller number of their descendants who still thought of themselves as Jews in the late sixteenth and seventeenth centuries held on to a few customs, but on the whole they lived lives relatively undifferentiable from those of their Christian neighbors. They went to church regularly, took communion, kept icons of the saints in their homes, and prayed for the salvation of their souls through the intercession of Jesus (or sometimes Moses). Of the vast range of Jewish customs detailed in the corpus of Jewish law, the *halachah,* they tended to preserve just a few. Of the festivals, they kept only the Passover seder and the Yom Kippur fast, and perhaps Purim, which they also observed by fasting. They revered the Sabbath, which they tended to observe by cleaning their house and clothes, abstaining from work, and lighting candles. And they clung to their familiar Jewish food.

Sephardic Cuisine and the Inquisition

There are no Jewish or crypto-Jewish cookbooks from this period. Instead, hints about Jewish cuisine and an occasional recipe are scattered through a variety of medieval documents, including the most unlikely of sources: Inquisition trial testimonies. The explanation has to do with the way in which the Inquisition operated.

When the Inquisition began inquiries in a particular region, inquisitors would first publicly read and publish an Edict of Grace, which gave people a certain number of days in which to confess their Judaizing activities, or to inform the Inquisition whether any of their neighbors were practicing crypto-Jews.[1] People who came forward voluntarily during this "grace period" would have their willingness to cooperate taken into consideration as the investigation proceeded. If they did not cooperate, the full rigor of the law would be brought to bear. To aid in the identification of Judaizers, comprehensive lists of Judaizing customs were published. These compilations advised citizens to be on the lookout for any activities which indicated that *conversos* were continuing to observe the Jewish Sabbath or festivals.

> . . . *any Christian persons, living or dead, present or absent, natives, residents or inhabitants of this said royal city of Las Palmas or other cities . . . who . . . [keep] . . . the Sabbaths . . . [by] cooking on the said Fridays such food as is*

*required for the Saturdays and on the latter eating the meat thus cooked on Fri-
days as is the manner of the Jews; . . . cleansing or causing meat to be cleansed,
cutting away from it all fat or grease and cutting away the nerve or sinew from the
leg; . . . not eating pork, hare, rabbit, strangled birds, conger-eel, cuttle-fish, nor
eels or other scaleless fish, as laid down in the Jewish law; and upon the death of
parents . . . eating . . . such things as boiled eggs, olives and other viands. . . .[2]
who have porged or deveined the meat they are preparing to eat, soaking it in
water to remove the blood, or who have removed the sciatic vein from a leg of
mutton or from any other animal. . . . Or who have eaten meat during Lent or
on other days forbidden by the Holy Mother Church, without needing to do
so. . . . Or who celebrate the Festival of unleavened bread, beginning by eating
lettuce, celery or other bitter herbs on those days.[3]*

Ironically, these same lists of customs advised later generations of *conversos,*
who had great difficulty in obtaining information about normative Judaism, precisely what they had to do to continue their Jewish practices. It
stands to reason that any special meat preparations and Sabbath or festival
foods were considered prime indicators of Judaizing. This is why the depositions are filled with statements like those from the servant girl Francisca,
who reported in the 1490s that her mistress, María Alvarez, ordered her to
pick out the vein and trim off all the fat with her thumbnail;[4] or the 1621
report by a family member that Isabel Núñez cooked the Jewish way,
koshering her meat and avoiding pork, and that for Passover she made her
own matza.[5] Most of the recipes in this book are based upon this sort of
testimony.

Thus, the recipes given in the trials do not resemble those of modern
cookbooks. They tend merely to list ingredients, and sometimes give a
sketchy indication about how a particular dish might be prepared. Often
they refer to "seasonal" greens. Rarely do they mention specific spices, for
these dishes were understood both by the trial deponents and their audience to be part of a tradition of Iberian cooking that blended Jewish,
Christian, and Muslim elements that, because it was common to everyone,
did not need to be particularized in detail. The trial testimony points only
to what was different about the allegedly Jewish recipes; but it has to be understood against the background of common Iberian culinary practice.

Jewish, and crypto-Jewish, cuisine tended to differ from that of its
neighbors in three ways that derived from ancient Jewish legal traditions.
First and most important, of course, it avoided foods prohibited by the Jewish dietary traditions: no shellfish, no eels, no rabbit, no pork. Second, Jews
and Judaizing *conversos* koshered their meat in accordance with those tradi-

tions. And last, they developed several special Jewish foods for consumption on the Sabbath and the principal festivals. The traditional foods of the first and second generation of converts echoed Iberian Jewish cooking as it was practiced in the years just prior to the expulsions.

Eating in Medieval Iberia

By and large, with the exceptions just noted, Iberian Jews ate mostly whatever their Christian and Muslim neighbors ate. The Roman cuisine of late antiquity was pan-Mediterranean. The sixth-century Iberian author Isidoro's list of foods is in line with what was being produced throughout the rest of the Mediterranean. It reflects an agricultural wealth whose staples were wheat, olives, and grapes. Protein came from beef or lamb, or from the bounty of the sea.

With the Islamic invasion in 711, and over the next eight centuries of Muslim occupation, culture on the Peninsula became heavily Islamicized. The preservation of Arabic food vocabulary even today vividly demonstrates the degree to which medieval Iberians of all cultures acquired a taste for the exotic foods that the Muslims had brought, products like rice (*arroz*), oranges (*naranjas*), artichokes (*alcachofas*), and almonds (*almendras*), seasonings like saffron (*azafrán*), caraway (*alcaravea*), and capers (*alcaparras*). They ate tangy meatballs (*albóndigas*). They covered their dessert pastries with sweet sugar sauce (*almíbar*, made from *azúcar*), or soaked their fruit in *alcohol*. The staples tended to be Mediterranean. The predominant meat was lamb. The preferred flavorings came from the Islamic tradition. The adoption throughout Europe of some Islamic culinary treats such as saffron, oranges, sugar, and almonds attests to the popularity of the exotic products introduced from the East.

Iberian medieval cookbooks survive from both the Christian and Islamic traditions. We have a few Arabic-language cookbooks from the southern portion of the Iberian Peninsula. There are Christian cookbooks from the northern areas beginning from the fourteenth century. One feature of the cookbooks surviving from the Middle Ages is that they cater to the nobility. For example, the late fifteenth-century *Manual de mugeres,* in addition to recipes, contains directions for making cosmetics. The paucity of references in these books to some common foods, such as garlic and onion, further reflects the upper-class nature of these written sources. In middle- and lower-class cooking, these ingredients would have been prevalent, and this is reflected in our other extant source material, the medieval household accounts and corporate records that mention meals and food purchases.[6]

Reading through the Arabic cookbooks and those from the northern part of the Peninsula one senses both similarities and differences in palate between the northern and southern regions of the Peninsula. The Arabic recipes in general provide a wider range of seasonings and flavors. Mixing more than one kind of meat in a single stew also seems to be more typical of the Islamic south. The north tended to preserve the culinary habits of the late Roman culture, the southern cuisine was much more heavily Islamicized. A clear example of this is the word for "olive": in the north it is *olivo,* from the Latin; in the south, *aceituna,* from the Arabic. Medieval southern Iberian cooking relied more heavily on Islamic culinary practices, as, for example, the habit of double-cooking some dishes, first frying and then stewing the main ingredient, or vice versa.

The cookbooks published in the northern part of the Peninsula reflect three centuries of continuing culinary culture that had its roots in the Mediterranean Roman tradition with later adaptations of Islamic tastes and practices. In the *Libre de sent soví* (fourteenth century), Nola's *Libro de cozina* (ca. 1520), and Granado's *Libro del arte de cocina* (1599), we can see similarities in general modes of preparations and in several specific recipes. Granado copied the majority of Nola's recipes and added a copious number of his own. References to stews and desserts with similar ingredients and preparations in other documents in Castile and Portugal confirm this largely homogenous tradition. The fact that the authors used similar titles for some of their sauces, such as *almodrote* and *capirotada,* points to a well-established and well-accepted cuisine. Later authors, such as the seventeenth-century lexicographer Covarrubias, who defined many of the terms used in the medieval cookery works, bear out the pervasive nature of this culinary tradition.

A Note About the Published Resources

In our attempts to re-create these Ibero-Jewish dishes and to better understand their culinary contexts, we have consulted several ancient and medieval cookbooks and supplementary medieval materials. Here is a list, in chronological order, of the sources to which we refer most often in our cookbook. The editions we have used are cited in the culinary bibliography.

Apicius, *De re coquinaria* (80 B.C.E. to 40 C.E.)

Apicius was a wealthy gastronomer whose fame lay in the fortune he spent on food. Four medieval manuscripts are extant of the recipes attributed to him, which were then printed a handful of times through the seventeenth century. None of these manuscripts gives recipes for pastries or other breads, which suggests that the extant manuscripts may not be complete.

Dioscorides, *Materia medica* (first century C.E.)

This is the most influential of the ancient herbals, with numerous versions in Latin and many in modern European languages.

Isidoro, *Etimologías* (sixth century)

Isidoro's *Etimologías,* Europe's first Christian encyclopedia, discusses the word origins of the terms for everything on earth, from agriculture to zoology. Along the way he occasionally gives an insight into practices relating to cuisine. His reliance on scholarship of the ancients—some of it not wholly trustworthy—is characteristic of medieval writing.

Ibn Butlan, *Tacuinum sanitatis* (eleventh century)

The *Tacuinum* is a consideration of the effects of plants, animals, minerals, and winds on humans. It was written by the Muslim Ibn Butlan (sometimes spelled Botlan), who studied in Baghdad before he became a Christian and died in a monastery in Antioch. It was very popular in Europe and was translated quickly into Latin; many copies were made throughout the Middle Ages.

Ibn al Awam (twelfth century)

An Andalusian author who wrote a book in Arabic on agriculture. Occasionally his remarks refer to practices or produce found in Iberia. The work was translated into French in the late 1800s and into Spanish in this century.

Baghdad Cookery-Book (ca. 1236)

In the late 1930s, A. J. Arberry translated a manuscript that describes some royal banquets at the courts of the Baghdad caliphs and that contains one hundred fifty-nine recipes for a wide range of foods. The recipes are ordered by whether they are "plain" or "sweet," fried or baked, and so forth. Although recently some researchers have found some faults with the translation, it is still one of the prime sources for understanding medieval Islamic food.

Cocina hispano-magribi/Al-Andalus (thirteenth century)

In the mid-1960s, Ambrosio Huici Miranda translated into Spanish a lengthy Arabic manuscript containing five hundred forty-three recipes. He concluded that the mansucript was written by an Andalusian author probably in the first half of the thirteenth century. The recipes vary from very brief to long, involved procedures. They cover fish, fowl, meat, vegetables, fruits, sweets, and syrups. Recently some scholars have found problems with some of the translations and the order in which the recipes appear, but to this date Huici Miranda's is the only Romance-language translation of this important Andalusian culinary manuscript.

Desde Estella a Sevilla (1352)

In late May of 1352 the King of Navarre dispatched emissaries to the court of Pedro I of Castile in Seville. The twenty-six men were gone for two months, half of that time on the road. Their account book, published in 1974, lists day by day exactly what was purchased and how much it cost.

Forme of Cury (ca. 1390)

Several medieval English cookbooks are accessible. *Forme,* attributed to the master chefs of King Richard II, contains about two hundred recipes. Its recipes have been modernized for the American kitchen.[7] Some of the recipes demonstrate just how thoroughly Islamic cooking had migrated north.

Goodman of Paris, *Le Ménagier de Paris* (1393)

This treatise by an older man for his very young, new wife is instructions to help her learn to manage a household and to comport herself. Among the diverse subjects he covers are appropriate menus for several feasts, reasonable prices to pay merchants, and recipes for many specific dishes. We have used a 1928 translation which, although incomplete, is easily accessible (Power), as well as an authoritative edition of the French text (Brereton/Ferrier).

Libre de sent soví (fourteenth century)

This collection of recipes is the earliest that has been found for Catalán cuisine. There are two extant manscripts; the most complete contains two hundred twenty recipes, divided into foods for meat and meatless days. The cookbook is fairly extensive in its recipes, with, for example, directions for preparing fifty varieties of fish.

Enrique de Villena, *Arte cisoria* (1423)

Villena was a Spanish nobleman whose interests in science and arcane knowledge led him to write several works, some of which were burned as heretical. Among the survivors are the *Arte de trouar,* the earliest Spanish study of the rules of poetry, and a treatise on astrology. His *Arte cisoria,* or *The Art of Carving,* is the first book written in Spanish about how to carve and serve at a noble's table. This kind of didactic material was not uncommon in the Middle Ages and there are similar works in English. The single surviving manuscript was printed in 1766. The *Arte cisoria's* twenty chapters cover aspects of the carving profession from the kinds of knives to be used and the comportment of servants to precise, detailed instructions about how to carve specific birds, fish, fruits, and so forth.

Bartolomeo de Sacchi di Piadena, *De honesta voluptate* (1475)

A Vatican librarian composed this treatise about the importance of food to the body's health and how to prepare it. The work contains ten books. Foods, spices, herbs, fish, and meats are discussed briefly with regard to their properties. He often gives recipes.

Manual de mugeres en el qual se contienen muchas y diversas reçeutas muy buenas (ca. 1475–1525)

This manuscript (Mss. Parmense 834), found in the Biblioteca Palatina in Parma, Italy, contains recipes and helpful hints for the upper-class woman, including information about cosmetics, medicines, perfumes, breath sweeteners, and, most important for our book, cooking. The selection is eclectic; many recipes are for sweets or conserves such as marzipan and cookies (*vizcochos*), but there are also recipes for capon and for blood sausage.

Gabriel Alonso de Herrera, *Agricultura general* (1513)

This lengthy agricultural manual by the Salamancan professor and confessor to Cardinal Cisneros provides useful data about what food crops were current in his day.

Roberto de Nola, *Libro de cozina* (ca. 1520)

The author and date of this important northern Iberian Peninsula work are problematical. It is generally believed that about 1520 this book was published in Barcelona with the title *Libre del coch,* but some scholars suspect an earlier edition, perhaps as early as 1477. There is no information about the author, who may have been a cook in the Spanish court in Naples. However, this book was extremely popular: ten editions were published in quick succession. The book is a collection of two hundred forty-three recipes with information about spices and herbs and information for cooks and servers.

Portuguese cookbook (ca. 1550)

A Portuguese manuscript (Codice I.E. 33 of the National Library of Naples) was probably taken to Naples in the mid-sixteenth century when Princess Maria went to Italy to marry Ottavio Farnese of Parma. The first page of the manuscript gives the title *Tratt. di Cucina Spagn.*, or "Treatise on Spanish Cooking," a title seemingly added by an Italian librarian who did not notice that the manuscript was written in Portuguese. Newman first transcribed the manuscript in 1964. Since then there have been two facsimile editions. The forty-two folios have many gaps, so that one cannot ascertain with certainty what kinds of recipes are missing. The extant manuscript contains recipes for meat (twenty-six), eggs (four), milk (seven), and conserves (twenty-four), plus a few others for remedies and for fattening chickens.

Diego Granado, *Libro del arte de cocina* (1599)

Perhaps because Nola's cookbook (see above) had not been edited in several years, Diego Granado published *Arte,* in which he copied all of Nola's recipes and added many of his own, for a total of seven hundred sixty-three recipes. The author calls himself an "official" of the Madrid court's kitchen, but no biographical information is available about him.

Sebastián de Covarrubias, *Tesoro de la lengua castellana o española* (1611)

Covarrubias wrote the first dictionary of the Spanish language. His descriptions not only summarize earlier sources—frequently ancient writers such as Dioscorides—but also refer to common practices and proverbs of his own time. His definitions of foods often list ingredients and modes of preparation.

Modern Sephardic Cooking

Readers of modern Sephardic cookbooks will note both similarities and differences in the recipes given here. To begin with, in modern parlance, the term *Sephardic* has come to mean anyone who is non-Ashkenazi, and thus includes Yemenis, Iraqis, and Iranians who have never been influenced by Iberian food customs.[8] But even when *Sephardic* is used in its more traditional sense of a Jew whose ancestors' home was in Iberia, modern Sephardic cooking is significantly different from its Iberian origins. Many of the Sephardic Jews who left Spain settled in the Ottoman Empire, with another large group in the Maghreb, particularly Morocco. The cooking of these communities today is heavily influenced by local traditions in North Africa or the eastern Mediterranean. Moreover, cooking of the last three centuries has been radically altered by four New World foods—tomatoes, potatoes, corn, and chile peppers—none of which was available to medieval Iberian cooks.

A Note About the Contributors

For the most part, the converts who unwittingly contributed the recipes to this book—via the pens of the Inquisition scribes who recorded their confessions and the allegations of the servants and neighbors and family members who testified against them—were ordinary people. Not the rich and famous. Not the powerful men who influenced the tragic course of events on the Iberian Peninsula. But middle-class shopkeepers and artisans and village administrators and their wives and families. Contrary to the false stereotypes about distinctive *converso* names, most of these cooks had the same last names as their old-Christian neighbors: González, Núñez, Rodríguez, Fernández, or García.

The list of contributors is skewed toward Spain, for reasons having to do with the locus of the authors' principal research in recent years. But some of the contributing *conversos* lived in Portugal and some in the far-flung Iberian colonies of Mexico and Brazil. Although *conversos* lived in hundreds of municipalities in the Iberian world, our contributors are clustered in certain communities—Almazán, Ciudad Real, Guadalupe, Toledo, Coimbra, Mexico City. This is because the Inquisition archives from those cities are easily accessible, many in published form, and because the inquisitors in those towns seemed to have been particularly sensitive to the role that culinary habits play in sustaining religio-ethnic identity. The contributors described meals prepared between about 1450 and 1677. Of the sixty or so different informants, thirty-six witnessed the expulsions firsthand and had vivid memories of the rich Jewish culture of late fifteenth-century Iberia. Some of the later informants showed a weakened adherence to *kashruth* and a greater assimilation to the cuisine of the majority culture. One recipe even includes pork.

Beyond the testimonies recorded by Inquisition scribes, we have found recipes in three other sources. One is an Andalusian cookbook from the thirteenth century that describes certain recipes as "Jewish dishes." A second source is a chronicler contemporary to the Spanish expulsion, Andrés Bernáldez, who in his virulent hatred of the Jews and Jewish culture details several Jewish culinary habits which he found particularly disgusting, such as frying meat in olive oil. Another good source is the scurrilous court poetry of the late fifteenth century that in mocking Jewish and *converso* customs gives lists of dishes which their society considered to be typically Jewish.

The Inquisition records, both published and archival, are frequently incomplete, and much of our curiosity about what happened to these people will never be satisfied. We know the outcome of the trials of only about half of the five dozen new-Christians profiled in this book:

seven contributors were burned at the stake;

two others had their bones exhumed and burned after their deaths, which permitted the Inquisition to confiscate their estates and rendered their descendants unable to enter certain professions;

one was sent to row in the king's warships;

ten were given lesser punishments that included such things as fines, house arrest, public whipping, temporary banishment, public shaming by wearing a penitential garment branding the wearer as a heretic, or the recitation of a certain number of prayers or attendance at church services;

three were set free for insufficient evidence.

The others have vanished into the mists of history, leaving behind only a few fascinating anecdotes about the Judaizing customs that got them into trouble with the Inquisition,
  and these recipes.

Cooking Medieval
in a Modern Kitchen

In re-creating these recipes from the fifteenth, sixteenth, and seventeen centuries, we have used standard American measurements, utensils, and cooking techniques. We have not roasted meat over an open flame, nor have we banked coals around clay pots filled with Sabbath stew. The recipes in this book were developed in our late twentieth-century kitchen, with ovenproof glass and ceramic casseroles, enameled pots and pans, and cast-iron skillets and Dutch ovens, with an occasional use of the microwave oven for quick heating of ingredients. We have opted for modern food processors, blenders, and grinders to pulverize spices and mix ingredients. Our directions assume that you will use similar equipment.

Ingredients

Medieval recipes tend to be sketchy, and what was obvious to medieval cooks, and therefore had no reason to be written down, is often obscure today. Consequently, the exact nature of some ingredients will likely never be completely known or completely duplicable. Here are some governing assumptions and the resultant modern approximations of ingredients:

Cheese

Medieval Iberian cookbooks call for several kinds of cheese, including "fresh cheese" and "Catalán cheese." We use two broad varieties of cheese which approximate but which do not correlate exactly to what probably was available to medieval cooks. For fresh cheese we prefer farmer cheese, *queso fresco,* carried by many Hispanic groceries. If that is not available, we suggest cream cheese and/or cottage cheese, blended to a smooth texture. For hard cheeses, we recommend the Spanish Manchego cheese, which is usually available in specialty cheese shops. If that is not obtainable, then Italian Romano or Asiago cheeses are acceptable.

Eggs

Eggs present a minor quandary. They are ever-present in medieval recipes, but there are no indications about what kind of eggs were to be used or what size. In the United States almost all cooking is with chicken eggs, but we cannot presume that the same held true five hundred years ago. Still, in these recipes we use large chicken eggs.

For those who must regulate their intake of cholesterol, we suggest that you try the recipes using half of the number of eggs and replacing the other half with "Egg-Beaters" or "Second Nature," unless otherwise indicated.

Flour

The most common medieval flour was stone-ground wheat flour. The more it was sifted the whiter it became. We have found no references to kosher flour. Our recipes use standard white flour or, when so indicated, a combination of three to one of white flour and stone-ground whole wheat flour.

Herbs and spices

A variety of herbs grew in every medieval household garden. During the growing season, they were used fresh and we have done likewise. Some herbs, like rosemary and oregano, can be used dried. Others, especially cilantro, cannot. We are fortunate in that today's supermarkets generally carry fresh green herbs and we recommend their use.

Medieval cooking used lots of spices and multiple flavors in a single dish. We have experimented to create pleasing combinations, but you may find that certain spices are not to your liking. You can reduce the amounts of those spices. Generally, we have used whole spices (e.g., caraway, cumin seed), grinding only enough for the specific recipes, unless otherwise indicated. We have found that using preground spices (such as dried ginger, cumin, or even pepper) diminishes the intensity of the dish's flavor.

Some medieval flavorings (such as galingale, lavender, or grains of paradise) do not appear on the typical supermarket shelf. But they are purchasable from mail order herb suppliers throughout the United States and many are available in natural food stores or co-ops.

Saffron deserves a special mention here. In medieval Iberian cooking it is called for in prodigious amounts to add both flavor and color. Often its flavor is combined with several other spices. However, it tends to be costly. We have suggested its use only in those recipes in which its effect will not get lost. If you wish to further enhance the yellow color of some recipes, especially stews, try turmeric or safflower tied in a muslin bag.

Leavening agents

Medieval bakers either used a fermented vegetable starter or a live yeast culture, which they kept going much as is done with a modern sourdough starter. Since potatoes come from the New World, potato starters were un-available. We have used packaged dry yeast.

Legumes

Much like today, chickpeas and many varieties of beans were dried so that they could be preserved and eaten year round. As today, they were reconstituted by boiling or by soaking them for several hours and rinsing them before cooking. In many recipes, for convenience's sake, we have substituted canned chickpeas, drained and rinsed.

To prepare dry beans or chickpeas quickly for cooking: boil the beans for two minutes in sufficient water to cover them. Set aside for one hour. Drain.

Meats

Kosher meat was available to crypto-Jews prior to the expulsion. Afterward most kosher slaughtering was done at home away from prying eyes. There are many references to salting and soaking any meat before using it and to removing fat and veins. Recipes prepared with kosher meat will differ somewhat from those where the meat has not been soaked and salted. See page 161 for our directions for soaking and salting.

Meat parts (innards)

In the Middle Ages much more of an animal was consumed than is the common practice in modern, middle-class American kitchens: every part that was edible was eaten. Specialty butcher shops still sell tripe, heart, kidneys, livers, and chicken feet. Many ethnic markets carry a large variety. Still, it may be difficult to convince your butcher that yes, you really do want chicken necks with the skin. In those recipes whose main ingredients may be difficult to find, we suggest alternatives.

Oil

Always olive oil. We recommend the use of "extra-virgin" olive oil for those occasions when the oil is not to be cooked (e.g., on a salad).

Salt

Medieval references to salt indicate that many times a cook would buy a cone of salt and scrape off the necessary amount when needed. We have used coarse-ground kosher salt or sea salt. The recipes indicate if the salt is to be ground finer. Many recipes call for quantities of salt that today we consider unhealthy. If you choose, you may reduce the amount of salt listed.

Sugar

As with salt, late medieval cooks bought cones of sugar and scraped off the needed amount, sifting it to attain finer sugar powders. Most medieval sugar was probably brown, although we have used white sugar or a combination of white and brown sugars in our recipes.

Thickeners

Modern cooks tend to use cornstarch or flour to thicken stews, casseroles, and some fruit desserts. Medieval and Renaissance cooks, like the author of the *Sent soví,* Nola, and Granado, used a variety of thickeners, sometimes more than one in a single recipe. On days when meat was not prohibited, beaten eggs or egg yolks was one popular thickener. Other times poultry livers, especially chicken livers, either raw or previously cooked, were ground and cooked into a stew. On meatless days, or when a white color was more desirable, almond milk was a popular thickener. Two other thickeners, based on starch, were also quite common. The first is *almidón* (or *amydon*), a paste made of wheat steeped in water for several days, then dried. Apparently small bricks of *amydon* were at the chef's side in the kitchen, to pulverize and mix into stews and pottages.[1] A thickener made of rice flour was used somewhat less often on the Iberian Peninsula.[2] By far the easiest, cheapest, and most common thickener was bread crumbs or bread soaked in vinegar. If the cook wished to have a white or light-color dish, the bread was soaked in vinegar and tempered with white wine. If the dish was meant to be dark, toasted bread was soaked in vinegar and tempered with red wine.[3] The *Al-Andalus* cookbook also occasionally mentions "flour" in an obvious thickening process.

For this cookbook, we occasionally suggest a specific thickener when its use reinforces the dish's flavor. This is especially true for mild white dishes for which almond milk is best. For certain recipes from the *Al-Andalus* cookbook, the directions include thickening with chicken livers and we have followed the thirteenth-century work's instructions. Other times a vinegar-soaked bread adds depth of flavor to the stews. On other occasions, especially with the Sabbath stews, we leave it to the cook's own preference. Here are general instructions for various medieval thickeners. The quantities suggested here should thicken a stew meant to serve four people.

Bread thickener

1. Toast 2 pieces of dry stale bread (whole wheat is good). Do not use commercial bread crumbs.

2. Pulverize the toasted bread in a grinder. You may have to do this in two batches.
3. Place the crumbs in a nonreactive bowl. Pour 3 tablespoons white or red wine vinegar and 2 tablespoons white or red wine over the crumbs. Let the crumbs soak up all of the liquid, making a very thick paste. Let the mixture sit for about 10 minutes.
4. Slowly pour 1 cup of the hot stew liquid into the bread mixture. Mix thoroughly with a fork, dissolving all lumps.
5. Gradually stir the mixture into the stew pot. Simmer gently, stirring occasionally, for about 8 minutes or until the stew thickens to the desired consistency.

Flour paste[4]

1. Place 2 tablespoons flour (white flour or a combination of white and whole wheat) in a small bowl.
2. Slowly add 2–3 tablespoons cold water and dissolve the flour completely.
3. Slowly mix in ⅓–½ cup of the hot stew liquid into the flour and water mixture.
4. Stir the flour and liquid mixture back into the stew and simmer until the desired consistency is reached.

Rice flour

1. Take 6 tablespoons uncooked rice and pulverize it in a grinder. You may have to do this in two batches.
2. Place the rice flour in a small bowl. Stir in 9 tablespoons cool liquid (water or almond milk).
3. Mix in ½ cup of the hot stew liquid.
4. Slowly stir the rice mixture into the simmering stew, about ¼ cup at a time, and cook for about 8 minutes, or until the stew thickens to the desired consistency. The pulverized rice will swell in cooking, adding a subtle granular texture to the stew.

Vinegar

Vinegar is a basic ingredient of medieval cuisine. We know that vinegar, as well as wine, *agraz* (a liquid made of unripe green grapes), and orange juice from the sour, Seville oranges were used to give a special tang to the foods. In every recipe we indicate which souring agent we have used. Generally speaking, we prefer balsamic vinegar because its fermentation process, in wood casks, probably resembles the fermentation and storage of medieval vinegar. But we also use red wine vinegar in certain recipes.

Sabbath Stews

Many of the recipes reported to the Inquisition tribunals were for Sabbath meals. The ingredients did not necessarily evoke suspicion. Instead, it was the manner in which the meal was cooked. The defining element of the Sabbath meal is that it is prepared before sundown on Friday and then not touched again until time to be eaten on Saturday. Often the pot was sealed and put on the side of the fire, near banked coals, and kept warm until it was time to serve it on Saturday afternoon. Others were eaten at room temperature. In medieval times and still in modern North Africa the pot is sealed with a collar of dough of flour and water which bakes on tightly, keeping the juices in the pot.[5]

For purposes of this cookbook, we have prepared nearly all of the dishes as if they were to be served at the time of preparation, or refrigerated to be eaten cold or to be reheated later. Only occasionally do we replicate the Sabbath stew preparation. In general, any recipe can be held for a Sabbath meal by following these few directions:

1. Use an ovenproof cooking pot with a tight lid, such as a cast-iron Dutch oven.
2. Prepare the stew, adding all ingredients, including spices and herbs.
3. Follow the recipe directions until the stew's meat or main ingredient is nearly tender.
4. Cover and place the cooking pot in the oven and keep it at 200° until ready to serve.

Almond Milk

Makes about 2 cups milk

Almond milk was such a common ingredient in medieval recipes in Spain and elsewhere that no one seems to have written down precisely how it was to be made. It was used both as a thickener and to provide nourishment on those occasions when animals' milk was not possible. Our best information suggests that it was made by steeping ground almonds in a liquid, perhaps broth or water, or even wine.[6]

> 1 cup sliced almonds
> 2 teaspoons sugar
> 2 cups chicken broth, water, or wine

1. Grind the almonds very finely. Place them in a medium bowl. Stir in the sugar.

2. In a medium saucepan, heat the liquid to nearly boiling over medium heat. If using bouillon cubes, boil the water and add the cubes and remove from heat. Stir to dissolve and let sit about 5 minutes. Reheat to very hot over medium heat.

3. Pour the hot liquid over the ground almonds. Stir and let steep about 15 minutes, stirring occasionally.

4. Strain and separate the liquid from the almonds. Discard the almonds.

NOTE

It is best to make the milk the day you intend to use it. However, it can be stored 1 or 2 days in the refrigerator.

Almorí

Almorí (Arabic: *murrí*) appears to have been a strong mixture of rotted unleavened breads, salt, herbs, and spices, tempered with water. Lexicographers believe that the Arabism (from *al* and *morí*) has a root in the Latin *muria* (salt liquor, brine),[7] from which derives the modern Spanish *salmuera*, pickling brine.[8] It was a staple in medieval Islamic cooking, often used as a coating for fowl or as a paste to add to oil when frying.

Both the twelfth-century *Baghdad Cookery-Book* and the thirteenth-century *Al-Andalus* cookbook mention *almorí* frequently in such a way as to

*Cooking
Medieval
in a Modern
Kitchen*

19

indicate that the cooks of the time knew the mixture well.[9] Other Arabic manuscripts also refer to *almorí* and other concoctions called *kamakh* and *bunn,* whose use seems to have been widespread and common. Although it had disappeared from use by the end of the Middle Ages, the eighteenth-century Spanish *Diccionario de autoridades* still records it, listing "flour, salt, honey, palm hearts, and other things" as *almorí*'s ingredients. It further states that "it was an esteemed and medicinal food."[10]

The basic ingredient of *murri* was *budhaj,* an unleavened dough made from barley flour. It was placed in a vessel and left to rot. Then it was combined with wheat flour, salt, and some herbs and again left to rot. Toward the end of the process, when the mass had turned black, water was added and the mixture was left for another prolonged period. Sometime during this process other herbs and spices were added. Finally, when the mixture had ripened to its appropriate state, the liquid was drained and used in cooking.

Arberry's translation of the *Baghdad Cookery-Book* in the late 1930s included two recipes for *budhaj* and *murri* which had been appended to the manuscript. His version features the herb pennyroyal as a basic ingredient. Since Arberry's translation, only Perry has dealt seriously with this culinary mixture. Perry believes that *fudhanj* is more properly "rotted barley dough" than "penny-royal."[11] He has actually made and taste-tested the rotted *budhaj,* and cautions strongly *not* to eat it, since it is highly carcinogenic.[12]

For our cookbook, we have preserved *almorí*'s arrays of spices without attempting to re-create the carcinogenic rotted mass. Our first version, with pennyroyal, reflects Arberry's interpretation of *almorí*. Version two is a combination of spices occurring frequently in the medieval Islamic *almorí* recipes. The first two versions can be used interchangeably, although with quite different flavor results. The third recipe, with nigella, combines the principal spices found in a thirteenth-century version of *murri*.[13] Since the original *almorí* was obviously a liquid or paste, we generally combine the aromatic herbs with a tempering agent such as honey and/or vinegar. The cooked version of the third *almorí* recipe should be used the day it is made or shortly thereafter. It is a remarkably tasty enhancer of meat broths.

Pennyroyal Almori

Makes about ¾ cup

⅓ cup bread crumbs	1½ teaspoons cinnamon
2 tablespoons sea salt	1 tablespoon fenugreek
1 tablespoon dried pennyroyal leaves (see Note)	

1. Finely grind the ingredients together until they are well combined.
2. Store in an airtight container. The mixture will store indefinitely, but it is better used within a month, since the spices lose potency over time.

NOTE

Important: Pennyroyal *oil* is toxic. The dried leaves are not. They are found in the medicinal herbs section of natural food stores.[14] If you wish, substitute dried mint leaves. Or use the next recipe.

VARIATION

Substitute dried mint leaves for the pennyroyal leaves.

Simple Almori

Makes about ¼ cup

2 tablespoons bread crumbs	1½ teaspoons fennel
1 tablespoon sea salt	1 teaspoon safflower (optional)
1 teaspoon cinnamon	

1. Finely grind the ingredients together until they are well combined.
2. Store in an airtight container. The mixture will store indefinitely, but it is better used within a month, since the spices lose potency over time.

Nigella Almorí

Makes about ¾ cup

3 tablespoons matza flour or ground
    matza
3 tablespoons bread crumbs
2 tablespoons salt
1 tablespoon nigella (see Variation)
1 teaspoon dried thyme
1 teaspoon coriander seeds

1 teaspoon caraway seeds
1 teaspoon fenugreek
1 teaspoon anise
1½ teaspoons cinnamon
1½ teaspoons fennel
1½ teaspoons safflower (optional)

Dry preparation

1. Finely grind the ingredients together until they are well combined.

2. Store in an airtight container. The mixture will store indefinitely, but it is better used within a month, since the spices lose potency over time.

Baked preparation
Makes about 6 tablespoons

1 tablespoon honey
4 tablespoons nigella almorí

4 tablespoons white vinegar

1. Preheat the oven to 325°. In a small saucepan over low heat, briefly warm the honey. Mix the *almorí,* vinegar, and warmed honey in a small nonreactive baking dish.

2. Bake the mixture for 20 minutes. Remove it from the oven. The top will look somewhat crusty, but the interior will be gooey. Use it when it cools, or refrigerate it, covered, for up to 3 days.

VARIATION

Nigella (*Nigella sativa*) is sometimes called "black cumin" or *kalonji*. It is a staple in Indian cooking, often seen as the black seeds in *nan* bread. If you cannot find nigella, an acceptable substitute is a finely-ground combination of

1 teaspoon oregano
1 teaspoon pepper
1 teaspoon poppy seeds

Cilantro Juice

Makes about ⅓ cup

Cilantro was a staple in medieval recipes of the Iberian Peninsula, especially the southern area, which had been influenced by Islamic cooking. Often the dried seeds are used, but the most important parts of the plant are the fresh green leaves and stems. Many recipes call for cilantro juice, which is often used in Moroccan cooking today. It is best made at the moment of its use, but if you must you may make a batch and freeze it in ice-cube trays.

1–1½ cups tightly packed chopped fresh cilantro leaves

3 tablespoons water

Puree the ingredients in a food processor.

Salsa Fina

Makes 3 tablespoons

Several fixed mixtures of spices were stocked by medieval Iberian cooks. Both Nola and *Sent soví* list the basic ingredients of this popular mixture called *salsa fina*.

4 teaspoons dried ginger
3 teaspoons cinnamon
1 teaspoon pepper
½ teaspoon ground cloves

½ teaspoon mace
½ teaspoon ground nutmeg
¼ teaspoon crushed saffron threads

1. In a mortar or electric mill, combine all the ingredients and grind them to a fine powder.
2. Store the mixture in a tightly closed container.

Vegetable Broth

Makes 10–12 cups

The vegetable broth we use for stews and as a base for sauces is made up of only those vegetables and herbs that would have been available in medieval Iberia. Thus tomatoes and peppers are excluded. Outside of that, we invite you to make your own broth based on what you find in your market vegetable section. Here is one of many possibilities:

2 medium onions, chopped	1 leek, well cleaned and sliced
2 cloves garlic, chopped	1–2 cups watercress
3 tablespoons olive oil	2 cups chopped mushrooms
2 bay leaves, fresh if possible	1 cup chopped celery
3 cups chopped cabbage	½ cup chopped lettuce
2 cups sliced carrots	½–1 cup chopped fresh parsley
1 cup sliced white turnip	10–12 cups water

1. In a large stewing pot, fry the onions and garlic in the olive oil over medium heat until the onions are translucent, about 5 minutes. Add the bay leaves and continue to fry until the onions are golden, about 8 minutes total.

2. Add the vegetables and herbs to the pot in any combination, totaling about 12–15 cups.

3. Add enough water to just cover. Bring to a boil. Turn down the heat, cover, and simmer for 1½–2 hours. Remove from the heat. Let cool.

4. Strain the broth from the vegetables. Discard the vegetables.

5. Freeze the broth in small containers (approximately ½ cup size) for easy use. We freeze the broth in ice-cube trays and store the frozen cubes in a plastic bag.

Recipes, Stories & Commentary

Salads and Vegetables

Salads tend to be eaten raw, while vegetables are usually cooked, but the line of demarcation between the two has always been a thin one. Beets, peas, and spinach, for example, are served both cold and hot; they can stand alone as a main dish or be mixed with other ingredients. Lettuce can be eaten cold in a salad or fried in oil, and its stalks can be boiled with lots of sugar to make a conserve.[1]

Spanish culinary traditions and terminology complicate matters further. Spanish categories overlap: an *hierba* is a grass or an herb; a *legumbre* is a vegetable, but especially a legume; *verdura* gives the sense of something green; while an *hortaliza* is almost anything that grows in the *huerta,* or garden. All of these terms were used in the Middle Ages, sometimes interchangeably. Enrique de Villena's *Arte cisoria* (*The Art of Carving*) lists twenty "*yerbas,*" including thistle, carrots, lettuce, turnips, onions, garlic, borage, purslane, fennel, caraway, and mustard.[2] The seventeenth-century dictionary writer Covarrubias even uses the same two examples—lettuce and radishes—to illustrate two different categories, *verduras* and *hortalizas*. For Covarrubias, the *legumbre* has fruit that develops in a pod, while *hierba* denotes produce without stalks that can be either cooked in stews or served raw in salads.[3]

In the late Middle Ages and Renaissance, salads must have been ubiquitous. The occasional references suggest that they included a wider variety of ingredients than are common today. Covarrubias defines "salad" (*ensalada*) as "different herbs, meats, salted [ingredients], fish, olives, conserves, condiments[,] egg yolks, borage, sugared almonds, and a great diversity of things. . . ."[4] He also tells us that its name derives from the custom of sprinkling the miscellany with salt (*sal*).[5] The single salad recipe in the late fourteenth-century cookbook from the kitchens of English King Richard II lists more than a dozen different ingredients, including some still-common greens and herbs such as parsley, garlic, onions, and watercress, and others not quite so common: fennel, leeks, borage, mint, rue, and purslane.[6] Renaissance literary references tell us about "sliced lettuces and carrots with oregano"[7] and "onion . . . artichoke . . . and chopped cucumber."[8] Sources such as these suggest that anything green and edible raw could be thrown into a salad, but that a salad was not limited to greens. Other ingredients depended only on what was seasonably available. In the temperate regions of the Iberian Peninsula, including the humid north where varieties of chard are common, people could count on salad greens during much of the year. Though rarely cited, seasonal varieties of lettuce were undoubtedly common in salads. People then believed that lettuce contained properties that calmed lust and thus it was the symbol for continence.[9]

No matter what went into the salad, salt, vinegar, and oil were its constant dressing, and this is still the norm on the Spanish table. The account ledger of a sixty-eight-day journey in 1352 from Estella to Seville lists the purchase of vinegar on forty-three occasions generally accompanying some reference to salad makings, such as lettuce, radishes, and rocket. According to a Spanish proverb, "To make a good salad, four men are needed: for the salt, a wise man; for the oil, a prodigal man; for the vinegar, a stingy man; and to mix it, a crazy man. . . ."[10] Granado's recipe for cooked white beans insists that if they are to be served as a salad one must add vinegar and oil.[11]

Elsewhere during the rest of the year, people largely consumed cabbage and root vegetables such as carrots, parsnips, and turnips. One popular proverb states, "There's nothing better than turnips with cabbage."[12] Radishes were so common that they gave their name to several Iberian towns, such as the Salamancan and Leonese Rabanal. Other proverbs substantiate the radish's popularity: "A tender radish, no matter the size, is good" and "There is no good life without radishes and candles."[13] Covarrubias adds that radishes help people suffering from jaundice.[14]

The list of vegetables common in Roman Iberia was expanded when the Muslims introduced Eastern products, notably the chickpea and the eggplant.[15] The *Al-Andalus* cookbook gives a good sense of the vegetables commonly consumed in Islamic Spain. Its "garden recipe" is for a green dish to be made from whatever happened to be in the garden. The author lists for summer: chard, squash, eggplant, fennel, and melon; for spring he suggests lettuce, fennel, fresh beans, spinach, chard, and cilantro. The directions make clear that any combination of these also could be used to make a vegetable broth which was thickened with eggs.[16] The vegetables mentioned in the rest of his book, such as cauliflower, turnips, artichokes, squash, and spinach, are generally a part of a stew or a seasoning for meat. One notable departure is an emphasis on the eggplant, for which the *Al-Andalus* cookbook offers more than a dozen recipes.

A common characteristic of medieval cookbooks has been thought to be the scant attention they give to vegetables as stand-alone foods.[17] However, two Christian Iberian cookbooks, *Sent soví* and Granado's, devote space to Lenten dishes featuring vegetables, usually prepared as thick stews. In fact, Granado devotes an entire section to vegetable stews (*escudillas de yeruas*), with individual recipes for borage, chard, spinach, lettuce, chicory, malva, asparagus, squash, and chickpeas, some of which are made with meat broth and others with almond milk.[18] We also find recipes for artichokes, asparagus, leeks, squash, cabbage, and mushrooms.

The medieval table included whatever was edible in its season. In addition, some vegetables were stored, or preserved, for later consumption when it was too cold for the greens to grow. We may infer that greens and legumes growing around the house were not highly prized, but they were eaten and probably eaten in great quantities, especially on non-meat days in the Christian calendar.[19]

Jews and crypto-Jews shared the taste for salads and vegetables. There is no reason to believe that the salads eaten by the crypto-Jews differed in any way from those eaten by their old-Christian neighbors. On the other hand, based on the frequency of references specifically associating them with Iberian Jews, eggplant, greens like chard, and chickpeas, combining equally well with meat, fish, and fowl, seem to have been defining characteristics of medieval Sephardic vegetable cuisine.

Juana Núñez's Lechugas y Rábanos

Lucía Fernández alleged that for lunch Juana Núñez used to give them **"lettuce and radishes and cheese and cress** *and other things she does not remember."*[20]

Juana Núñez and her husband, Juan de Teva, a clothing merchant, practiced crypto-Judaism in Ciudad Real in the early sixteenth century. When the Inquisition's curiosity focused on the couple, Juan fled to Portugal. The Spanish Inquisition tried him in absentia and burned his effigy on September 7, 1513.[21] Juana was arrested on March 3, 1512, and her trial dragged on for two and a half years. Juana got along poorly with her neighbors, and the pettiness of their squabbles is evident in the malice with which they shared gossip about her with the Inquisition.

Malice aside, their testimony is rich in details about Juana's crypto-Jewish customs. For example, Juana and her closest women friends used to fast during daylight hours on Mondays and Thursdays. According to one neighbor, in the afternoons when Juana's sons Hernandico (twelve years old) and Antonito (thirteen years old) came home from school, to show their respect they would kiss their mother's hand in the Jewish fashion, and she would put her hand on their heads and draw it down across their faces, but without making the sign of the cross.

Above all, Juana tended to keep the Sabbath fully, on Friday sweeping and scrubbing her house, preparing food to be kept warm until Saturday, and taking a bath with her crypto-Jewish friends María González and Luisa Fernández and their daughters. She heated water in a large tub, into which she sprinkled rosemary and orange peels. After the bath, according to her servant Lucía Fernández, wife of the shepherd Francisco de Lillo, she used to hop straight into bed with her husband without quarreling the way they did on other weeknights. She had several strategies to abstain from working during the Sabbath. Again according to Lucía, her favorite was to pretend she had a headache and to throw herself down on some pillows until Saturday afternoon, when she routinely recovered and invited her women friends to her house for a social late afternoon to talk and snack and make jokes about the Catholic mass. It was at these Sabbath gatherings that Juana used to serve this salad.

The Inquisition found Juana guilty of Judaizing, but because so many of the prosecution witnesses were shown to be biased against her, Juana's sentence was relatively light: to remain under house arrest, to wear the penitential San Benito robe, to abstain from wearing jewelry or any adornment, and to make confession a minimum of three times annually. Ten months later, at Juana's petition, even these minor sentences were commuted.

Juana Núñez's Lettuce and Radish Salad

Serves 4–6

Salad

- 1–2 ounces watercress
- ½ head green lettuce
- 2 cups torn-up other greens, such as a combination of radicchio, red lettuce, romaine, endive, or fennel
- 1 tablespoon chopped fresh mint
- 3–4 radishes, sliced
- 1–2 ounces grated hard cheese, such as Romano or Manchego
- 1–2 teaspoons coarsely ground sea salt

Dressing

- 1–2 teaspoons balsamic, cider, or red wine vinegar
- 3 tablespoons olive oil

1. Remove the stems from the watercress. Chop the leaves into bite-size pieces.
2. Tear the lettuce into bite-size pieces. Toss all the greens together in a large bowl.
3. Top with the radishes and cheese.
4. Sprinkle with the salt.
5. Make the dressing: Pour the vinegar into a jar; add the olive oil. Cover and shake vigorously.
6. Pour the dressing over the salad and toss well before serving, or pass a cruet at the table.

Salads and Vegetables

31

María Sánchez's Verduras

María Sánchez testified that on Saturday in Guadalupe she had seen "lots of conversa *women sitting by the doors of their houses eating* **greens with vinegar**.*"*[22]

María Sánchez, the widow of the butcher Diego Ximénez of Guadalupe, was herself tried in 1485–86. The most damaging testimony came from her daughter Inés, who was also a prisoner. She told inquisitors that her mother had most likely confessed to all their Judaizing customs except three: that after the baptism of her son Diego she had scrubbed off the chrism; that she frequently donated oil for the lamps in the synagogue in Trujillo; and that she had taken the crucifix that her now-deceased husband had hung at the foot of their bed and had thrown it in the privy. Inés reported that when she went into her mother's cell she found her despondent, moaning that she would be killed for what she had confessed. Inés said that she had asked her mother if she had mentioned the crucifix to the inquisitors, to which María replied, "Daughter, nobody knows it but you; so tell me if you talked about it, for if you didn't I won't say anything."[23] The fact that we have this datum proves that this attempt at collusion failed.

A principal witness against María was a serving girl who had become a confidante of one of María's daughters. The daughter explained to her in great detail how in the time before the founding of the Inquisition the local crypto-Jewish community was accustomed to observing the Sabbath, and how in the afternoons they used to gather in the doorway of someone's house to talk and munch on greens with vinegar.

María went to the stake on November 20, 1486.[24]

We have seen that the Spanish term *verdura* encompasses any edible green grown in the garden. The greens could have been eaten raw or cooked, sprinkled with vinegar or, perhaps, vinegar and oil. It is common in modern-day Spain to sprinkle vinegar over cooked green vegetables such as chard. Because we already have a number of clear references to salads that were eaten with vinegar, we have opted to interpret this reference to greens as a vegetable dish. Since we cannot be sure if the greens were cooked or not, we offer two recipes for this dish.

María Sánchez's Greens

As a Cold Dish
Serves 4

1 large bunch of greens (see Variations)
2 tablespoons other finely chopped
   fresh green herbs (see Variations)

1–2 tablespoons balsamic or red
   vinegar
½ teaspoon coarsely ground sea salt

1. Wash the greens and pat them dry. Cut them into bite-size pieces and place them and the herbs in a large bowl. You should have about 8 cups.
2. Sprinkle with the vinegar and sea salt.
3. Mix well and serve.

As a Hot Dish
Serves 4

1 large bunch of greens (see Variations)
1–3 tablespoons olive oil
2 tablespoons other finely chopped
   fresh green herbs (see Variations)

1–2 tablespoons balsamic or red
   vinegar
½ teaspoon coarsely ground sea salt

1. Wash the greens and pat them dry. Chop them into medium-size pieces.
2. In a medium skillet, heat the olive oil over medium heat. Toss in the greens and herbs and stir-fry briefly. Sprinkle the vinegar over the greens and stir it in. Continue to fry just until the vinegar has been absorbed, about 2 or 3 minutes.
3. Sprinkle with the salt and serve immediately.

VARIATIONS

Any green or combination of flavorful greens is possible. It is best to balance peppery or spicy flavors, like turnip, lovage, or mustard greens, with more bland ones, such as lettuces, radicchio, or spinach.

The herbs add diversity to the greens. Here are some possibilities:

2 tablespoons chopped chives or onions
1 teaspoon chopped fresh marjoram
½ teaspoon chopped fresh oregano

½ teaspoon chopped fresh dill or fennel
1 tablespoon chopped nasturtium leaves
2 teaspoons chopped fresh basil

María Alvarez's Acelgas Ahogadas en Aceite

In the Sorian city of Almazán in 1505, María Alvarez allegedly prepared **"Swiss chard,** *parboiling it in water and then frying it with* **onions** *in oil, and then boiling it again in the oil. And then she threw in water and* **grated bread crumbs and spices and egg yolks;** *and she cooked it until it got very thick."*[25]

Medieval recipes generally distinguished between spices, herbs, and greens. Greens grew locally and were eaten as what we today term "vegetables," generally in meat stews. The leaves of other plants, used for flavoring or for salads and not for bulk, were known as herbs.[26] These were grown in the garden, or picked on the mountainside, where even today wild thyme, rosemary, oregano, and anise scent the boots of the Iberian hiker. Spices, on the other hand, tended to be the seeds, bark, or roots of plants. Some popular spices—mace and grains of paradise, for example—were not native to Iberia and had to be imported. Because they were exploited commercially and represented a significant expense, they show up in household accounts and were often mentioned specifically by cookbook writers. Other spices, such as caraway, mustard, and cumin, were cultivated on the Peninsula.

Any devotee of medieval cookbooks will notice four things with regard to these flavorful additions. The first is that they are used everywhere: on meats and fish, in sauces and gravies, in pastries and soups. If a dish is prepared in six stages, each stage is likely to contain spices. Second is the enormous quantity of individual herbs and spices used. When medieval recipes specify amounts, which is rare, the measures given for seasonings astound the modern cook.[27] A cook faithful to the quantity of just the saffron specified in the *Al-Andalus* cookbook may need to take out a second mortgage. Third is the variety used, both in individual recipes and in the aggregate. An eggplant recipe in the *Al-Andalus* cookbook calls for dried and fresh cilantro, pepper, caraway, cumin, fennel, garlic, saffron, salt, citron leaves, rue, mint, and thyme.[28] Nola's sardine recipe requires pepper, ginger, saffron, almonds, pine nuts, parsley, and peppermint.[29] Last, and most problematical for the modern cook, is that medieval spices seemed to have been used in a number of fixed combinations so well known to cooks that there was rarely any need to list them individually in the recipe's directions. Some common combinations were given names: *salsa fina* contains ginger, cinnamon, pepper, cloves, mace, nutmeg, and saffron.[30] "Duke's powder" (*polvo de duque*) combines white sugar, cinnamon, ginger, and cloves.[31] Another version adds nutmeg, galingale, and cardamom as well.[32] Another mixture listed in Nola, *salsa de pago,* consists of ginger, cinnamon, cloves, grains of paradise, and saffron.[33] One of Nola's recipes for a roast stuffed chicken calls for ten separate seasonings (cinnamon, cloves, raisins, almonds, mint, parsley, saffron, sugar, rose water, and marjoram) plus an unspecified amount of *salsa fina*. The specific contexts of the generic references to "spices," which appear in hundreds of medieval recipes, must have been transparent to their audience, even though they are often opaque today.

Individual spices, and many herbs, were thought to have specific properties related to the body's four humors. They were important not only as flavorings but also to keep the body's essential fluids in balance. Many had medicinal properties as well, which led taxonomists like the lexicographer Covarrubias to define spices as "those drugs which come from the Indies with which we flavor stews, like clove, cinnamon, ginger and pepper; not only these, but any other medicinal substance which is sold by pharmacists. . . ."[34] Despite the modern myth, spices were not used in medieval kitchens to mask the unpleasantness of spoiled meat.[35]

Herbs and spices were known and used in antiquity: the Bible mentions several and the Talmud dozens more.[36] The wealthy Roman Apicius used them profligately. Locally grown products were probably always part of every region's cuisine, but there is good evidence that from as early as the tenth century Western Europeans had developed a craving for Eastern spices. An Iberian Muslim visiting the German city of Mainz, in the year 978, remarked about the quantity of spices for sale in the markets there and the role of the Jews in importing them from the Orient by way of Kiev. With the exotic tastes of the returning crusaders, the spice markets boomed. Jewish merchants participated in the Mediterranean and Indian Ocean spice trades in the eleventh through the thirteenth centuries, in the African spice trade in the fifteenth century, and in the American trade, which added so many new flavors to Europe, in the sixteenth.[37]

Iberia's Christian cooks did not have to go as far as the crusaders to acquire the taste for the highly spiced Islamic cuisine. Andalucía was a perfumed garden. As the *Al-Andalus* cookbook put it: "The knowledge of the use of spices is the principal base of the dishes of the kitchen, because it is the scent of cooking, and one builds on top of it."[38] The large-scale use of saffron as a colorant and of nuts, particularly ground almonds, are Islamic characteristics which northern European cooks also quickly adapted.[39] Three other aspects probably derive from the Islamic palate: the heavy use of sugar as a sweetener, of citrus fruits, and of scented essences like rose water or orange-blossom water to perfume the food.

It is unlikely that Iberian Jewish cooking was in any way special in its use of herbs and spices. The Inquisition's informants keyed on the principal ingredient of the main dish, its relation to the Jewish or Christian calendar of ritual, and a few foods—chard, chickpeas, eggplant—that old-Christians associated with Semitic cuisine. Spices did not attract their attention. Thus, given the pervasive imprecision with which most of the contributors reported these recipes to the Inquisition, two problems confronted us in preparing this book. Which spices to use? And in what amounts?

Our solutions were based on the following assumptions. Keeping the general principles that we have just outlined in mind, we searched for analogous recipes in cookbooks contemporary to Inquisition times. We concluded that in the kitchens of the socio-economic class of our contributors, the easily available Iberian seasonings would have been used a lot. These include thyme, rosemary, and oregano, caraway, and cilantro (dried and fresh leaves, as well as seeds), mustard, anise, fennel, citron, and saffron. Certain imported spices, like pepper and cinnamon, probably were available everywhere and were within the reach of the average budget. The account books of the Navarran travelers show near-daily purchases of garlic, pepper, and vinegar, and frequent purchases of mustard sauce.[40] The extant late medieval Iberian cookbooks also cite these ingredients in abundance and mention a host of others—like galingale, grains of paradise, and cubebs—somewhat less often. Spices appearing in more than 10 percent of *Sent soví*'s recipes are saffron, pepper, and ginger; those appearing in more than 20 percent of Nola's recipes are cinnamon, ginger, pepper, and saffron.[41]

Finally, as we prepared our recipes, we looked for some indications of quantities. When none existed, the proof was in the pudding, so to speak. We experimented with a variety of amounts until we found a balance of flavors which would not occlude the dish's main ingredients.

María Alvarez's Boiled and Fried Swiss Chard

1 large bunch of Swiss chard (about 60
  leaves and stems)
5–6 tablespoons olive oil, plus more if
  needed
1–1½ cups finely chopped onions
2 teaspoons caraway seeds

1 teaspoon cinnamon
1 tablespoon Salsa Fina *(page 23)*
10 egg yolks, beaten
⅔–¾ cup water
⅔ cup ground bread crumbs

1. Wash and drain the chard leaves and stems. Chop them into 1-inch
   pieces. Simmer them for 15 minutes in a large, covered pan of water.
   Drain and press out the excess water. This should make about 3 cups
   of greens.

2. In a large skillet, heat the olive oil over medium heat. Add the onions
   and stir-fry until just transparent, about 4 to 5 minutes.

3. Add the chard and continue to fry. If the oil is completely absorbed,
   add 1–2 tablespoons more.

4. Grind the spices together. Add them to the frying chard and mix them
   in evenly.

5. Mix the egg yolks and water. Add the bread crumbs to the liquid and
   stir briskly.

6. Stir the egg yolk mixture quickly into the frying chard. Move the skillet
   back and forth over the heat so that the resulting omelet won't stick.

7. Reduce the heat to low and continue cooking for about 5 minutes, or
   until the omelet is firm. With a spatula, turn the omelet over and cook
   another 5 minutes. Serve warm.

VARIATION

This dish can also be baked. Complete the first 5 steps of the recipe.

6. Remove the frying pan from the heat and allow the chard to cool.
7. Preheat the oven to 350°. Pour 1 tablespoon oil into a medium ovenproof
   glass casserole or two small ones. Put the casserole(s) into the oven to heat.
8. Combine the chard with the egg yolk mixture in a bowl and then pour it
   into the heated casserole(s).
9. Bake for 20 minutes, or until the bottom of the casserole begins to turn
   golden brown. Serve hot or cold.

*Salads and
Vegetables*

Mayor González's Cazuela de Huevos y Zanahorias

Juana García

testified that Mayor

González cooked

*"a **casserole of eggs***

and carrots and

spices and other

***things**" on Friday*

and ate it cold on

Saturday.[42]

Pedro Núñez Franco and his wife, Mayor González, lived in a large house in Ciudad Real next to a convent. Juana García, wife of the laborer Miguel Rodríguez of Las Casas, a village near Ciudad Real, had a fourteen-year-old son, Miguel, who served in the Núñez Franco household. One Friday in 1510, just before Christmas, when Juana went to visit her son, she observed Núñez Franco slaughtering a goose in the Jewish fashion by cutting its throat.

During the visits to her son, Juana made note of several other Judaizing customs of the González-Núñez Franco family. On Fridays they kept a lamp burning all night long, and she reported hearing Mayor ask the serving girls to put a new wick in the lamp. She said that she heard Pedro Núñez Franco singing in bed, but that she couldn't understand the words. She also related that she had seen a group gather at the home for a Sabbath meal, and she listed by name the thirteen people at the table.

Another Friday she saw Mayor González prepare this Sabbath dish for the family. When questioned further, she stated that it may also have had meat in it, but that she personally had not seen it.[43]

Even though inquisitors found little evidence of Mayor's Judaizing after 1483, nonetheless she was sentenced to life imprisonment and confiscation of property. This was later reduced to certain penances, and eventually commuted altogether.

Mayor González's Casserole of Eggs and Carrots

2 cups baby carrots

2 cups Vegetable Broth (page 24)

2 hard-boiled eggs, coarsely diced

2 eggs, beaten

2 green onions, thinly sliced (about 2 tablespoons)

½ cup grated Romano cheese

½ teaspoon ground dried cardamom

¼ teaspoon cloves (optional)

½ teaspoon salt

½ teaspoon pepper

1 tablespoon bread crumbs or matza meal

1. Boil the carrots in the vegetable broth for 10 minutes, or until fork-tender. Drain, reserving 2 tablespoons of the liquid. Cool. Slice the carrots lengthwise in half or in thirds.

2. In a bowl, combine the carrots, hard-boiled eggs, and onions. Add the beaten eggs.

3. Preheat the oven to 350°. In another bowl, mix the cheese and spices. Add the bread crumbs and stir. Pour the dry mixture into the carrot mixture and combine.

4. Lightly grease an 8-inch round or square (glass) ovenproof baking pan. Place the mixture in the pan and level it out. It should be about 1 inch thick. Bake 45–60 minutes, or until the bottom just begins to brown.

5. Refrigerate until ready to serve, at least 6 hours.

NOTE

This dish can be served hot as well.

VARIATIONS

This casserole recipe is the most basic one.

Try adding either or both of the following ingredients in step 2:

½ cup raisins

¼ cup sliced olives

Sprinkle 1 tablespoon cinnamon-sugar over the top before baking.

Salads and Vegetables

Juan Sánchez Exarch's Hamín de Berzas

The converso Juan

Sánchez Exarch

was accused of

"ceremonially (i.e.,

with religious intent)

eating a Sabbath

dish called **hamín,**

made of **chickpeas**

and spinach or

cabbage."[44]

Juan Sánchez Exarch's trial began in Teruel in October of 1484. The first nineteen of the fifty-three articles of his indictment give a good picture of the breadth of Judaizing activities in the region just prior to the 1492 expulsion.

1. Sánchez Exarch keeps the Sabbath as the Jews do.

2. Specifically, on the Sabbath he eats food cooked on Friday and warmed over.

3. He eats this food, called *hamín*, ceremonially.

4. He lights clean lamps on Friday nights as the Jews do.

5. On the Sabbath he puts on clean clothes and clean tablecloths on the table.

6. On the Sabbath he abstains from selling and making contracts or handling money.

7. On the Sabbath he won't walk, but he walks about on Sunday to show his scorn for that holy day.

8. On the Sabbath he meets with the Jews.

9. He celebrates the Passover, on that day eating matza, celery, and lettuce, as the Jews do.

10. He gets unleavened bread from the Jewish neighborhood on the Passover.

11. He buys new dishes for the Passover.

12. He does everything else the Jews do on Passover.

13. He celebrates the Festival of Booths.

14. He makes a hut of branches outside his house; if he can't do it there, he goes to the home of a Jewish relative or a bad Christian to construct the hut, and eats almond pastries with them.

15. He also celebrates the Festival of the Horn,[45] of Haman, and of Taamuz when the holy temple was lost.

16. He keeps the fasts of *Quipuz*, called the Pardoning Fast, and of Haman, and of Taamuz, and then in the evening breaks his fast with beef or chicken.

17. He does not observe the holidays of the Church, nor keep the Christian fasts.

18. He believes more in Moses than in Jesus, and prays in Hebrew, swaying back and forth, facing the east.

19. He washes his hands before praying.[46]

After a two-year trial and an extensive confession in which he confirmed these and other practices, Sánchez Exarch was condemned to death in 1486. His children and grandchildren were disqualified from ever holding public office or entering the clergy

Juan Sánchez Exarch's Cabbage Stew

Serves 4

1–1¼ pounds green cabbage
6 tablespoons olive oil
6 cloves garlic, diced
2 (19-ounce) cans chickpeas, drained
1 cup broth

½ teaspoon salt
½ teaspoon pepper
1 teaspoon ground coriander
1 teaspoon ground cumin

1. Wash the cabbage and drain it. Cut it into 1–1½-inch pieces.

2. Heat the oil in a large stew pot over medium heat. Add the garlic and fry it until it begins to turn golden, about 6 minutes.

3. Add the cabbage. Stir-fry for 4–5 minutes over medium heat, until the cabbage begins to wilt.

4. Add the chickpeas, broth, salt, pepper, and spices. Cover the pan. Turn the heat to low.

5. Simmer for 1 hour, stirring occasionally. For less broth, uncover the pan the last 15 minutes of cooking. Serve hot.

NOTE

Although the Sánchez Exarch family ate this dish as a Sabbath stew, it can be cooked a shorter time (10–15 minutes) for a crisper cabbage.

Isabel Vélez's Olla de Acelgas con Queso

Isabel's father was evidently a first-generation convert who made his living as a toll collector. A servant noted that before going to bed he used to mutter phrases in Hebrew, which he followed with the Latin "Our Father."[48] A neighbor woman named Teresa, who served in the house, noted that when family members sat down to eat "she never heard them say any Christian prayers like the 'Ave María,' the 'Our Father,' the Creed, or the 'Hail Mary,' nor had she seen them cross themselves."[49]

When Isabel's father, Pedro Vélez, was dying, he reputedly asked to be buried in the Jewish fashion in virgin soil.[50] The neighbor Teresa noted that he had not received the last rites, and that no one in the family had recited any Catholic prayers as he lay dying.

The Church's Edicts of Grace, which included checklists of customs indicative of heresy, generally listed a number of Jewish funerary customs. This edict, from 1639, was promulgated in Mexico:

> [Judaizing is suspected] if when some person is at the point of death, he turns to the wall to await death and then [the corpse] is washed with warm water, shaving the beard and under the arms and other parts of the body, and attiring it with clean linen, under drawers, and shirt and cover, which is folded over the top, and putting a pillow with virgin soil under the head, or money in the mouth, or a misshapen pearl or some other thing. Or singing some funeral dirge or throwing out the water from the large jars and emptying all the containers with water in the house of the deceased and all other houses of the area as a Jewish custom; eating fish and olives on the floor behind the doors; not meat because of sorrow of their loss; not leaving the house for one year in accordance with the observance of the laws. Or if they are buried in virgin soil or in a Jewish cemetery.[51]

In their cross-examination of witnesses in the Pedro Vélez investigation, the inquisitors went right down the list. "No," the servant Teresa answered, "I did not see him wrapped in his shroud because I was not present, nor do I remember if they poured the water out of all the pitchers in the house when he died. . . . I did see that when it was time to eat they set a bushel basket covered with a cloth on the floor near the door, where I never saw them eat on any other day. And I saw them bring from the house of Luis Vélez, his son-in-law, the tailor, a new-Christian . . . a pot of chard and cheese and bread crumbs. . . . They also brought with them the dishes they served it on, and they brought them secretly, and when they went in . . .

*In Almazán in 1501, an anonymous witness reported that when Isabel Vélez's father died, the family sat at a low table near the door, and ate "a **casserole** made of **chard and bread crumbs and cheese**," which Isabel had prepared at home and brought to her father's house.[47]*

Salads and Vegetables

Luis Vélez said, 'Give me those dishes; I don't want people to see what we have hidden here.'"[52]

Typical of Iberian Jewish funerals was a communal meal eaten in the house of the deceased following the burial. The food most commonly served was hard-boiled eggs, in accordance with the dictates of the legal compendium *Kol Bo* (1490), which says that they are "symbolic of the roundness of the world and the mourning which comes to us all."[53] Also common was the consumption of fish, which is reported at funerals of Judaizers from the 1480s and over the next two hundred years.[54] Even more important seems to have been the specific prohibition against eating meat, the consumption of which was a sign of ostentation and not mourning. After funerals in Majorca in the 1670s, Judaizers ate rice fried in olive oil, which they called "funeral food."[55] Juan de Chinchilla testified in 1484 that at funerals in Ciudad Real the Christians would sit "at their table where they ate chicken, and the converts on the floor ate chickpeas and eggs."[56] At funerals in the 1630s the Mexican Váez family ate raisins, almonds, salad, home-made bread, and chocolate, but never any meat.[57] And the Vélez family in Almazán prepared this dish of chard and cheese.

We have found evidence of one other culinary custom related to dying. In Mexico in the 1640s crypto-Jews in the Machorro clan often fasted on the anniversary of a loved one's death. The night before the fast they ate a soup made of bread soaked in water and salt.[58]

Isabel Vélez's Chard and Cheese Casserole

2–3 tablespoons olive oil
2 cloves garlic, diced
1 medium onion, chopped
6 cups chopped chard (about 15
    stalks), chopped in 1-inch pieces

¼ cup grated hard cheese, such as
    Manchego or Romano
¼ cup fine bread crumbs
½ teaspoon salt
6 thin slices Cheddar Cheese (about
    3 ounces), to top the casserole

1. Heat the oil in a medium-size ovenproof pan. Add the garlic; stir-fry 3 minutes. Add the onion and continue to stir-fry until the onion is translucent, about 5 minutes. Add the chard. Stir gently until the chard reduces by half, about 10 minutes. Remove from the heat.

2. Preheat the oven to 325°. Mix the cheese, bread crumbs, and salt in a bowl to combine them evenly.

3. Smooth the chard mixture evenly into the pan. Stir half the cheese mixture into the chard. Pour the rest of the cheese mixture on top. Top with the Cheddar slices.

4. Bake in the oven 10 minutes, or until the cheese is melted. Serve hot.

VARIATION

This basic recipe invites variations. It is likely that several spices were used in its preparation in the Vélez household. Try adding 1–2 teaspoons *Salsa Fina* (page 23).

*Salads and
Vegetables*

The Cota Wedding Berenjena con Acelguilla

"At the wedding," conversos *were served ". . . lots of eggplant and Swiss chard seasoned with saffron."*[59]

L ate fifteenth-century *conversos* were evidently so fond of eggplant that the satirical literature of the day is filled with pointed references to this predilection. Typical is the burlesque poem by Rodrigo Cota about a *converso* wedding at which the guests were served this vegetable.

The courts that grouped around fifteenth-century Castilian kings included a number of poets and court fools who entertained the monarch, the nobility, and each other with scurrilous satiric poetry that insulted women, the handicapped, *conversos,* and other marginalized members of their society, often using some topical event—a boar hunt, a dance, a wedding—as a pretext for skewering people who were well known at court. Many of the poets and fools themselves were *conversos,* and everyone in that milieu knew enough about Jewish customs to understand the burlesque allusions to Jewish practice. These poetic jibes, later gathered into songbooks known as *Cancioneros,* often provide interesting anthropological data about contemporary customs, including Jewish cooking.

The sixty-five-stanza poem that alludes to this dish poked none-too-gentle fun at *conversos* who attended the wedding of the grandson of Diego Arias Dávila,[60] the notorious *converso* finance minister of King Enrique IV of Castile, to a girl related to the family of Cardinal Pedro González de Mendoza. Rodrigo Cota, who was not invited to the wedding, decided to make his pique public with this poem. The recipe is in stanzas 41–42.

En la boda desta aljama	At this Jewish wedding party
no se comió peliagudo	bristly pig was not consumed;
ni pescado sin escama	not one single scaleless fish
en quanto'l marido pudo;	went down the gullet of the groom;
sino mucha verengena	instead, an eggplant casserole
y açafrán con alçelguilla.	with saffron and Swiss chard;
Quien "¡Jesu!" diga en la çena,	and whoever swore by "Jesus"
que no coma albondiguilla.	from the meatball pot was barred.

The Cota Wedding Eggplant with Chard

Serves 6

1 medium eggplant (about 2 pounds)
2 tablespoons salt
1 large bunch of Swiss chard (about 50
   leaves and stems)
2 tablespoons olive oil
½ teaspoon saffron threads

1 medium onion, sliced
½ cup water or Vegetable Broth
   (page 24)
1 teaspoon salt
¼ teaspoon white pepper

1. Peel the eggplant and cut it into ¼-inch-thick slices. Soak it 30 minutes
   in heavily salted cold water (about 2 tablespoons salt to 3 cups water).
   You may have to put a weight on the eggplant to keep it from bobbing
   to the surface. Rinse it thoroughly three or four times. Press out as
   much liquid as possible between paper towels.

2. Wash the Swiss chard. Cut the large stems into 1-inch lengths.

3. Heat the olive oil and saffron in a large frying pan over medium-low
   heat until the oil begins to turn yellow, about 4 to 5 minutes.

4. Sauté the onion and chard stems in the saffroned oil until they are
   translucent, about 10 minutes. Add the eggplant slices.

5. Add the water or broth. Cover. Boil for 8 minutes. Turn the heat to
   low and simmer for 15 minutes more. Meanwhile, chop the chard
   leaves into 1-inch pieces.

6. Add the chopped chard leaves, cover, and simmer for an additional
   3 minutes. Season with salt and pepper. Serve hot.

Berenjenas con Huevos

Conversos *were*

frequently accused

of eating "**casseroles**

of **eggplant with**

eggs."[61]

The eggplant (*berenjena*) belongs to the rather large horticultural family of *Solanum,* which also includes the potato and nightshade. *Melongena* is the term that designates the eggplant, and there are several varieties. It was known in the eastern Mediterranean before the tenth century.[62]

Eggplant appeared relatively early in the Hispanic Middle Ages as well. Legend has it that the Muslims who had conquered the Peninsula early in the eighth century brought a poisonous eggplant variety purposefully to kill the Christians.[63] Eggplant of the nontoxic sort is documented in Iberia in the twelfth century. The thirteenth-century *Al-Andalus* cookbook contains more than a dozen eggplant recipes, including one called "Eggplant, Jewish Style."[64] Apparently the eggplant was cultivated first on the east coast of the Peninsula in Cataluña and then spread throughout the south. The fourteenth-century *Sent soví* has four recipes for eggplant[65] and Nola's early sixteenth-century Catalán cookbook gives six recipes. Sixteenth-century comments on the eggplant speak of varieties colored white, yellow, and purple. Perhaps the earliest reference to the eggplant in European non-Iberian sources is found in a 1570 Italian menu for Pope Pius V in which it was combined with various spices in a sauce accompanying fried veal liver and sweetbreads.[66]

Common lore held the eggplant in low esteem, as Covarrubias corroborated when he said that eggplants have insipid taste and bad texture and engender melancholy, making for a sad spirit.[67] What is crystal clear is that in Iberia the eggplant was closely associated with Semitic cultures. One of Nola's recipes is called *Berenjena ala morisca* ("Eggplant Moorish Style"). From as early as the fifteenth century, Toledo—considered the heartland of medieval Iberian Semitic culture—was proverbially linked to eggplant.[68] In the second volume of *Don Quijote* (1615) the imaginary Muslim chronicler Cide Hamete Benengeli is, by slip of Sancho's tongue, called "Cide Hamete *Berenjena*."[69]

The following recipe emphasizes the reddish-purple color of the eggplant in contrast with the yellow of the egg yolks.

Eggplant and Eggs

Serves 6

1 medium eggplant (about 2 pounds)
2 tablespoons salt
3 tablespoons olive oil
1 clove garlic, chopped

3 hard-boiled Vermilioned Eggs (page
76) (see Notes)
Salt and pepper to taste

1. Cut the unpeeled eggplant into 1-inch cubes. Place them on two layers of paper toweling. Sprinkle them with the salt. Leave for 20–30 minutes. With paper towels, firmly pat the eggplant as dry as possible.

2. In a large skillet, heat the olive oil over high heat. Add the chopped garlic. Stir-fry for about 2 minutes.

3. Add the eggplant and fry slowly over medium heat for 10 minutes, stirring often.

4. Shell the hard-boiled eggs. Cut into eighths.

5. In a serving bowl, mix the eggplant and eggs. Season with salt and pepper.

NOTES

Traditional hard-boiled eggs can be substituted with little loss of flavor.

This dish can be served hot or cold. If served cold, a vinegar and oil dressing can be drizzled over the top.

Salads and
Vegetables

Catalina de Teva's Cazuela de Berenjenas Rellenas

*On the Sabbath
the women of the
Alfonso Alvarez
family of Ciudad
Real used to lunch
on "a **casserole** of
stuffed eggplant
which was eaten
cold, and grapes,
and fruit."[70]*

Catalina de Teva was identified as a Judaizer in testimony given in the 1511 and 1513 trials of her friend María González, the wife of Pedro de Villarreal. María herself provided a good deal of information about the group of her friends who used to gather to spend the Sabbath together in one or another of their houses. Frequently the group included Catalina de Teva, Ximon de la Çarça's aunt Marina de Herrera, the spice dealer Diego Alvarez's wife Graçia de Teva, and the tax farmer Fernando de Alvarez's wife Leonor.[71] Among the information about this group that emerged in María's testimony are the following insights into the women's activities:

- The Çarças' black slave had complained to María that her mistress, Catalina de Teva, would not let her do the family wash on Saturday, and sometimes used to send her out to the vineyards for the day so that she wouldn't see what the Çarças were doing at home.

- Marina de Herrera used to read Jewish prayers from a little book, which she hid when María came in.

- Leonor Alvarez used to deck herself out for the Sabbath with a clean shirt and head scarf, and a festival sash. One day María González found her plucking her eyebrows. When María said she looked like a queen, or as if it were a festival Sunday, Leonor haughtily retorted that "women who had given birth to sons had the right to dress up."[72]

María testified that on one Sabbath afternoon in 1509 she had visited the home of Ximon de la Çarça, where she found his wife, Catalina de Teva, with her usual group, all dressed in their best clothes, relaxing and enjoying themselves and eating this eggplant casserole, which had been prepared the day before. Although the fruit cited in this reference seems to have been eaten as a snack, contemporary references suggest that fresh fruits in season were also added to vegetable casseroles, as we have done in the following recipe.

*A Drizzle
of Honey*

Catalina de Teva's Stuffed Eggplant Casserole

Serves 4

1 medium eggplant (about 2 pounds)
3–4 tablespoons olive oil, plus more if needed
1 clove garlic, finely minced
1 stalk celery, finely sliced
¼ cup sliced mushrooms
¼ teaspoon dried sage, crumbled
¼ teaspoon dried rosemary

¼ cup ground almonds
1 pear, diced
1 apple, diced
¼ cup broth
2 teaspoons red wine vinegar
2 tablespoons bread crumbs
½ cup water

1. Cut the eggplant in half lengthwise. Scoop out and save the seeds and pulp. Set the two cavities aside, cut side down. Chop the pulp finely.

2. In a large skillet, heat the olive oil over medium low heat. Add the garlic and fry gently for about 3 minutes. Add the celery, mushrooms, and eggplant pulp and seeds. Fry about 5 minutes, until the celery is fork-tender. Add more oil if necessary.

3. Meanwhile, mix together the sage, rosemary, and almonds. Pour them into the frying mixture and combine well. Add the diced apple and pear, the broth, vinegar, and bread crumbs. Continue to cook another 5–6 minutes, until the flavors meld and the stuffing mixture begins to hang together.

4. Preheat the oven to 350°. Place the eggplant cavities, side by side, cut side up, in an ovenproof casserole. Fill them with the stuffing mix. Add the water to the bottom of the casserole dish. Cover with aluminum foil.

5. Bake 20 minutes. Take off the aluminum foil and bake another 10 minutes, until the stuffing becomes firm.

NOTE

This dish may be served hot or cold. If you intend to serve it cold, put the baked eggplant on top of pieces of paper towels so that they may absorb any water. Cover lightly with plastic wrap and refrigerate.

VARIATION

You may substitute ⅓ cup diced dried apricots or ⅓ cup raisins for the apple.

Salads and Vegetables

51

Isabel González's Berenjenas con Cebolla

Isabel González, tried by the Inquisition in Ciudad Real in 1511, allegedly "used to cook on Friday for the Sabbath **stews** *... with* **eggplant and onions and coriander and spices.** *"* [73]

Beatriz and Isabel González, the daughters of Fernán González, voluntarily confessed to Judaizing during the first wave of trials in Ciudad Real in 1483–84. Among the particulars of their confessions are that they koshered their meat; that they dressed up for the Sabbath and lit candles; and that they celebrated Yom Kippur and Passover. During their trials they successfully pled for mercy, claiming that their extreme youth had led them to imitate the adult Judaizers in their family without giving the matter serious thought.

Beginning in 1511, the Ciudad Real Tribunal reopened cases against suspected relapsed heretics and indicted the González sisters again. This time, however, the Inquisition had to try them in absentia, because when the sisters became aware of the investigation, they fled to Portugal where Beatriz's husband Juan de la Sierra had a business selling saltpeter to King Manuel I. By then Isabel was a widow, for her husband, Rodrigo de Villarrubia, had been tried and burned by the Inquisition in the late 1490s. One witness reported that Isabel considered her husband a martyr and believed that false testimony had condemned him. Whenever she spoke of him she burst into tears. [74]

There is no question that the family continued to self-identify as Jews and to practice as many Jewish customs as they were able. Catalina Martín, who served in the González house for three years, reported, for example, that "they celebrated Friday nights and Saturdays, when they did no work, and they put on clean shirts and holiday dresses and they decked themselves out like it was a Sunday, or a [Christian] festival; and on Saturdays they did no cooking, and would not even let [her] or a black slave who worked for the family make a fire." [75] They would not eat from any utensil used by their servants, nor would they drink from a jar that the servants might have used. They would not let their clothing and the servants' clothes be washed in the same tub. Catalina also described how Beatriz and Isabel used to pray, their shoulders covered with linen cloths, lowering and raising their heads and swaying forward and backward. [76]

A Drizzle of Honey

This recipe for Sabbath eggplant casserole is part of Catalina Martín's testimony against the sisters.

Isabel González's Eggplant and Onion Stew

1 medium eggplant (about 2 pounds)
2 tablespoons salt
2 cups chicken broth (see Variations)
2 medium onions, quartered
1 (1½-inch) stick cinnamon
3 whole white cardamom pods (see
    Variations)

½ teaspoon ground dried coriander
    (see Variations)
1 teaspoon dried cilantro leaves
¼ teaspoon ground cloves (see
    Variations)

1. Peel the eggplant. Cut it into ½-inch-thick slices. Soak for 30 minutes
   in salted water (about 2 tablespoons salt to 3 cups water). You may have
   to put a weight on the eggplant to keep it from bobbing to the surface.
   Rinse the eggplant three or four times in cold water, and press the slices
   between paper towels to remove the excess liquid. Cut the eggplant
   slices into ¾-inch cubes.

2. Place the eggplant in a saucepan with the chicken broth. Add the onion
   quarters. Bring to a boil, reduce the heat to low, cover the pan, and simmer for 25 minutes, stirring occasionally.

3. Remove the lid. Stir in the five seasonings, and continue to simmer for
   another 30–40 minutes.

NOTES

Serve over rice or couscous.

This dish is good served hot or cold.

VARIATIONS

This stew may be thickened by adding 1 piece of toasted bread that has been
soaked in 4 tablespoons white vinegar (see pages 16–17 for more about
thickeners).

Instead of the cardamom, coriander, and cloves, substitute:

1 teaspoon ground caraway seeds and ½ teaspoon ground fennel seeds
or
½ teaspoon ginger and ½ teaspoon pepper

For the chicken broth you can substitute meat stock or vegetable broth.

*Salads and
Vegetables*

Aldonza Laínez's Olla de Nabos con Queso

*Aldonza Laínez of Almazán served some workmen "a **casserole** made of **turnips and grated cheese.**"*[77]

Once day in the spring of 1504 several workmen had come to Aldonza's house for lunch before going up to plow their vineyards. When Aldonza had her black slave, Angelina, spoon out this dish, the workmen laughed at her, pointing out that she could not serve cheese during Lent.

In addition to disregarding Lenten rules, Aldonza evidently preserved a number of Jewish customs. One neighbor saw her "seated at the entrance to her . . . kitchen, with a white linen cloth spread out over her knees, covering her skirt, and on it a whole leg of lamb, or of goat, and a knife next to it, and it was cut open; and she was holding it with one hand and with her nails or the fingers of the other she was digging out all of the fat and the large vein."[78] Another remarked how Aldonza pinched her nose whenever she smelled pork cooking and boiled any utensils that might have come in contact with pork. Martín de Ortega heard Aldonza say she did not have to go to mass because she had a prayerbook at home, and that when her family were Jews they had everything they needed, but now they lived in poverty. A neighbor named Olalla heard Aldonza say of her daughter Orobuena, who had died before the family converted, that "she wished her well in paradise,"[79] the implication being that having died as a Jew she would have to be in hell, not paradise. Another woman, who used to go to Aldonza's house to spin thread with her, said that once she heard her lamenting her change of religion and sighing, "Old Testament, alas, Old Testament. . . . Cursed be the one who prohibited the Old Testament."[80] Still another neighbor heard her cursing the expulsion of the Jews, which she called an "evil day."[81]

Aldonza Lainez's Turnip and Cheese Casserole

Serves 4

1½ pounds turnips (1 large white
   turnip or 4–5 smaller purple-
   topped turnips)

Spice Mixture

¼ teaspoon galingale

½ teaspoon caraway seeds

¼ teaspoon cinnamon

½ teaspoon salt

4 ounces cream cheese, softened

½ cup cottage cheese

¼ cup grated Manchego or Romano
   cheese

1 egg, beaten

¼ cup coarsely ground bread crumbs
   (optional)

1. Preheat the oven to 350°.

2. Pare the turnip(s). Slice thinly by hand or with a food processor. In a large pan of water, parboil the slices for 6–8 minutes over medium heat. Remove and drain.

3. Combine the four spices and grind them together.

4. In large bowl, combine the cheeses, egg, spice mixture, and bread crumbs, if you are using them. Stir until well mixed. Add the drained turnip slices. Spoon into an ungreased 9 × 12-inch glass ovenproof casserole dish.

5. Bake about 35 minutes or until it begins to turn golden brown on the bottom. Serve hot.

NOTE

The purple-topped turnips impart a slightly peppery flavor to this casserole.

VARIATION

Add any of the following for variety in step 4:

1 tablespoon capers

3 tablespoons ground almonds or pistachios

3 tablespoons chopped fresh cilantro

*Salads and
Vegetables*

Cebollas con Almodrote

The Spanish term *almodrote* apparently derives from the Latin *moretum,* related to the word mortar. The first-century Roman cookbook attributed to Apicius contains this recipe for "Mortaria" or "Moretaria": "Mint, rue, coriander, fennel, all fresh, lovage, pepper, honey, *liquamen.* If needed, add vinegar."[83] By its form, *almodrote* might also logically be an Arabic term, and this has been confirmed by modern lexicographers,[84] even though the thirteenth-century *Al-Andalus* cookbook written in the southern part of the Peninsula does not use the term to refer to any of its many sauces.

In medieval Cataluña, *almadroc* was a dish that included garlic and cheese. Nola offers a recipe for *almodrote,* a sauce for partridges, composed of cheese, garlic, eggs, and broth.[85] *Sent soví's* two recipes for *almedroch* are similar to Nola's sauce and, as *Sent soví's* editor Grewe suggests, they are much like the modern garlic *ali-oli* sauce.[86] The late sixteenth-century cookbook by Granado copies Nola's recipe, calling it *capirotada,* and adds several variants, with garlic present only in the version called "common *capirotada.*" Granado's recipes are particularly helpful because he lists the spices by name. Covarrubias describes *almodrote* as "a certain sauce made from oil, garlic, cheese and other things,"[87] but the examples he chooses come from Latin sources, not Arabic.

To conclude, it appears that at least by the fifteenth century in the Iberian Peninsula, the aspect of grinding green ingredients in a mortar had been lost for *almodrote,* even though lexicographers still recognized the Latin etymological debt. Instead, the Iberian variants of *almodrote* centered on garlic and cheese. In Guadalupe in the 1480s, Fray Gonçalo Bringuylla was reported to have eaten "eggplant with *almodrote*" one Friday. The witness who named the dish responded to an inquisitior's query by saying that he didn't know "if it had cheese or garlic in it."[88]

Several modern Sephardic cookbooks contain eastern Mediterranean recipes called *almodrot* and *almodrote.* These are hot vegetable casseroles made with a generous amount of eggs and cheese, but without vinegar or garlic.[89]

Onions in sauce are also still popular throughout the Levantine Sephardic world, but they are not related to or called *almodrote.*[90] The modern recipes usually contain a sweet-sour sauce of lemon and sugar and sometimes are based on tomato paste.

. . .

It is difficult to know whether the popular fifteenth-century Castilian crypto-Jewish dish was served hot or as a cold salad. As a result, we offer four recipes for this dish. The first is the basic *almodrote* sauce. The second, a kind of salad that is served cold, and the third, a salad served hot, emphasize the green nature of the dish. The fourth, based on the ingredients listed by Covarrubias and Granado, is intended to be served hot as a vegetable.

Almodrote

Makes 2 cups sauce

1 cup grated Romano cheese or a
    combination of Romano and
    Parmesan
¼ cup bread crumbs
3 cloves garlic, chopped

6 hard-boiled egg yolks
2 tablespoons olive oil
1 cup warm Vegetable Broth (page 24)
    or water
Salt and pepper to taste

1. In a food processor, mix the cheese and bread crumbs. Add the garlic, making sure the garlic gets thoroughly minced and combined.

2. Add the egg yolks and combine thoroughly. Gradually add the olive oil.

3. Continue mixing, adding the broth slowly, 1 tablespoon at a time (14–16 tablespoons should make a sauce the consistency of creamy dressing).

4. Season with salt and pepper.

NOTES

Refrigerate the sauce, tightly covered, until ready to use, up to 1 week.

Allow the sauce to come to room temperature before using.

If the sauce has thickened, slowly thin with cool broth or water to the consistency of a creamy dressing.

VARIATION

For an even spicier sauce, use four cloves of garlic.

Onions in Almodrote

As a Cold Salad
Serves 4

1 tablespoon olive oil
2 cups frozen pearl onions
2–3 cups chopped fresh mixed greens,
    including 1–2 cups chopped
    lettuce, ¼ cup chopped mint,

¼ cup chopped cilantro, ¼ cup
chopped fennel greens, ¼ cup
chopped lovage or celery greens, ⅛
cup chopped parsley (see Variation)
½ cup Almodrote (page 58)

1. In a medium skillet, heat oil over medium heat. Add the pearl onions. Fry 4–5 minutes, stirring often, until no more than two teaspoons of liquid remain in the pan and the onions begin to brown.
2. Cool the onions. Put the greens into a large bowl. Toss the cooled onions with the greens when ready to serve. Drizzle the *Almodrote* sauce over the top. Serve.

NOTE

If the sauce has thickened, slowly thin with cool broth to the consistency of a creamy dressing.

VARIATION

Other greens may be substituted.

As a Hot Salad
Serves 4

1 tablespoon olive oil
2 cups frozen pearl onions
2–3 cups chopped fresh mixed greens,
    including 1–2 cups chopped
    lettuce, ¼ cup chopped mint,

¼ cup chopped cilantro, ¼ cup
chopped fennel greens, ¼ cup
chopped lovage or celery greens, ⅛
cup chopped parsley (see Variation)
½ cup Almodrote (page 58)

1. In a large skillet, heat oil over medium heat. Add the pearl onions. Fry 4–5 minutes, stirring often, until the onions just begin to brown.
2. Warm the *almodrote* sauce gently, either over low heat in a small pan or at medium power in a microwave oven for 45 seconds. The sauce should be very warm but not boiling.

3. Add the greens to the frying onions in the skillet. Stir-fry 1–2 minutes over medium heat, until the greens are wilted. Turn them into a serving bowl and top them with the *almodrote*. Combine and serve immediately.

VARIATION

Other greens may be substituted.

As a Hot Vegetable
Serves 4

2 tablespoons olive oil
1 clove garlic, finely chopped
2 cups thinly sliced onions (see
  Variation)
½ teaspoon cinnamon
¼ teaspoon nutmeg

⅛ teaspoon cloves
½ teaspoon salt
¼ teaspoon pepper
½ cup Vegetable Broth (page 24)
4–5 tablespoons Almodrote
  (page 58)

1. Heat the olive oil over medium heat in a small skillet. Add the garlic and fry 2 minutes.

2. Add the sliced onions and stir-fry another 6–8 minutes, until the onions turn golden brown.

3. Add the spices and salt and pepper. Fry another minute, continuing to stir, making sure that the onions are coated with the spices.

4. Add the broth and boil on medium heat for about 6–8 minutes or until most of the liquid has evaporated. Stir frequently.

5. Turn the heat off. Stir in the *almodrote* sauce. Serve immediately.

NOTES

You can prepare steps **1–4** and refrigerate the onions for several hours or overnight.

Reheat the onions before adding the *almodrote* sauce.

VARIATION

Frozen pearl onions can be substituted. Fry them until most of the liquid has evaporated and the onions begin to brown.

Isabel García's Olla de Garbanzos

The chickpea (Spanish: *garbanzo*, Latin: *Cicer arietinum*) was a widespread staple in the ancient Mediterranean and the East. Roman writers Columella and Pliny both describe it. The first-century Roman cookbook writer Apicius devotes three recipes to the chickpea. The twelfth-century Iberian author Ibn al Awam mentions it in his book on agriculture, and the thirteenth-century writer and teacher Albertus Magnus describes red, white, and black chickpeas.[92] Several medieval treatises, such as the *Tractatus de modo preparandi*[93] and Chiquart's *On Cookery*,[94] tout soups made with chickpeas as being good for the infirm. The *Tacuinum sanitatis* contains an illustration of a sick person in bed waiting for the soup that is being made in the kitchen.[95] Yet chickpeas seem to have been favored primarily in the Mediterranean region, for English cookbooks of the same era do not contain recipes using them.

Even in Iberia chickpeas seem to have been more popular in Castile than in Cataluña or Portugal, since the medieval Portuguese cookbook apparently does not contain references to the chickpea.[96] Nola does not feature the chickpea, while the later Catalán cookbook by Diego Granado uses it sparingly[97] Among the recipes in the *Manual de mugeres,* clearly intended for noble circles, there is only one recipe that contains chickpeas. Its title, *Olla morisca* or "Moorish Pot," suggests that chickpeas were Muslim food, not normally eaten by Christian nobility. Although the thirteenth-century *Al-Andalus* cookbook calls the chickpea a food of country people and gluttons,[98] it features chickpeas in several recipes and it contains a recipe for a soup made with chickpea broth meant for those who have been fasting. All this leads us to believe that the chickpea was a staple of the lower classes and therefore not worth featuring in a cookbook for a more refined audience.

But the reality of *converso* cooking is that the chickpea was pervasive. A good, cheap source of protein, grown on the Peninsula, it is mentioned by witnesses as a basis for soup, in vegetable casseroles, with onions (as in this recipe), and in stews with beef, lamb, and fish. Here are two versions of Isabel García's recipe, using spices that were typical in the stews of the time and that contain sweet and sour flavors. The second recipe contains pomegranates, since they often appear in cookbooks of the period as a flavoring for vegetables.

In a 1520–23 trial, Isabel García, a *conversa from* Hita, was accused of making a one-pot Sabbath dish of **"chickpeas, onions, spices, and honey."**[91]

Isabel García's Chickpeas and Honey with Cilantro

Serves 4

1 (16-ounce) package frozen pearl onions or 2 medium onions, diced (see Notes)
1 fresh bay leaf (optional)
2 tablespoons olive oil
2 (19-ounce) cans chickpeas, drained
1 tablespoon dried thyme, ground
¾ teaspoon ground cardamom
¼ cup honey
¾ cup chopped fresh cilantro

1. In a large pan, sauté the onions and bay leaf, if you're using it, in the olive oil over medium-high heat 6–8 minutes, until the onion is golden.

2. Add the drained chickpeas, thyme, and cardamom. Cook over medium-low heat only until heated through (about 6 minutes). Remove the bay leaf, if you've used it.

3. Stir in the honey and simmer for 5 minutes, stirring occasionally.

4. Stir in the chopped cilantro and serve at once.

NOTES

The frozen pearl onions afford a nicer texture than the fresh onions, but they do not brown as readily.

This dish may be served hot or cold.

Isabel García's Chickpeas and Honey with Pomegranate

Serves 4

1 (16-ounce) package frozen pearl
    onions (see Notes)
2 tablespoons olive oil
1 (30-ounce) can chickpeas, drained

1 tablespoon honey
¼ teaspoon fresh ginger
¼ teaspoon cloves
Seeds and juice of 1 pomegranate

1. In a large pan, sauté the onions in the olive oil until golden, about 6–8 minutes.

2. Add the drained chickpeas, honey, spices, and the seeds and juice of the pomegranate. Simmer for 10 minutes over medium–low heat.

NOTES

The frozen pearl onions afford a nicer texture than the fresh onions, but they do not brown as readily.

This dish may be served hot or cold.

Salads and Vegetables

María González's Habas

As a rule the inquisitors applied torture only in cases where they thought a witness might be lying, or had not been fully forthcoming in his or her testimony. This, unfortunately, was the case with Pedro de Villarreal's wife, María González, who testified in several of the Judaizing cases in Ciudad Real in 1513. This particular allegation, about Judaizers snacking on fava beans on the Sabbath, was extracted under duress. One of the most frequently used tortures involved putting a thin cloth over the person's mouth, and then pouring in a pitcher of water, which forced the cloth into the throat and created a sensation of drowning. At intervals the cloth was roughly removed so that more questions could be asked. Here is a fragment of the verbatim testimony in María González's case, written down in third person without quotation marks by a scribe who was present at the questioning:

> *She said that everything that she had said about Costanza Núñez was true, and that she had truly seen her observing the Sabbath in Fernando de Córdoba's house. . . . She said why are they questioning her more, for she has already told the truth, and she wants only to die, and that she has told the truth for the sake of her soul. She was cautioned several times to tell the truth, for it would be better not to have been born than to tell a falsity. She said that she has not lied about anybody, and oh, God, have pity on her. Another pitcher of water was ordered. She said, I tell the truth, I have told the truth, I have already told you the truth, I speak the truth, what I have said is true, I tell you truly, I do not lie, I have not lied, I speak the truth. The jar was emptied. She repeated, I have told the truth.*[100]

A moment later María evidently wavered, for she confessed that she had lied previously in saying that one of her mother's books really belonged to Fernando de Córdoba. With that, the questioning continued.

> *Their Graces ordered the water to be brought and the cloth put in place. She said, Stop, I will tell you the truth. I tell you that I really couldn't stand the sight of Lorenzo Franco's wife; I wanted to see her ground to dust. She [María] was asked if what she said about her was true, and she replied that lots of what she said about her was because she was her enemy, except when she reported that one Sabbath in Rodrigo de Chillón's house they spent the afternoon idly eating fava beans; the other things she said because she wished her ill, because she is an evil woman.*[101]

Thirty-four days after this testimony was given María González was condemned to be burned at the stake, not so much for her Jewish customs, the sentencing document makes clear, as for retracting her confession and for withholding evidence. The sentence was carried out on September 7, 1513, in the Plaza de Zocodóver in Toledo.

This reference to beans is too vague for us to know how the beans were prepared or served. The fourteenth- and sixteenth-century Catalán cookbooks have a few recipes for beans. One of Granado's recipes instructs the cook to add vinegar and oil and pepper if the beans are to be served as a salad. One of Nola's recipes, made with almond milk, is clearly a sweet pottage. Therefore, for this dish we are offering two versions: the first as a cold salad and the second as a sweet vegetable dish.

María González's Beans

As a Cold Salad
Serves 2

½ cup dry white beans (see Note)
1¼ cups water
2 broth cubes (beef or vegetable)
½ onion, quartered

1 clove garlic, quartered
1 tablespoon olive oil
5 teaspoons balsamic vinegar
½ teaspoon black pepper

1. In a medium pot, combine the beans, water, broth cubes, onion, and garlic. Simmer covered for 2–2½ hours, or until the beans are tender.

2. Drain the beans. Add the oil, vinegar, and pepper. Stir. Refrigerate, preferably overnight. Serve cold.

NOTE

See how to prepare the dry beans, page 15.

VARIATION

The addition in step **2** of ¼ cup sliced celery, ¼ cup sliced carrots, and/or ¼ cup fresh peas or the like, will add interest to the dish.

As a Sweet Dish
Serves 2

½ cup dry white beans (see Notes)
1–1¼ cups Almond Milk (page 19)
1 teaspoon sugar
½ teaspoon salt

½ teaspoon black pepper
¾ teaspoon ground (dry) ginger
½ teaspoon cinnamon
1 teaspoon rose water

1. Combine the beans, almond milk, and sugar in a medium saucepan. Simmer covered for 2 hours or until just barely tender. There should be a little liquid in the bottom of the pan.

2. Add the spices and simmer another 10 minutes. The liquid will thicken.

3. Add the rose water. Simmer another 2 minutes. Serve.

NOTES

See how to prepare the dry beans, page 15.

For a creamier dish, mash the beans with a spoon when adding the spices.

Marquesa Badia's Faves Tenres

Marquesa, the wife of Pau Badia, was one of several *conversas* tried in Barcelona in 1491. There was little doubt that she was guilty as charged, for when she was arrested she confessed in great detail to her Judaizing activities.

Marquesa was thirty-eight years old when she was arrested. She told her inquisitors that from the time she reached the age of discretion, when she was eleven or twelve, until she was married at age sixteen, her mother had instructed her in the ways of the Law of Moses, and that for the first ten years of her marriage she had remained fairly observant. During her Judaizing years she always fasted for twenty-four hours on Yom Kippur, until the sight of the first stars told her the fast was over, and then the family broke the fast with chicken or fish. They also observed the Fast of Esther, and on Sukkot visited the booths of her Jewish neighbors. And she said that she used to recite a prayer that began "God of Abraham, Isaac and Jacob, have mercy on me and on all sinners. Amen."[103]

Like many people arrested by the Inquisition, Marquesa admitted having done the things she was accused of, but tried to shift the blame to someone else, preferably a relative who was already deceased and whose body was thus beyond the Inquisition's reach. Marquesa said that her mother's family kept the Sabbath strictly, and that although she had often wanted to work on Saturdays, her mother would not let her. She claimed that she herself had sometimes eaten scaleless fish, or rabbits, and that when her mother caught her she scolded her severely. Marquesa said that on Passover her mother ate unleavened bread for all eight days, but that she and her siblings only ate it the first day, because they were afraid that their servants would accuse them of not being good Christians. During her years at home Marquesa adopted her mother's scornful attitude toward all things Christian. She admitted that if they went to church it was only to give the appearance of being good Christians, for they did not really believe in the Catholic sacraments. For the same reason she and her mother and brothers used to show themselves at the front window when the Christian processions passed in the street. On saints' days they would visit the appropriate local shrine, but only to fool their neighbors, and afterward they would laugh about it. Marquesa claimed that her mother had told her that the reverence shown to the statue of Mary proved that Christians worshiped a hunk of stone.

*"She says they kept the Jewish Festival of the unleavened bread which lasts eight days and that her mother during all eight days always ate unleavened bread, and rice, and fish, and **tender beans** and properly slaughtered chicken, but she never ate meat from the butcher shop."*[102]

Salads and Vegetables

67

In short, she admitted to the acts, but said that they were not really her fault, because she and her sisters were too young to break from their mother's control, and that later, "when they were all married they lived a good life, and no servant in their homes could accuse them of having done anything wrong."[104]

The inquisitors bought her argument, for they recognized that many second-generation *conversos,* once they became adults, tried to acculturate as best they could and leave behind the ingrained customs of their unassimilable parents. Marquesa and her sisters were excommunicated and forced to publicly abjure and renounce all their past heretical practices, but then they were welcomed back into the bosom of the Church.

Our recipe for tender beans is found in *Sent soví.*[105] In contrast to María González's sweet beans, *Sent soví*'s *faves tenres* are more sweet and sour.

Marquesa Badia's Tender Beans

Serves 2

½ cup dry white beans (see Notes)
1½ cups water
1 cup Almond Milk (page 19)
1 teaspoon olive oil
1 teaspoon salt
¼ teaspoon pepper

1 teaspoon dried marjoram
1½ teaspoons dried basil or
    1 tablespoon chopped fresh
½ teaspoon grated ginger
3 tablespoons chopped fresh parsley
2 tablespoons balsamic vinegar

1. Place the beans and water in a medium pan, cover, and simmer gently for 20–30 minutes until they are fork-tender.

2. Remove them from the heat. Drain the beans in a colander. Return them to the pan and add the almond milk. Add the oil, salt, pepper, marjoram, basil, and ginger.

3. Heat the mixture over medium heat just until it boils. Remove it from the heat and stir in the parsley and vinegar. Serve.

NOTES

See how to prepare the dry beans, page 15.

This recipe is also good when made ahead and reheated or even served cold.

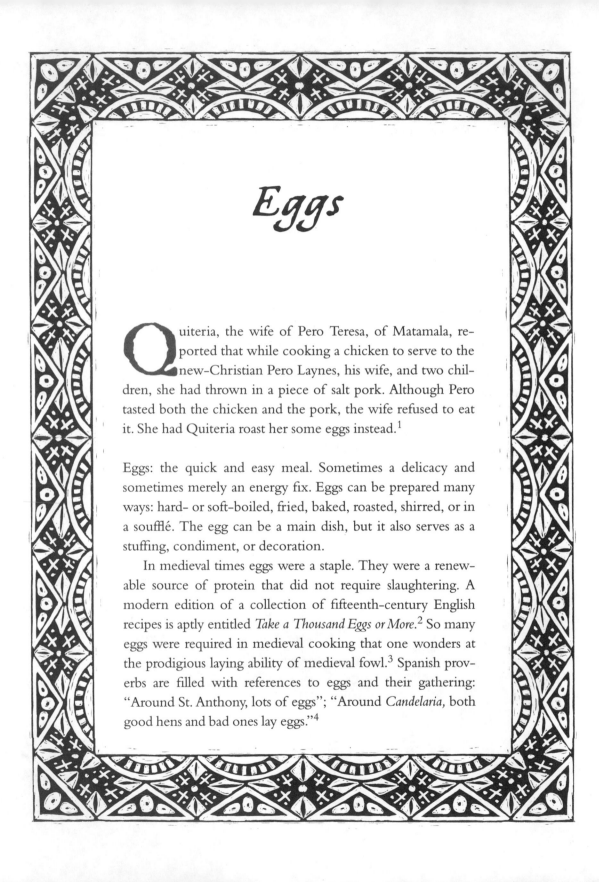

Eggs

Quiteria, the wife of Pero Teresa, of Matamala, reported that while cooking a chicken to serve to the new-Christian Pero Laynes, his wife, and two children, she had thrown in a piece of salt pork. Although Pero tasted both the chicken and the pork, the wife refused to eat it. She had Quiteria roast her some eggs instead.[1]

Eggs: the quick and easy meal. Sometimes a delicacy and sometimes merely an energy fix. Eggs can be prepared many ways: hard- or soft-boiled, fried, baked, roasted, shirred, or in a soufflé. The egg can be a main dish, but it also serves as a stuffing, condiment, or decoration.

In medieval times eggs were a staple. They were a renewable source of protein that did not require slaughtering. A modern edition of a collection of fifteenth-century English recipes is aptly entitled *Take a Thousand Eggs or More*.[2] So many eggs were required in medieval cooking that one wonders at the prodigious laying ability of medieval fowl.[3] Spanish proverbs are filled with references to eggs and their gathering: "Around St. Anthony, lots of eggs"; "Around *Candelaria,* both good hens and bad ones lay eggs."[4]

Eggs have always been both ordinary and special. In Apicius's first-century cookbook, several recipes for eggs appear in the delicacies chapter.[5] Medieval cookbooks from England, France, and Italy contain numerous recipes for egg main dishes and call for their use in the preparation of sauces, casseroles, and stews.[6] Frequently, eggs were used to thicken a dish or to add color, an important concern. The cookbooks of the Iberian Peninsula are completely consistent with the rest of medieval Europe with respect to the importance of the egg in cooking. They all call for large amounts of eggs, sometimes a dozen or more in a recipe designed to create only a small dish. Whole eggs, egg whites, or egg yolks are regularly required for meat, chicken, and vegetable dishes.

It is not surprising that modern cookbooks usually have a section devoted to such a versatile food. Yet although all of the medieval Christian Iberian cookbooks contain dozens of recipes incorporating eggs, only the Portuguese cookbook and the *Libre de sent soví* group these recipes together in a recognizable division.[7] For Nola, eggs generally play a supporting role, with the one notable exception of a dish that resembles the present day famous and ever-present Spanish *tortilla*—without the New World potato, of course.[8] The *Al-Andalus* cookbook, too, has few dishes in which the egg is the primary ingredient, with one striking exception being a recipe for what we today would call deviled eggs.[9]

Curiously, medieval recipes generally indicate solely to "add eggs," or give directions for specific numbers of eggs (e.g., "six eggs," or "six egg yolks"), but very few specify what kind or size of eggs are called for. Modern cooking presumes large chicken eggs, but there is no reason to eschew other possibilities. The various illustrated manuscripts of the medieval *Tacuinum sanitatis* also show goose, partridge, and ostrich eggs being gathered.[10]

References to eggs in the Inquisition testimonies corroborate that they were a part of everyday meals in all places and for all occasions. The quick-roasted eggs for Pero Laynes's wife indicate that the eggs were fairly plentiful and on hand. The specially colored vermilioned eggs point to decorative possibilities that were already popular among medieval Christians at Easter time.[11] Eggs were always included in crypto-Jewish funeral meals, as their round shape suggested an existence without beginning or end and hinted at rebirth or resurrection. And the numbers of hard-boiled and raw eggs used to stuff meats or fish and to add to other dishes give us an idea how thousands of eggs could be consumed in larger households in little time. For Jews, the egg has the additional advantage of being self-contained. When cooked in its own shell it is not contaminated and thus is kosher.

Juan de León's Huevos Asados

Part of the traditional preparations for Yom Kippur is a thorough cleansing of both house and body. Testimony in Mexican Inquisition trials in the early seventeenth century is particularly rich in details about personal hygiene. Witnesses in the trial of Tomás Treviño Sobremonte, for example, explained how on the afternoon preceding Yom Kippur his mother would heat water in their kitchen, fill a large tub, scrub herself from head to toe, put on a clean dress, and then have him come in to use the water to bathe in a similar fashion.[13] In the 1640s for the circle of crypto-Jews that grouped around the Machorro family, personal hygiene was transformed into an important social event. On the morning preceding Yom Kippur the women of the group would gather in one of their homes to scrub each other down. Salomón Machorro (aka Juan de León) and other male friends would go to one of Mexico City's bathhouses, called *japones,* and there bathe themselves thoroughly, put on their clean clothes, and then have a picnic lunch, including eggs roasted on the bathhouse fire.

The Treviño community was eradicated in the *Gran auto de fe* on April 11, 1649, Mexico's bloodiest, in which one hundred nine crypto-Jews were condemned to death. Though Machorro/León was spared the stake, he was condemned to eight years' service rowing in His Majesty's galleys as a slave.

Juan de León's Roast Eggs

Serves 4

12 eggs (see Note)

2 tablespoons chopped fresh parsley   *1–2 tablespoons red vinegar*

1. Place the eggs near coals on a grill or a fireplace. Turn them occasionally to ensure all-round roasting. Leave for 12–15 minutes.
2. Crack the shells and wash off the eggs. Slice them in half and place them on a plate. Sprinkle them with the parsley and vinegar.

NOTE

You may first wrap the eggs individually in aluminum foil so the shells won't get dirty.

Eggs

Pedro de la Caballería's Huevos Haminados

Despite their *converso* background and crypto-Jewish practices, the immensely wealthy Caballería family (named Benveniste before their conversion) played a major role in Aragonese politics. Pedro served as financial minister to the Aragonese King Joan II, and his son Alfonso was vice chancellor.

In May of 1492, Moshe Algamiz talked with inquisitors about the Caballerías. He recalled how one year, when the plague was ravaging the capital city of Zaragoza, Pedro de la Caballería had taken his wife, his sons, Jaymico and Paulico, and his daughters, Violant and María, to spend the summer in a mountain town called Villanueva. Algamiz, then fifteen, was serving an apprenticeship to the Jewish weaver Abraham Leredi. One day, "practicing archery near the house, [Algamiz] went into Leredi's garden through a back gate and climbed over the adobe wall into the house, where Leredi and Caballería were celebrating the Sabbath." Algamiz said that Caballería "often went there on Saturdays, and hardly ever on other days . . . and he used to sit down at the table and eat with Leredi the Jewish meat and Sabbath stew and red eggs, and he drank the Jewish wine and ate the other foods that the Jews ate and joined in reciting the Grace after meals."[15]

In the environment of the 1490s, with Inquisition spies everywhere, clearly both men recognized the risks they were taking. According to Algamiz, Caballería asked Leredi—in Hebrew—not to inform officials of his visits, to which Leredi replied, "My lord, have no fear, I won't disclose it. But I would prefer that you not keep visiting like this. I would be delighted for you to come by during the week to talk with me about the Jewish Law, but not on the Sabbath."

Algamiz reported another conversation in which Caballería commented on the advantages of having converted. Leredi had asked, "My lord, why did you convert so quickly, being as you are so learned in our law?" Caballería's answer was sharply to the point: "Silence, fool! Could I, as a Jew, ever have risen higher than a rabbinical post? But now, see, I am one of the chief councillors of the city. For the sake of the little man who was hanged,[16] I am accorded every honor. . . . Who hinders me, if I choose, from fasting on Yom Kippur and keeping your festivals and all the rest? When I was a Jew I dared not walk as far as this;[17] but now I can do as I please." When Leredi criticized him for his answer, Caballería retorted: "Now I have complete freedom to do as I like; those old days are gone."[18]

· · ·

Eggs are commonly cited in connection with the Sabbath, funerals, Purim, and Passover. *Huevos haminados* were a favorite dish of *conversos* of that time in Huete (Guadalajara) who prepared them by boiling eggs with onion skins, olive oil, and ashes, imparting a vermilion color and delicate onion flavor to the eggs.[19] In Soria around the time of the expulsion, *conversos* prepared eggs similarly by boiling them in clay pots with onion skins.[20] This is still a favorite dish of Sephardic Jews of Turkey, who follow the same recipe.[21]

Pedro de la Caballería's Vermilioned Eggs

12 eggs

Loose yellow or red onion skins (about 6 cups)

12 white eggs
½ cup white vinegar

1. In a large nonreactive pot, place half the onion skins; then add the eggs and the rest of the onion skins. Pour in the vinegar and add water to completely cover. Cover the pot.

2. Slowly bring the water to a boil over medium heat and then turn down the heat to very low. Cook over low heat for 1 hour.

3. Take the eggs out of the pot. With a spatula, gently crack each egg once or twice. This allows the dye process to penetrate the egg whites. Return the eggs to the water. Continue to cook over very low heat for another 2 hours.

4. Remove the eggs from the water. Drain. When cool, refrigerate.

5. Peel the shells and wash off the eggs in cold water just before serving.

NOTE

We sugggest refrigerating the vermilioned eggs no more than 24 hours.

María González's Cazuela de Huevos y Queso

When María, the wife of Pedro de Villarreal of Ciudad Real, was arrested, she not only confessed to maintaining a thoroughly Judaized household, she also implicated many of her friends and neighbors in her activities. María tried to be surreptitious about her Judaizing activities. On the Sabbath when she visited her friends she took needlework with her to fool any curious neighbors into thinking that she was working. When someone noticed that a joint of meat had had the sciatic vein removed, María blamed it on the cat.[23]

This recipe serves as the basic egg casserole to which *conversas* as well as present-day Sephardic cooks add(ed) a variety of vegetables, among which eggplant, spinach, and carrots are common.[24] Originally, these egg dishes were prepared on top of the stove: thus the term *fritada,* fried. Later, with the increasing commonality of the home oven, the dishes were baked, and in many places the term for these dishes changed to *cuajada* (coagulated).[25] Both names persist today and are largely interchangeable. In one American Sephardic cookbook recipes for both *fritada* and *cuajada* have almost identical ingredients and directions.[26]

The common denominator is eggs, several of them, usually whipped to make the dish lighter. The egg casserole is not unique to Sephardic or Jewish cuisines. Apicius, the Latin first-century epicure, offers one recipe, instructing that the egg and milk be mixed to make a "smooth" product and then cooked "over a slow fire."[27] Two thousand years later in twentieth-century Spain a similar omelet, the *tortilla,* is fried in a skillet and is served as a bar snack, an hors d'oeurve, or an evening meal.

The second element universal to the many *fritada* recipes is cheese. Modern Greek Sephardis often use feta, which adds a strong salty flavor to the dish. For French and Balkan Sephardis, cantal cheese, sometimes called kachkaval, is a favorite.[28] Farmer cheese or sharp cheeses are more common in American kitchens. The medieval cookbooks of the Iberian Peninsula also used cheese relatively often in casserole dishes. Nola's Catalán cookbook calls for *queso rallado,* shredded or grated cheese, or for fresh cheese, but it is obvious that other kinds of cheeses were known. In one recipe Nola specifies *mantecoso,* a cheese like those made in "Lombardy, or in Parma, or Brussels, or Lascauallo, or cheese from Aragon and Navarre and some parts of Castile. . . ."[29] The Portuguese cookbook also frequently calls for cheese.

María González used to make "casseroles of eggs and cheese and parsley and calantares and spices, and sometimes she made them with eggplant and sometimes with carrots, according to what was in season, and . . . they used to eat those casseroles cold."[22]

Eggs

77

There are many ways to combine cheese and eggs and spices. Nola gives three recipes: *Queso assadero,* which incorporates beef broth and uses only one egg for each serving; *Fruta de sartén,* which calls for sweet spices; and *Fruta de queso fresco,* using fresh sheep's cheese and a little flour. After having been fried, this last dish is topped with something sweet.[30] The *fritadas* or *cuajadas* of Sephardic cooking generally include some combination of cheese with eggs and may be served either hot or cold, whereas the other medieval recipes seem to prefer the dish served warm.

One key to the popularity of the Sephardic *fritada* is its ability to accept a variety of other ingredients to form almost any vegetable casserole. The eight modern Sephardic cookbooks we consulted all contain at least one *fritada* recipe incorporating vegetables such as tomatoes and eggplant. Other additions include carrots, spinach, squash, and leeks. The cookbook by the Los Angeles Sephardic Sisterhood, Temple Tifereth Israel, has an entire chapter devoted solely to these casseroles.

We offer two recipes for María González's casserole. The first is the basic egg and cheese *fritada,* made spicy with the use of feta and Manchego or Romano cheeses. The second uses milder cheeses so as not to overwhelm the vegetable flavor, in this case the eggplant. We have selected our spices based on those used in Nola's cheese and eggplant recipe, which he calls *moxi,*[31] and an eggplant recipe from the *Al-Andalus* cookbook.[32] The same cookbook has a recipe for a seasoning mixture which gives specific measurements: "Pepper one part; caraway two parts, dry cilantro three parts."[33] We tried this combination and found the flavors delightful for an egg casserole, but since the amounts given were so strong that they overwhelmed everything else in the casserole, we have adjusted the proportions.

María González's Eggs and Cheese Casserole

The Basic Recipe
Serves 4

¼ pound hard cheese, such as
 Manchego or Romano
⅓ pound semisoft cheese, such as Portuguese queijo natural *(see Notes)*
¼ cup crumbled fresh feta cheese

1 tablespoon olive oil
4 eggs *(see Notes)*
¼ teaspoon saffron threads, crushed
 (optional)

Spice Mixture

½ teaspoon pepper
¼ teaspoon ground cumin

¼ teaspoon ground cloves
½ teaspoon cinnamon

⅓–½ cup chopped fresh parsley

1. Preheat the oven to 350°. Grate the hard cheese and cut the semisoft cheese into small chunks. Combine the three cheeses in a medium bowl.

2. Pour the olive oil into a deep 8-inch-diameter ovenproof casserole. Place the casserole in the oven until the oil is very hot, about 5 minutes.

3. Meanwhile, beat the eggs. Stir in the saffron. Add the eggs slowly to the cheese mixture and combine well.

4. Stir the ingredients for the spice mixture together. Combine the spice mixture and the parsley with the eggs and cheese.

5. Remove the heated casserole from the oven and pour the egg and cheese mixture in the dish. Return it to the oven. Bake for 30 minutes or until the casserole is golden brown.

6. Refrigerate and serve cold.

NOTES

The secret of this dish is the combination of the hard and semisoft cheeses. For the soft cheese, use Munster, farmer cheese, cream cheese, or drained cottage cheese. For the hard cheeses and strong flavor, combine fresh feta and Romano.

This casserole is also tasty when served hot or reheated.

VARIATION

For a lighter casserole, whip the egg whites separately and fold them in last.

Substitute ¼ cup fresh chopped cilantro for half of the parsley in step 4.

María González's Eggs and Cheese Casserole with Eggplant

Serves 4

1 medium eggplant (about 2 pounds)
1 tablespoon olive oil
4 eggs

¼ teaspoon saffron threads, crushed (optional)

Spice Mixture

½ teaspoon pepper
¼ teaspoon ground cumin
¼ teaspoon ground caraway seeds

¼ teaspoon ground coriander seeds
¾ teaspoon cinnamon

1 cup cubed semisoft cheese, such as farmer cheese, cut into ½–1-inch cubes

⅓ cup chopped fresh parsley

1. Preheat the broiler. Prick the eggplant several times with a fork. Place the eggplant under the broiler and cook it until the skin is charred and the pulp is soft, turning it several times, about 20 minutes. It is important that the eggplant pulp be very soft. Remove the eggplant from the broiler and when it has cooled, peel it, using a fork and knife.

2. To reduce the liquid, place the pulp in a strainer. Mash the pulp to extract the liquid. Leave for about 30 minutes.

3. Preheat the oven to 350°. Pour the olive oil into a deep 8-inch-diameter ovenproof casserole. Place the casserole in the oven until the oil is very hot, about 5 minutes. At the end of that time you should be ready to bake the casserole.

4. Meanwhile, separate the eggs. Place the yolks in a medium bowl and beat them until creamy. Set the whites aside to beat later. Add the saffron to the egg yolks, if you're using it.

5. Stir the ingredients for the spice mixture together and add them to the egg yolks. Add the mashed eggplant and combine thoroughly. Add the cheese and parsley and mix.

6. In a medium bowl, whip the 4 egg whites until stiff. Fold them into the eggplant mixture. Take the casserole out of the oven. Pour the mixture into the casserole dish and return it to the oven.

7. Bake 30–35 minutes, or until the casserole is set and golden brown.

8. Serve (see Notes).

NOTES

For a larger eggplant, add another egg.

You need not whip the egg yolks and egg whites separately, but it makes the dish lighter.

This casserole is good hot or cold, but the flavors are best if it is served at room temperature.

VARIATION

Any vegetable can be substituted for the eggplant in this recipe.

Fish

A good American supermarket may offer ten species of fresh fish. An inland market in Spain may display thirty, while in the seaside markets the number may reach higher. One random April morning in Cádiz in 1981 the authors counted and photographed sixty-eight species for sale. A glance at a map shows that Iberia is a peninsula surrounded on five of six sides by water. Half the coast is Mediterranean, half Atlantic. Bays and estuaries and salt lagoons abound. While lakes are uncommon, several major river systems drain to the coasts, and rare is the village more than a day's walk from a river.

All evidence points to the fact that for most medieval Iberians, fish was not a luxury but a staple. Fishing fleets harvested the coastal waters and bays. Monasteries and municipalities squabbled over the rights to dry and salt and market fish. Each foot of river frontage was jealously defended as a potential income source. Fish and fishing were taxed and provided a healthy income to the conceders of fishing rights. On the estates of nobles, special tanks held freshwater fish alive until they were needed for serving.[1]

Literary evidence supports this sense of abundance. To cite just one example, in his fourteenth-century *Libro de buen amor (The Book of Good Love)*, the poet archpriest Juan Ruiz, who lived in the Castilian town of Hita, reports an allegorical battle between Meat and Lent, in which most of the Lenten troops are fish. Surprisingly, although Hita is about as landlocked as you can be in Iberia, about half of Ruiz's fish come from the ocean. He lists two dozen varieties, some of which are kosher (amberjack, barbel, dace, herring, mullet, red bream, salmon, sardines, shad, trout, tuna), and others which are not (conger eel, crab, crayfish, cuttlefish, dogfish, dolphin, common eel, lamprey, lobster, octopus, oyster, and whale). Other evidence confirms the widespread availability of ocean products. In the 1490s the new-Christian Jeronymite monks of the inland monastery of Guadalupe were reported to dine on tuna.[2]

The few surviving contemporary cookbooks also list numerous fish by name. The *Al-Andalus* cookbook cites six: eel, hake, red mullet, sardines, shad, and sturgeon, as well as numerous other recipes merely for "fish." To these Nola adds sixteen more: barbel, bogue, bonito, dendex, lamprey, moray, octopus, oyster, pandora, red bream, salmon, sole, squid, swordfish, tuna, and weever, as well as just plain "fish."

Fish could be eaten at any time, but consumption soared on the many meatless days prescribed by the Christian liturgical calendar, especially the forty days of Lent. Typical are the 1438–69 accounts of the Valladolid confraternity, where fish appears on the menu only during the days of abstinence.[3] Jews and crypto-Jews might eat fish at any time as well, but it was especially popular after funerals and to break the holiday fasts.[4]

Jewish and crypto-Jewish cooks in Iberia were constrained in their choices by the rules of *kashruth,* according to which the permissible fish must have both gills and scales. This eliminates perhaps half of the seafood routinely consumed by Christian Iberians: octopus and squid, eels, scaleless fish like rays, skate, shark, and catfish, and all varieties of mollusks and crustaceans. But even with the remaining half, no *conversa* cook ever lacked for variety.

Isabel González's Cazuela de Pescado y Sardinas

*On Friday Isabel González allegedly used to cook "**casseroles of fish and sardines**" for the Sabbath.*[5]

The introduction to this section notes the staggering array of fish commonly available on the Iberian Peninsula in the late Middle Ages. In practice, however, housewives were likely to be limited to whatever fish was for sale in their market on a particular day. For this reason references to fish in recipes tend to be generic. While researching this book, it became clear to us that Iberian cooks thought of ocean fish in five general categories, that recipes or references to fish were by category, and that any fish within a given category could be substituted for another, according to availability. The five categories of ocean fish were:

1. Sardines. These were any small, tubular fish that could be grilled and eaten whole. The category includes sardines, anchovies, herring, mackerel, sea trout, and smelts. They were sometimes stuffed.

2. Flat fish. These bottom fish included flounder, plaice, halibut, and sole. They were likely to be served as fillets.

3. Salted fish. While presumably any fish could be dried and salted, the occasional specific references suggest that cod was generally used for this purpose.

4. Large ocean fish. The flesh of these strong-flavored fish when cut into steaks, or chunked, tended to hold its shape. The most common examples—tuna, swordfish, and salmon—were generally referred to in recipes by name. Since tuna and swordfish appear in recipes from central Iberia, and from Mexico City as well, their meat, too, may have been salted and dried.

5. Fish. This catch-all category of round fish includes any medium-size white-meat fish that could be cut into chunks and stewed. This was the most common ingredient of Sabbath fish casseroles. Common examples were bream, hake, haddock, cod, pollack, and grouper.

In addition to these ocean fish, we have found some specific references to freshwater fish, particularly trout. We suspect that away from the coasts most generic references to fish (category 5) were probably to freshwater species caught in local rivers.

In other words, if it swam and had gills and scales, Iberian Jews ate it. If it was small or flat they would pan-fry it. If it was medium size they might stuff it and grill it. If it was very large they might slice it into steaks to be fried or broiled, or chop it into pieces and stuff it into something else, like an eggplant. For stews almost any fish might do, and mixtures that included both fresh and salted fish were common. A Sabbath fish stew might be eaten hot on Friday night, with the leftovers served warm or cold the following day.

With these principles in mind, we have been guided by market availability in choosing fish for the following recipes, and urge users of this cookbook to do likewise.

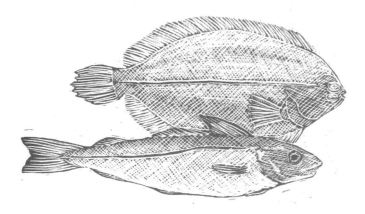

Isabel González's Fish and Sardine Casserole

Serves 4

½–1 teaspoon pepper (see Notes)

2 teaspoons salt

2½ teaspoons finely minced fresh ginger

½ teaspoon saffron threads, crushed

¾ cup boiling water

1½ tablespoons oil

1 pound fresh sardines or mackerel, cleaned and sliced in ¾-inch pieces

½ pound fresh white fish, such as haddock or pollack, cut into 1-inch pieces

2 tablespoons slivered almonds

2 tablespoons pine nuts

⅓ cup golden raisins

¼–½ cup water

2–3 tablespoons frozen orange juice concentrate

5 teaspoons apple cider vinegar (see Notes)

Thickener (see Notes)

Garnish

2 tablespoons chopped fresh dill

2 tablespoons chopped fresh mint

1. Mix the spices together. Pour the boiling water over them and let steep for 5-10 minutes.

2. Heat the oil in a stew pot over medium heat. Add both fish and stir-fry gently for about 3 minutes. Stir so that the fish will not stick to the pan.

3. Add the spice mixture with its water, the almonds, pine nuts, and raisins. Add up to ½ cup more water, just enough to barely cover the fish. Cover the pot and simmer for 20 minutes, until the fish is thoroughly cooked.

4. Remove the lid. Simmer 10 minutes more, until half the liquid has evaporated. Add the orange juice concentrate and vinegar. Continue cooking another 10 minutes to allow the flavors to blend.

5. Thicken the stew and cook for about 3 minutes. Remove from the heat.

6. Garnish with the dill and mint and serve immediately.

NOTES

The pepper adds piquancy; use less for a milder flavor.

For a sweeter version, omit the vinegar.

See pages 16–17 for thickening agents. The quantity depends on the thickener you choose.

A Drizzle of Honey

Rodrigo de Chillón's Cazuela de Berenjena y Pescado

In the early 1500s the Ciudad Real Judaizing community, composed of first- and second-generation *conversos* and their young children, had developed an intricate social network. Several women who testified in Inquisition trials around 1513 described the Friday afternoon and Saturday gatherings that cemented the community of *conversa* women. María González, wife of the butcher and landlord Rodrigo de Chillón, was a regular member of one of these groups, and when she hosted them in her own home she sometimes served the Sabbath dish described in this recipe.

These Sabbath gatherings were characterized by a number of activities. Pedro de Villarreal's wife, who was also named María González, and who was a cousin of Chillón's María González, reported that when they met on Friday afternoons at the home of Diego de Teva's wife—who was also named María González, what else?—they would talk and eat. Sometimes they even bathed together in the kitchen in a large ceramic tub in hot water scented with chamomile and other herbs, scrubbing first the little girls (Catalinica, aged eleven, and Juanica, aged eight) and then the older women. After they had bathed they would dress up in clean clothes which they had brought with them. On Saturdays Rodrigo de Chillón's María used to dress in purple damask cloth with a narrow sash of black velvet. On fast days they would chatter about how they managed to withstand their hunger pangs and what they would eat when sundown came. On Saturday afternoons in the summer they would sit and gossip while the men slept off the heavy Sabbath meal. During the winter it was harder to get out, and the group did not meet quite as often.[7]

Another regular of this group was Rodrigo de Chillón's mother, Inés de Mérida, who used to remind her friends how keeping the Sabbath properly was essential for the salvation of their souls.[8] The whole Chillón family found itself continually under suspicion, and Inés was actually tried twice. In September of 1513, after having confessed to various Judaizing activities, she was sentenced to house arrest under the care of her brother Juan de Mérida. In 1522, she was tried a second time, not as a relapsed heretic—which would almost inevitably have led to her execution—but for speaking ill of the Inquisition. On October 27 she was sentenced to be led by the town crier through the streets of the city on a donkey, with a noose around her neck, to be given one hundred lashes, and to be expelled from Toledo and Ciudad Real.[9]

In Rodrigo de Chillón's house the women prepared a Sabbath "casserole of eggplants and fish and eggs."[6]

Fish

87

Rodrigo de Chillón's Fish and Eggplant Casserole

Serves 4

5–6 tablespoons olive oil

2 cloves garlic, diced

20 thin slices eggplant, cut in half

8 thin slices onion

1 teaspoon ground dried coriander

1 teaspoon ground savory

4 sprigs of fresh parsley or arugula,
  chopped

3 hard-boiled eggs, diced

4 flat fish fillets (flounder or sole)
  (about 1 pound)

½ cup fresh lime juice

½ cup sweet white wine

1 tablespoon honey (see Notes)

1. Heat the olive oil over medium heat in an ovenproof frying pan. Add garlic and stir-fry 2 minutes.

2. Add the eggplant and onion slices and stir-fry until translucent, turning them several times, about 7 minutes. The frying may have to be done in two batches.

3. Put the cooked mixture in a medium bowl. Add the coriander, savory, parsley, and diced eggs. Stir to combine.

4. Preheat the oven to 325°. On a board lay the fillets out flat. Place 2 tablespoons of the eggplant mixture on top of each of the fillets. Roll up each fillet and fasten with toothpicks. Place them in the frying pan.

5. Combine the lime juice, wine, and honey and add to the frying pan. Shake the pan gently to mix. Surround the fish with the leftover eggplant mix. Cover the pan with aluminum foil. Bake 20 minutes.

6. Uncover and serve hot. The rolled fish will be firm all the way through.

NOTES

This casserole prepared as a Sabbath stew would simmer all night and be served warm.

This dish is mild and semisweet. To deemphasize the sweetness, omit the honey.

Steps 1–3 may be done ahead of time.

Mayor González's Cazuela de Pescado y Zanahorias

This dish was mentioned in testimony of Juana González, an old-Christian who managed the household affairs of Mayor González and her husband, Pedro Núñez Franco. She was one of the principal prosecution witnesses in the trials against them. When Juana González subsequently told the head of Ciudad Real's Franciscans that she had falsely denounced her employer in Mayor's 1511 trial, Juana was recalled by the Inquisition and reexamined under torture. She first swore that her recantation was true. Then—threatened with more pain—she reversed herself and reiterated the accusations made in her original 1511 testimony. Among other things she said she remembered how twenty-three years earlier, when she first went to work for the family, Mayor and her husband and their family kept the Sabbath. She reported how on Friday nights Mayor and Pedro used to go to bed earlier than usual, "lying down on some pillows next to the fireplace,"[11] while on other nights they were accustomed to working quite late.

Just prior to her death in 1516, Juana González once again recanted her testimony. But it made little difference, for by then the Inquisition had garnered sufficient corroborating evidence against Mayor González. In 1518 Mayor González was sentenced to life in prison, and her property was confiscated. Although two years later the sentence was commuted to a variety of penances, Mayor's property does not seem to have been restored. In 1516 her husband, Pedro Núñez Franco, was condemned to be burned at the stake.

*"On Fridays, [Mayor González's maid] used to make **casseroles of fish and carrots and spices and eggs,** and she made them because her mistress ordered her to, and her mistress and master used to eat them on Friday night and saved [some] for Saturday which they ate cold."[10]*

Fish

Mayor González's Fish and Carrot Casserole

Serves 4

5 tablespoons olive oil

2 cloves garlic, diced

1 bay leaf, fresh if possible

4 cups leeks, sliced 1-inch thick

1½ cups carrots, sliced ¼-inch thick

1¼–1½ pounds boneless whitefish
   fillet, cut into 1½-inch pieces

½ cup white wine

½–¾ cup water

2 broth cubes

Spice Mixture

2 tablespoons prepared mustard

1 teaspoon ground anise

4 teaspoons ground cumin seeds

1 teaspoon salt

3 hard-boiled eggs, sliced or quartered

3 tablespoons chopped fresh cilantro or
   fresh parsley (optional)

2 tablespoons fresh lime juice
   (optional)

1. Over medium heat, heat 3 tablespoons of the olive oil in a stew pot. Add the garlic and bay leaf and stir-fry for 3–4 minutes. Add the leeks and fry for 4 minutes. Add the carrots and stir-fry an additional 4–5 minutes, until the vegetables are tender. Remove all this to a plate.

2. Add 2 tablespoons olive oil to the pot. Fry the fish over medium heat, stirring so that it does not stick, until its juices begin to appear.

3. Stir the carrot and leek mixture in with the fish. Add the wine, water, and broth cubes. Bring to a boil over medium heat. Turn the heat down to simmer.

4. Meanwhile, combine the spice mixture ingredients in a small bowl. Stir them into the stew. Simmer the stew, uncovered, for about 20 minutes. The liquid will decrease by about half. Discard the bay leaf.

5. Add the eggs and continue to simmer another 10 minutes.

6. Just before serving, add the cilantro or parsley and the lime juice.

NOTES

Serve over rice.

The stew may also be eaten cold. Add the cilantro or parsley and lime juice just before serving.

Isabel Núñez's Caldo de Garbanzos y Pescado

In 1621, one hundred twenty-nine years after the expulsion of the Jews, thirty-eight-year-old Isabel Núñez, the widow of Francisco Paulo, was arrested after having been denounced as a Judaizer in Ciudad Rodrigo by one of her deceased husband's bastard teenage sons. The boy accused Isabel of a host of Sabbath observances: cleaning her home thoroughly on Friday, sweeping the floor from the outside in, putting clean sheets on her bed, and lighting Sabbath candles with the words "Lord Adonay, bring me luck; Lord Adonay, free me from my enemies. . . ." He said she and his father called the holy images "idols," and when they were reading religious books and came to the name Jesus, they ripped out the page and threw it away. In church they avoided pronouncing the name Jesus by substituting the name Cristóbal Sánchez and—still according to her husband's bastard son—she made fun of the Eucharist and spit it out after the priest had given it to her. He reported that Isabel and her family were well aware of the risks of employing old Christian servants, because they threatened them that if they ever spoke of anything they had witnessed in the house, Isabel would sew their mouths shut.

The boy said that Isabel was committed to Jewish cooking, and that she koshered her meat by salting and soaking it. The boy added that she could not stand the taste, sight, or even the smell of salt pork. On Passover she baked her own matza, and they broke their Yom Kippur fast with the Sabbath recipe given here.

In repeated testimony, sometimes under torture, Isabel denied all charges, protesting that she could not be a crypto-Jew because she frequently ate pork. Her lawyer called fifty-four character witnesses in her behalf, despite the fact that many of these were *conversos* and therefore automatically suspect. Even though their chief witness had been very specific about Isabel's Judaizing customs, the inquisitors decided that they did not have enough evidence to convict her. So, after two and a half years of incarceration, she was set free.

*Isabel Núñez of Ciudad Rodrigo made a Sabbath stew "of **fish and chickpea broth**."* [12]

Fish

Isabel Núñez's Fish and Chickpea Stew

Serves 4

½ teaspoon saffron threads
1 cup hot water

2–3 tablespoons olive oil

Spice Mixture

½ teaspoon pepper
4 teaspoons thinly sliced fresh ginger

½ teaspoon salt

1 pound halibut, cut into ½-inch
    cubes

Herb Mixture

4 teaspoons chopped fresh chives
2 teaspoons chopped fresh oregano

2 teaspoons dried coriander
2 tablespoons dried parsley

2 (15-ounce) cans chickpeas, drained
⅔ cup raisins

1. Crush the saffron and place it in a microwave-safe bowl (if using a microwave) or in a pan (if using a conventional stove). Add the 1 cup water and heat just to the boiling point. Stir once. Set aside.

2. Pour the olive oil into a medium stew pot. Heat over medium heat.

3. Combine the spice mixture ingredients. Add them to the hot oil and fry 1–2 minutes, stirring constantly so that the mixture does not stick.

4. Add the fish cubes and continue stirring and frying for 5 minutes, until the fish is coated with the spice mixture and is beginning to firm.

5. Combine the herb mixture in a small bowl. To the fish, add the chickpeas, raisins, herb mixture, saffron, and water, and enough additional water just to cover the mixture. Cook covered over very low heat 2 hours or more, stirring occasionally. The dish will have the consistency of a thick soup.

6. Serve in bowls.

Ruy Díaz Nieto's Pescado Mixto Mexicano

Ruy [Rodrigo] Díaz Nieto was a Portuguese Judaizer from Oporto, who emigrated with his family to Ferrara, Italy. In 1590 he secured a papal bull authorizing him to raise money to ransom from the Turks various new-Christian captives, including two of his sons. The fund-raising was difficult, and Díaz Nieto returned to Madrid to ask Philip II for permission to go to the New World to try to raise the money. He took with him to Mexico letters of introduction to principal members of the crypto-Jewish community there. The Mexican crypto-Jews were impressed with Díaz Nieto's commitment to Judaism and his knowledge of Jewish prayer and practices, and soon referred to him as "the old saint."

Perhaps even more observant than Ruy was his son Diego, arrested first in 1596 and again in 1601. Diego's case, one of the most extensive in the Mexican National Archives, dragged on for years. At one point Diego revealed under questioning that he had never been baptized, and the shocked inquisitors, realizing that swearing on the New Testament would have little importance to Díaz Nieto, extracted from their files a Jewish oath by which they made him swear.

The Díaz Nieto case is full of revealing details about the family's practices and Mexican crypto-Judaism at the beginning of the seventeenth century. Diego significantly upgraded the traditional practices of Mexican crypto-Judaism by regaling his Mexican friends with details of Jewish observances in Italy. He taught them to wash and salt their meat and which parts of the animal were forbidden to eat. He taught them the blessings attendant on daily rituals such as the washing of the hands. Diego knew all of the *Amidah* prayer and numerous other prayers in Hebrew by heart. He lectured on the nature of the Messiah. He brought to Mexico a calendar of festivals and informed his colleagues about the proper ways to celebrate Yom Kippur, Passover, and Purim. In 1596 Diego was sentenced to a year in prison. On his release he resumed his active role in Mexico's crypto-Jewish community. He was rearrested and reconciled in the *Auto de fe* of 1605.

In his 1601 trial Diego also implicated his father Ruy Díaz Nieto, whose own subsequent trial provides much additional information about crypto-Jewish customs, particularly with regard to the Sabbath. Ruy's personal hygiene on Fridays in preparation for the Sabbath always included trimming his hair. He refused to work in his tailor shop on the Sabbath, and

*The Mexican Ruy Díaz Nieto used to prepare on Friday afternoon a Sabbath meal of **"chickpeas, eggs, salt fish, fresh fish, and tuna, all stewed together,"** portions of which he sent to his friends.*[13]

Fish

93

once when a customer asked for a new cowl to be delivered the next day he replied, "Daughter, don't you see that tomorrow is Saturday?"[14] Ruy Díaz Nieto was given a hundred lashes, made to forfeit all of his property, and condemned to life in prison. But even in prison Ruy continued to light and bless a Sabbath candle every week, and in September of 1603 with two of his crypto-Jewish colleagues, he tried to celebrate Sukkot in jail.[15] Ruy's trial includes this description of a Sabbath fish stew.[16]

Ruy Díaz Nieto's Mexican Fish Stew

Serves 4–6

¼ pound boneless dried cod (bacalao)

1 large tomato

2 tablespoons olive oil

2 cloves garlic, diced

1 medium onion, sliced

1 ancho chile, diced

⅓–½ cup dry white wine

½ pound fresh tuna, cut into 1-inch cubes

½–¾ pound fresh whitefish, such as cod, scrod, or hake, cut into 1-inch cubes

1 (19-ounce) can chickpeas, drained

3 hard-boiled eggs, cut into eighths

¼ cup loosely packed chopped fresh cilantro

Garnish

1 hard-boiled egg, sliced

4–5 sprigs of cilantro and/or parsley

1 avocado, diced (optional)

Juice of 2 limes

The day before serving:

1. Desalt the dried cod. Soak it in water for 24 hours, changing the water three or four times.

The day of serving:

2. Drain the dried cod. Cut into 1-inch square pieces. Boil for 10 minutes in water to cover. Remove and drain the fish. Reserve the liquid.

3. Preheat the broiler. Wash and quarter the tomato. Place it under the broiler for about 5 minutes, or until it is well browned. Remove it, peel the skin off, and dice the pulp. Set it aside.

4. In a large skillet heat the olive oil over medium heat. Add the garlic and fry it for 2 minutes. Add the sliced onion and chile and stir-fry for 3 minutes, separating the pieces of the onion.

5. Push the onions to the side. Add the dried cod, wine, diced tomato, and ⅓ cup of the reserved fish stock. Simmer for 10 minutes.

6. Add the tuna. Simmer for 5 minutes more. The tuna will lose its pinkness.

7. Add the whitefish, the chickpeas, and the hard-boiled eggs. Simmer for an additional 5 minutes or until the fish is cooked through.

8. Turn off the heat, stir in the chopped cilantro.

9. Serve hot. Pass the egg slices, cilantro sprigs, avocado if you're using it, and lime juice.

Fish

95

Juan de León's Escabeche

Juan de León and his Mexican converso *friends used to break their fasts with "**fish marinade** . . . olives, cheese, bread, fruit, and wine."*[17]

Salomón Machorro, whose Christian name was Juan de León, was a baptized Italian Sephardi who emigrated to Mexico from Livorno, Italy, at age twenty in July of 1639. Because of his dedication to Judaism, and his knowledge of how Judaism was practiced openly in Mediterranean countries, he soon became one of the leaders of the crypto-Jewish community in Mexico, as had Ruy Díaz Nieto a generation earlier. León was arrested in Querétaro in 1642 and brought back to the capital, where he languished in prison for eight years, gradually revealing the details of his life. He had been born and baptized in the Andalusian city of Antequera. When he was four, his parents took him to Livorno, where he was educated in Hebrew—against his will, he told inquisitors—in the Jewish schools. He testified that when he was twelve, his parents punished him when they found him attracted to Christianity, and they sent him with an uncle on a business trip to the Turkish city of Izmir to learn how Judaism was practiced there. At sea he was captured by Algerian pirates and spent four years in Algiers, worshiping in Algerian synagogues, until he was finally released. Finding that his father had emigrated to the Indies, he set sail for Mexico in 1639. He never found his father, who seems to have died at sea.

In Mexico, Machorro/León taught crypto-Jews how properly to wash their hands, to bury the dead, how to burn the parings from their fingernails, the rules of feminine hygiene, the ceremonies attendant on Yom Kippur, Passover, and Purim, and the proper words to the *Shema*. Despite the reports of dozens of witnesses who had observed these behaviors, Machorro/León was sentenced not to be executed, but to be paraded through the streets of the city, given three hundred lashes, and sent to row as a galley slave for eight years. What saved him from the stake was his public oath to follow the dictates of Catholicism and to abjure all forms of heresy, as well as his willingness to denounce to his inquisitors the names and activities of sixty-eight members of his crypto-Jewish community.

Escabeche, the dish cited in the León trial, is an astringent liquid that can be used either as a preservative or a sauce. Versions have been known since the times of the Roman Apicius.[18] The word *escabeche* derives from the Arabic (*as-sikbaya* or *sikbaj*). There are recipes both in the *Baghdad* and *Al-Andalus* cookbooks in sections on "sour" or "fermented" dishes, which are meat stews cooked in sauces whose main ingredient is vinegar.[19] Nola's recipe for *escabeche* seems in the Roman tradition, for it picks up Apicius's vinegar, raisins, and spices. Since it was used to soak previously cooked fish or meat, it is more of a sauce than a marinade.[20] Granado combines both Roman and Islamic traditions. In his several *escabeche* recipes, the fish or fowl is first cooked before placing it into a simmering spiced vinegar broth. Finally, it is put in a basket lined with bay leaves. According to Granado, *escabeche* can conserve partridges for up to three months.[21] It is Covarrubias's 1611 definition that most closely approximates modern *escabeche:* a preparation to conserve fish, made out of white wine, lemons, and bay leaves.[22]

In the Americas, especially Mexico and Peru, it is still common to "cook" raw fish in a marinade of lime or lemon juice, adding spices and herbs for flavor. This dish is called *ceviche.* Since Juan de León lived in Mexico, we have adapted a Mexican *ceviche* for this dish, and have included several New World foods: tomato, chiles, and avocado.

Juan de León's Fish in Marinade

Serves 4

½ pound fresh sole, cut into 1-inch-square pieces

½ cup fresh lime juice

1 large tomato

2 cups water

2 tablespoons olive oil

¼ cup finely diced red onion

2 tablespoons diced drained mild green chiles

2 tablespoons chopped fresh cilantro

2 tablespoons minced fresh oregano

1 teaspoon finely ground sea salt

½ cup diced avocado

Garnish

2 tablespoons chopped fresh cilantro or fresh parsley

3 tablespoons diced avocado

1. Marinate the fish in the lime juice in a medium covered glass dish in the refrigerator for 5–8 hours. Turn at least twice.

2. Two hours before serving: Boil the water in a saucepan. Plunge the tomato in the water for 15 seconds. Rinse the tomato in cold water. Quarter it, remove the skin, and squeeze out and discard the seeds and juice. Dice the remaining part of the tomato. You should have about ½ cup of diced pulp.

3. Combine the diced tomato and the rest of the ingredients, except the garnishes, in a medium bowl. Pour them over the marinated fish. Marinate 1½ hours longer in the refrigerator.

4. Serve in small bowls and pass the garnishes.

María González's Sardinas Rellenas

ood was likely to get *conversos* into trouble with the Inquisition for four separate reasons. Two have to do with choice of menu. First is what one chose to eat: some dishes were considered by their communities to be Jewish dishes, so that anyone observed cooking them was naturally suspect. Second is what one chose *not* to eat: Jewish dietary prohibitions were well known, so that anyone who in any way avoided eating pork, rabbit, scaleless fish, and the like was liable to be accused of Judaizing. The other two reasons have to do with timing. Special meals made in proximity to any occasion marked on the Jewish calendar were cause for suspicion: one-dish meals prepared on Friday to be warmed over for the Sabbath, or feasts preceding or following one of the Jewish fasts, or the Passover *seder* dishes were obvious indicators of non-Catholic behavior. The last reason has to do with the Christian liturgical calendar, which prohibited the consumption of certain foods on certain days or at certain times of the year. Anyone who ignored these prohibitions also ran a great risk.

What were the Christian prohibitions? To begin with, theologians distinguished between fasting and abstinence. Fasting was not eating at all during daylight hours, or in some circumstances reducing intake to one meal a day. Abstinence concerned the avoidance of certain luxurious foods, or foods that within the conceptual framework of the four humors tended to warm the body, and thus to decrease its ability to focus on spiritual values. The principal foods in this category were meat and its by-products like fat and grease, eggs, or dairy products such as milk, butter, and cheese.[24]

When were fasts imposed, or certain foods proscribed? Meat was banned every Friday, in commemoration of the crucifixion. Lent, the forty days before Easter, required abstinence from meat. Ash Wednesday, the first day of Lent, was a fast day. Other abstinence days, tied both to the Christian liturgical and ancient Roman agricultural calendars, marked the beginning of each season of the year. These were: the Wednesday, Friday, and Saturday after the third Sunday of Advent, or in some countries the day before Christmas; the first Sunday of Lent; the week of Pentecost; and the day after the Feast of the Holy Cross on September 14. Some Christians also observed the days before the Assumption of the Virgin (August 15), and before the saints' days of Philip (May 1), James (July 25), and John the Evangelist (December 27).[25]

There are a couple of practical consequences of these rules. The first is

María González confessed in 1513 in Toledo to eating **"fried sardines stuffed with hard-boiled eggs"** *on Friday, even though the consumption of eggs on Friday violated the dictates of the Church.*[23]

Fish

99

the enormous popularity, and expense, of fish during Lent. European law books abound with injunctions against fishmongers gouging their clients during the weeks before Easter. European literature and art are filled with images of Lenten fish locked in battle with the fleshy armies of Carnival.[26] Another consequence is that many medieval cookbooks—Nola's and Granado's are good examples—contain special sections devoted to Lenten recipes, which feature fish or vegetables.

Since fasting and abstinence were viewed as exercises in spiritual focus, it was deemed inappropriate to put anyone's health at risk. Thus exemptions from fasting or abstinence were routinely granted to pregnant or lactating women, growing children, beggars, the sick, and people whose work demanded intense physical effort, such as walking pilgrims.[27]

The inclination of Judaizing new-Christians, particularly those of the expulsion generation who in the early days of the Inquisition did not always fully understand the consequences of their acts, was to pay no heed to the Christian fast or abstinence days. They might even joke about it. Once, during Lent, Aldonza Laínez astonished some laborers, who had stopped by her house for lunch before going out into the Laínez fields, by ordering her slave Angelina to top the turnip stew with grated cheese. Then, seeing the laborers' startled reactions, she burst into laughter.[28]

But the joking soon stopped, as *conversos* came to realize that violation of these prohibitions incurred deadly risk. The numbers of denunciations for these lapses make it clear that old-Christian snoops considered them telltale indicators, even if there had been no specific Judaizing intent.[29] As a result, the Judaizers who deliberately broke the rules took great pains to cover up their violation of the Christian abstinence days. Typical is this 1621 report from Toledo in which a black slave named Felipa informed about her master and mistress whose Judaizing, curiously, did not involve avoidance of pork or of blood:

> She said that she had observed that during almost the whole of Lent her masters ate meat, without being sick or having permission . . . and she herself thought ill of that, because they always ate it in secret, and that in order to be able to eat it they first fed their servants and her and sent the servants downstairs and her upstairs . . . but that when working in the kitchen she had put a spoon into the stew pot and had seen morcilla sausages inside, or meat. . . . [30]

Quite naturally, the first reaction of any Judaizer accused of violating one of these prohibitions was to claim infirmity. Pedro Caballero, of Almazán, said that the reason he had eaten fowl during Lent was because he had a wounded leg. His neighbor, Ruy Díaz de Alvez, said that he was too thin, and that the priest had given him permission. María García claimed that she had been pregnant. Pedro Laínez claimed dizzy spells. Diego López's daughter Isabel said she had eaten eggs only because she had a headache. Franco Núñez excused himself because of a venereal disease.[31]

María González's Fried Stuffed Sardines

Serves 2

2 mackerels or large sardines (about ¾
    pound each) (see Note)
1 tablespoon chopped fresh tarragon
1 tablespoon chopped fresh cilantro

Salt and pepper to taste
2 hard-boiled eggs
2 tablespoons olive oil

1. Split, clean, and bone the fish. Wash and pat dry the fish cavity.

2. Sprinkle the cavity with the tarragon, cilantro, salt, and pepper.

3. Slice the eggs. Stuff the fish cavity with them. Close the cavity and secure with toothpicks.

4. Heat the olive oil in a large skillet over medium-low heat. Fry the fish about 10 minutes on each side. Gently shake the skillet occasionally to keep the fish from sticking to the skillet. When they are done, they will be crispy on the outside and firm all the way through.

NOTE

On the Iberian Peninsula, meal-size sardines are common in the markets.

Isabel Rodríguez's Truchuela

Inquisition documents that mention cuisine quite naturally focus on the one telltale dish or method of preparation that denotes Jewish practice. Rarely do we find a description of an entire meal, such as Isabel Rodríguez's trout dinner or the description of the meals that Juan de León and his Mexican *converso* friends ate before and after their Yom Kippur fast around 1650. They preceded the holiday with "sweets, fruit, and chocolate," and they broke the fasts with "salad, eggs, sweets, and chocolate." In Mexico Gaspar Váez broke his 1640 Yom Kippur fast with "eggs, salad, pies, fish, olives, and chocolate," while the following year Blanca Enríquez and her mother broke theirs with "stewed fish, salad, fish pies, and boiled eggs."[33] They never ate meat before or after a fast, and as good colonial Mexicans they invariably started their meals with a cup of the native festive drink: chocolate[34]

It is difficult to generalize very much about *converso* menus based on these two references to special meals that broke or preceded religious fasts. We can see, however, that they have points in common, such as a fish course, and another of fruit, and something sweet. Many components of these two meals were finger food. The foods fall easily into modern-style courses: vegetable or salad, meat or fish, starch, dessert, and beverages. Since no one could work on Yom Kippur, the cooked foods were undoubtedly prepared a day ahead and then kept warm on a banked fire, or else eaten at room temperature.

We must look beyond the Inquisition material for Iberian traditions of menu planning, which were the context for *converso* cuisine. Culinary documents from the late Middle Ages throughout Europe are consistent on many points, and the hints found in Iberian archives do not suggest major variance with the rest of the continent. For example, in 1352 emissaries from the court of Navarre made a sixty-eight-day round-trip journey to Seville, and from their records of daily expenditures we can see that their typical meal comprised a salad, a serving of protein (meat, fowl, or fish), bread, and wine.[35] Fifteenth-century hospices in Burgos put out a similar meal of bread, wine, and a little fish or beef with a bowl of pottage.[36] In the mid- to late fifteenth century, at confraternity banquets in Toledo, Burgos, and Valladolid, some form of meat, especially lamb or goat, was preferred. A variety of fowl was also served in perhaps as many as 70 percent of the banquets. Fish was served only on those days when meat was prohibited by

Isabel Rodríguez, an eighty-year-old illiterate conversa *from Toledo, allegedly broke her Yom Kippur fast in 1677 with* **"trout, fruit,** *chickpea stew, olives, honeyed pastries, and chocolate with biscuits."*[32]

the Church. In addition, a pottage with legumes and vegetables was offered, although not often to the officials. Rice, especially with saffron or cinnamon-sugar, was very popular. Fruits were a typical dessert in Valladolid but all sorts of fried sweets were the favorite desserts.[37] By the seventeenth century, Madrid menus usually contained an appetizer—generally fruit—a main course or courses, which for all but the most elegant tended to be a one-pot stew of some sort, and a final course, which might consist of salad, olives, or some fried sweet.[38]

Of course, documents tend to record only the remarkable, which means that we find less information about the daily menus of common people than about noble households and the feasts they served on special occasions. For example, the menus of *Goodman of Paris* in the late fourteenth century indicate meals of multiple courses and several dishes for each course. He lists the menus of noble banquets so that his wife can pick among them and choose what she might serve when having company. His menus range from six courses, with thirty or so separate dishes, to more modest banquets of only three courses and twenty-four or so dishes. Each course offers a combination of items: beef, fish, tarts, fowl, and sometimes a vegetable or legume. Many courses include a pottage, and about half of each course's offerings are dishes that have strong sauces. Only the meals with six courses end with what we would term a dessert. One of the dinners culminates with a choice of pears, medlars, peeled nuts, hippocras wine, and wafers.[39] Cosman and others have reasoned that so much food at one time must mean that one was expected to taste some or all of the individual dishes, but not to eat substantially of any of them, much as at modern buffet receptions.

In Cataluña, Nola suggests a five-course meal that begins with fruit, followed by a pottage, a roasted dish, another pottage, and finally another stew. Nola offers several variations of this pattern and an occasional dessert.

The *Al-Andalus* cookbook suggests a menu of eight courses. It starts with something bland, perhaps cooked vegetables, or *tafaya,* a stew with meatballs.[40] This is followed by a peppery meat stew called *yinmli* and then an unspecified third course. Next come two strongly flavored dishes, one made with *almorí*[41] and the other with vinegar; then a dish made with honey, an almond-cinnamon-vinegar omelet called a *fartun,* and finally another honey-based dish. The element common to all is that they are cooked: there is no mention of raw or fresh foods.

Cervantes's hyperbolic description of the wedding feast of the wealthy Camacho is clearly within this multicourse banquet tradition, long on meat, fowl, cheese, and wine, and short on vegetables and starches:

> The first thing that offered itself to Sancho's eye was an entire young bull spitted on an entire elm tree and a middling mountain of wood burning on the fire where it was to roast; and around the fire six clay pots which could not have been fashioned in the way of common pots, because they were six half tuns, each of which could hold a side of beef: they swallowed and buried in their gullets whole sheep, leaving not one part visible, as if they had been doves; innumerable hares, already skinned, and chickens, plucked of their feathers, were hung in the branches ready to be buried in the pots; game birds and diverse meats were hung in the trees to be cooled by the air. Sancho counted more than sixty wine skins of more than two gallons each, all of them brimming, as he later discovered, with aromatic wine. Stacks of the whitest bread were piled as high as the mountains of wheat one finds heaped on the threshing floor. The cheeses, piled up like bricks, formed a wall, and two tubs of olive oil, larger than dryers' vats, served to fry the dough fritters, which two brave men with wooden paddles scooped out when they were fried, to swirl them in another tub of prepared honey, which was readied nearby. . . . In the hollowed-out stomach of the bull were twelve tender little suckling pigs which, sewn into place, gave it flavor and tenderized it. The spices of all sorts did not seem to have been purchased by the pound, but by the bushel, and they were all displayed in an enormous chest.[42]

Medieval menu planners thought not in terms of our seven basic food groups, but rather in terms of the four bodily humors, and the need to temper one food with another. Also important were the demands of digestion. The Italian author Platina, writing about 1477, explains:

> In serving food there is an order that should be observed. For the first course, it is recommended that one have all those things that act as a laxative and which are light and not filling, such as a few apples and pears and other such mild and pleasant things. In addition, one may serve lettuce and such, either raw or cooked with vinegar and oil; also eggs, especially soft-cooked, and some other confections which we call sweets, made from spices and pine kernels and either honey or sweet juice. These are to be served to the guests first of all.[43]

Toward the end of his book, Platina discusses those foods which should be eaten last in order to "seal the stomach" and to keep "the vapors from rising," things such as cheese, apples, or radishes. For Platina, as for others concerned with health in the Middle Ages, the humors had to be balanced; therefore the final course of a meal was designed to put hot and cold, wet and dry into harmony.

Trout was a favorite freshwater fish in the Iberian Peninsula. It appears frequently in the medieval cookbooks and is prepared several ways, including as fish croquettes.

Bitter chocolate, cultivated throughout Meso-America prior to the conquest, once it had been sweetened with Arabic sugar rapidly became the favorite drink of the Mexican colonists and by the late sixteenth century of Spaniards as well. An early friar of ethnographic bent gave this recipe:

> . . . grind the cacao first in this fashion: first time crush the beans; second time grind them more finely; and the third time grind them very finely. Mix them with kernels of corn, cooked and washed, and combine them with water in a glass. Strain them, and when they are strained, beat them up so that they raise a froth, which you discard. If it gets too thick, add more water.[44]

Chocolate made such a hit in Spain that it is not surprising to see it consumed by *conversos* as part of any meal that they thought special. Chocolate was thought to have medicinal qualities both as a tonic for energy, a stimulant for intellectual activity, and to firm up loose bowels. Christians consumed it during Lent, as it fortified them against the rigors of the Lenten fasts.[45]

By the late seventeenth century, the ubiquitous chocolate recipe in both Europe and the Americas was this one, jotted down in 1697 by an Italian visitor to Mexico: "Put with each pound of cacao a pound of sugar and an ounce of cinnamon . . . the quality of the drink depends on good cacao and the best cinnamon."[46]

Isabel Rodríguez's Trout

Serves 4

4 whole trout, cleaned and deboned
   (about ½–¾ pound each)

½ cup butter

Dredging

4 tablespoons white flour

1½ teaspoons salt

2 tablespoons whole wheat flour

¾ teaspoon pepper

2 tablespoons dried dill

4 teaspoons dried dill

⅓ cup fresh lime juice

Salt and pepper to taste

½ cup white wine

1. Wash the trout and pat dry.

2. Melt the butter over medium-low heat in a skillet large enough to hold the trout for frying.

3. Meanwhile, in a small bowl, mix the dredging ingredients and place them in a platter or dish large enough to hold each trout individually.

4. Place each trout on the platter with the dredging. Coat both sides of the trout. Open the trout and sprinkle about 1 teaspoon of the dill and salt and pepper evenly over the inside of each one.

5. Place the trout in the skillet. Over medium-low heat, braise the trout equally on both sides until the meat loses its pink color, about 6 minutes each side.

6. Turn the heat to medium-high and pour in the lime juice and wine and sizzle until the liquid has nearly evaporated, about 3 minutes. Carefully remove the trout and serve hot.

Fowl

American supermarkets offer fresh turkey in season and chicken all year. A few other fowl—capons, Cornish hens, and the occasional duck or goose—are in the frozen food aisle. Quail, pheasant, and partridge are fairly common meals at the Spanish table, and some bars in southern Spain serve whole fried thrushes as an appetizer.

Medieval Europeans routinely consumed a substantially wider variety of fowl. The list offered by Villena in his fifteenth-century *Arte cisoria* (*The Art of Carving*) includes a whopping twenty-nine different birds. This variety is corroborated by the recipes in the Catalán, Arabic, and French cookbooks as well as in lists found in medieval poetry. The fourteenth-century Castilian *Libro de buen amor (The Book of Good Love)* lists eight different birds at the dinner table. References in various Iberian medieval chronicles imply that fowl were a favored dish of the nobility.[1] Common among all of these sources are chickens, capons, doves, ducks, geese, partridges, peacocks, and turtledoves. There are occasional references to eating cranes, pheasants, pigeons, swallows, and thrushes.[2] Chickens and hens were favored by nobility and villagers alike. They were served at court at special banquets and they flocked in the barnyard.[3] Peacocks were a royal bird and royalty enjoyed them at their table. Some medieval recipes call for peacocks to be presented with their feathers reattached.[4]

In the extant peninsular cookbooks, some recipes are generic, suggesting that the type of bird does not matter: Nola merely instructs cooks to prepare *volatería* (flying things) or *pájaros* (birds). On the other hand, sometimes distinction mattered. The chicken family has several members and some documents carefully differentiate them, calling for *gallina* (hen), *gallo* (cock), or *pollo* (chicken). The bird's age is also relevant. Nola's recipes clearly distinguish between chicken and hen, for example, or young pigeon and pigeon. Young fowl are often prepared whole or by frying, roasting, or grilling, while older birds are usually stewed and chopped into pieces to incorporate into larger casseroles. Size was similarly important. Granado's cookbook has recipes for large and small domestic fowl and game birds. The *Al-Andalus* cookbook calls for chickens and hens, doves, partridges, pigeons, and thrushes. There the smaller birds are often fried and then prepared with sauces, while hens are usually stewed. Hen broth generally was a staple for stewing and a base for making other sauces.

Inquisition testimonies do not label particular recipes for fowl as being Jewish, perhaps because fowl recipes were so common that they did not distinguish the *converso* eating habits from those of their neighbors. Fowl do not appear to have been favored for Sabbath stews, though there are sporadic references to *adafina* of goose,[5] but they were commonly served to break fasts. In the documents, we have found references to chicken, doves, geese, hens, and partridges. All are served roasted, fried, and stewed; hot and cold; in casseroles and pies.

Pedro Laínez's Gallina con su Caldillo

*Pedro Laínez of Almazán was denounced for eating **"chicken with its broth"** during Lent.[6]*

A laborer named Diego, nicknamed the "trumpet," appeared before inquisitors on July 4, 1505. He told them that one night during Lent of 1500, after a hard day's work, he and some companions were sleeping in a building next to Pedro Laínez's house. Sometime in the middle of the night, just after the first cock crowed, they were awakened by a loud conversation in the street. A new-Christian named Luis del Peso was calling to Pedro Laínez and saying:

> *My lord, we're back from the vineyard. We can't work any more, it is freezing, and we're going to bed now so that we can go back in the morning and try to do something. You won't see us back here until nightfall. I have some fish and sardines and stuff wrapped up for the laborers, and I'm leaving you some stewed chicken with its broth . . . , and I've drawn some wine from your big wineskin into a pitcher and I'm leaving it for you, corked up tight.[7]*

The problem, as Diego and several of his neighbors pointed out to the inquisitors, was that Laínez was not sick, and so he had no business eating chicken during Lent.

Carrete Parrondo and Fraile Conde transcribe the testimonies of fourteen witnesses against Pedro Laínez. The following excerpts will give an idea of the *minutiae* on which many Inquisition cases were built.

- A *converso* named Alvaro said that once in a shouting match Pedro's son called Pedro a Jew.

- Antón de Barbas saw Pedro testing the edge of his knife for sharpness on his thumbnail before slaughtering a goat. Martín de Ortega confirmed that Pedro wouldn't slaughter an ox the way the Christians do, but rather cut the throat as the Jews do.

- Miguel Jiménez said that Pedro refused to lend him money to have some masses said, telling him, "Leave me alone with your masses and your foolish nothings."[8]

- Magdalena, the wife of Martín Jiménez, added that on festival days Pedro would lie in bed until after people were going home from mass.

- Catalina de Valdivieso said she had seen Pedro sway back and forth while praying from some books he kept in a cupboard. And besides, he wouldn't allow salt pork in his stew.

- María la Manzana added that the room with the cupboard had been the village synagogue back when there were Jews, and that she suspected that Pedro still kept a Torah there. She added that when she sneaked in to look she found the cupboard locked.

- Bernaldino de Mendoza said that he had seen Pedro wearing a fringed shirt, like the *tzitziyot* the Jews used to wear. Mendoza actually used and defined the Hebrew word in his denunciation.[9]

- María added another detail: that Pedro's wife Aldonza kept an image of the Virgin on the floor of her bedroom, and that when she prayed she turned her back to it. Juan de Pedro reported that Pedro himself disparaged the Virgin by referring to her as that "lady in a skirt."[10]

In re-creating this recipe, we have focused on the flavor of the broth, loosely adapting one of Nola's recipes for soup that calls for basil and cloves.[11] Basil was already being cultivated on the Iberian Peninsula by the twelfth century. Its Spanish name, *albahaca,* once again bespeaks the Arabic influence on medieval agriculture. In fact, two medieval peninsular Arabic treatises discuss its propagation and one, written by Ibn Bassal of Toledo, mentions it as an ingredient in medications, so basil's use in this broth for sick persons is quite logical. Nola's recipe is a broth for convalescents. For those at the point of death, Nola suggests dipping pieces of gold into the broth several times to enrich its flavor. We have chosen not to follow this last direction.

Pedro Lainez's Chicken with its Broth

Makes 7 cups broth; Serves 4

1 (3¾–4 pound) whole chicken,
    including innards
2 bay leaves, fresh if possible
Salt and pepper to taste
5 whole cloves
1 (1-inch) stick cinnamon

5 leaves fresh basil or ½–¾ teaspoon
    dried, plus 2 leaves fresh basil,
    chopped (see Variation)
About 6 cups water
3 tablespoons rose water (optional)

1. Remove the innards from the chicken. Wash the chicken and cut it into large pieces.

2. In a large stew pot, place the chicken pieces and bay leaves. Add salt and pepper.

3. Place the cloves, cinnamon, and basil leaves in a small gauze bag and put it in the stew pot.

4. Add enough water barely to cover, about 6 cups. Tightly cover the stew pot and simmer about 1¼ hours for a young chicken (2½ hours for a hen). Skim the fat from the top about halfway through the cooking time.

5. Take the chicken pieces out and arrange in a large, warm bowl. Keep warm.

6. Remove the gauze bag of spices and bay leaves and discard them. Bring the broth to a gentle boil. Add the 2 leaves of chopped fresh basil and rose water and simmer 5 minutes more. Pour the broth over the chicken pieces and serve.

VARIATION

Substitute any fresh herb for the basil (fennel or thyme, for example). We suggest using only one herb in order to impart a distinctive flavor to the broth. Adding celery or lovage leaves approximates what is traditionally done in American kitchens today, and will impart a much different flavor than the basil.

Mayor González's Buenas Gallinas

Spanish Inquisition procedure allowed the defendant to attempt to discredit the testimony of potential accusers by naming personal enemies whose testimony could be presumed to contain bias. Since the defendants did not know who their accusers were, it was to their advantage to list in detail as many enemies as possible along with convincing proof of their enmity. The so-called *tachas* lists graphically demonstrate the petty jealousies and hates that infused small-town Iberian communities. Here is a verbatim selection of *tachas* written down by the court scribe in Mayor González's trial in Ciudad Real in 1512–27:

- Diego de Villa's daughter Catalina [a serving girl in Mayor's house] . . . is Mayor's enemy because . . . one day Juana González caught Mayor's son Lorenço Franco kissing Catalina, and Juana was jealous, and told Catalina's father, who had to take her home . . . and because they had thrown her out she was their enemy. . . . And because her father took her without telling Mayor, the Gonzálezes did not pay Catalina her salary, then or later, so that both Catalina and her father are enemies.

- Juana González is their enemy because Pedro, son of Mayor González and Pedro Núñez Franco, had put out one of Juana's eyes with a lance. . . . Also they suspect that Juana González murdered Pedro, because though he was healthy she gave him some sugar one night and he woke up sick and died shortly thereafter.

- The wife of Miguel Rodríguez and their son Miguelito are enemies because when the son worked for them as a shepherd he killed a puppy, and because of it Pedro wounded [Miguelito] and he went home to his mother and complained and skipped work for many days, and his mother went around saying that it was Pedro's and Mayor's fault that her son had stopped working. . . . Besides, everybody knows that Miguel Rodríguez's wife is poor, and fond of testifying . . . and is a foul-mouthed, evil-tempered whore . . . who had even said that her own sister had had a child by a shepherd, which was not true.

- Juan Gallo was their enemy because . . . once, when Pedro Franco and a man named Araoz were fighting, Araoz picked up a rock and

Mayor González was fond of eating **"geese and other fowl"**[12] *and also* **"hens, chickens, and doves."**[13] *After the fasts of Esther she ate* **plump chickens.**[14]

Fowl

threw it at Franco and missed him and hit Juan Gallo in the mouth and knocked out his teeth.

- Miguel the butcher's widow was their enemy because . . . she was a bad woman who had slept carnally with Pedro Núñez Franco, who caught the pox from her.[15]

Roast chicken is featured prominently in contemporary cookbooks, and is cited frequently in association with *conversos*. We offer two recipes here for roast chicken. Both are stuffed and basted, but for different purposes. The first recipe emphasizes the colorful contrast between the yellow chicken and the green stuffing. The second calls for the chicken to be stuffed with chopped fresh fruit. In addition, both its basting sauce and stuffing contain a rich combination of spices meant to contrast sweetness and pungency. The second chicken's basting sauce is composed of a variation on the Arabic *almorí* ingredients that we use in other recipes for an aromatic and tangy flavor.[16]

Mayor González's Green Stuffed Roast Chicken

Serves 6–8

For Stuffing the Cavity

⅓ cup fresh lime juice

3 scallions, sliced in ½-inch-thick pieces

2 cloves garlic, diced

1 cup chopped fresh cilantro

1 tablespoon chopped fresh oregano
leaves, or 1 teaspoon dried

3 tablespoons chopped fresh parsley
leaves, or 1 tablespoon dried

1 tablespoon lime or lemon juice
concentrate, if needed

1 (5–7 pound) roasting chicken,
including innards

¼ cup flour

4 teaspoons coarsely ground sea salt

3 egg yolks, well beaten

At least 3 hours before cooking:

1. In a glass or ceramic container, combine the lime juice with scallions, garlic, and herbs. Make sure the greens get well moistened in the juice. If there is insufficient liquid, add up to 1 tablespoon of lime or lemon juice concentrate. Let the mixture sit for about 10 minutes.

2. Remove the innards from the chicken cavity. Discard or save for future use. Pull off, wrap, and refrigerate the fatty parts from around the cavity's opening. Wash the chicken inside and out and pat it dry. Place it in a large ovenproof glass baking pan.

3. Stuff the cavity with the herb concoction. Let it sit in the refrigerator 3–24 hours.

Cook the chicken:

4. Preheat the oven to 350°. Place the chicken in the oven and bake for 1 hour.

5. Meanwhile, take the pieces of fat that you removed when you cleaned the chicken and place them in a small frying pan to render the fat. Fry on low heat until the pieces are liquid. Discard the unrendered pieces. Reserve the fat.

6. Remove the chicken from the oven.

7. Mix the flour and sea salt together.

Fowl

115

8. With a basting brush, brush all sides of the chicken with the rendered chicken fat. Then baste it with the beaten egg yolks. Finally, gently spoon the flour and salt mixture over the top and sides of the bird.

9. Put the chicken back into the oven. Baste the chicken every 15 minutes (three to four times) with the pan juices.

10. When the chicken is done (see Notes), remove it from the oven and let it sit for 10 minutes.

11. Cut it into serving pieces and place them on a warm platter; spoon the stuffing around the pieces. Serve with the pan juices drizzled over the meat.

NOTES

A minimum marinating time of 3 hours is recommended; overnight is preferable.

We calculate a cooking time of 25 minutes per pound for the poultry. The chicken is done when the meat and juices are no longer pink.

This recipe calls for a lot of salt in the coating. If you prefer, cut the salt in half.

Mayor González's Roast Chicken Stuffed with Fruit and Basted with Almorí

Serves 6–8

Coating

8 tablespoons Nigella Almorí
  (page 22)
1 tablespoon cumin seeds, coarsely
  ground

1 teaspoon dried powdered thyme
8 tablespoons honey
1 tablespoon water

1 (5–7) pound roasting chicken,
  including innards

For Stuffing the Cavity

1½ cups chopped pears
1½ cups chopped apple
2 cups chopped mushrooms, such as
  bella
2 large cloves garlic, finely minced

1 teaspoon cinnamon
½ teaspoon cloves
1½ teaspoons dried ground ginger
1½ teaspoons dried lavender flowers,
  crushed

About 2 to 6 hours before cooking:

1. In a nonreactive bowl, combine the dry *almorí*, cumin, and thyme. In a small saucepan over medium-low heat, heat the honey and water together until they are hot but not boiling. Pour the liquid into the dry ingredients and combine thoroughly. Put the mixture in the refrigerator for about 10 minutes.

2. Remove and discard the innards from the chicken cavity. Pull off and discard the fatty parts around the cavity's opening. Wash the chicken inside and out and pat it dry. Place it breast side up in a large ovenproof glass baking pan.

3. Combine all of the stuffing ingredients in a large nonreactive bowl. Mix well. Stuff the cavity with the herb and fruit concoction. If there is some left over, refrigerate it, covered, until it's time to bake the bird.

4. Remove the *almorí* mixture from the refrigerator. With a sturdy spatula, coat the chicken, except the back, which is resting on the pan. Be sure to coat the legs and wings.

Fowl

5. Poke four or five toothpicks into the chicken. Cover the chicken loosely with waxed paper, using the toothpicks as stakes to hold it secure and off the *almorí*-coated chicken. Place the chicken in a large plastic bag and refrigerate it until it's nearly time to begin cooking.

Cook the chicken:

6. Preheat the oven to 325°. Remove the chicken from the refrigerator and discard the bag and waxed paper. If the *almorí* mixture has slipped off the chicken breast, spread it back on. Place the leftover stuffing mix around the sides of the chicken.

7. Put the chicken in its pan in the center of the oven. Cook until done, about 2½–3 hours (see Note). The *almorí* will turn golden brown and crusty. If it appears to be turning black, loosely cover the chicken with a piece of aluminum foil.

8. When the chicken is done, remove it from the oven and let it sit for 10 minutes.

9. Cut it into serving pieces and place them on a warm platter. Spoon the stuffing around the pieces. Serve with the pan juices drizzled over the meat.

NOTE

We calculate a cooking time of 25 minutes per pound for the poultry. The chicken is done when the meat and juices are no longer pink.

VARIATION

In place of the pears and mushrooms, add this combination of fruits and herbs to the apples and spices:

1½ cups chopped dried apricots
1 cup raisins
⅓ cup chopped fresh chives

Rábanos Buenos en Papillos Rellenos

Antón de Montoro, also known as the Rag Merchant of Córdoba, was one of the most accomplished, and bitterest, of the *converso* poet-fools at the court of Queen Isabel of Castile. As a well-known figure he was also the butt of many attacks, and the songbooks of his time include several comic debates between Montoro and his antagonists. One of these was triggered by the old-Christian poet Román, a nobleman who served as commander of one of the military orders and who was associated with the household of the Duke of Alba. Román complained that the upstart *converso* poets did not know their place, and should leave off Christian themes to write instead about Jewish customs. The poem gives a long list of subjects that Román finds suitable for *converso* rhymsters. For example, in the sixth stanza we find:

<table>
<tr><td>*Trobar por vuestros dineros*</td><td>Sing about your stacks of money,</td></tr>
<tr><td>*con razones no muy flacas,*</td><td>make your rhymes out of your riches,</td></tr>
<tr><td>*lindos garuanços cocheros*</td><td>sing of chickpeas, fat and sunny,</td></tr>
<tr><td>*y gentiles espinacas . . .*</td><td>and of tasty spinach dishes . . .[18]</td></tr>
</table>

The tenth stanza, which is the source of this recipe, pokes fun at several Jewish dietary customs:

<table>
<tr><td>*Trobar en rauanos buenos,*</td><td>Sing of radishes so sweet—</td></tr>
<tr><td>*porque nadie n' os reproche;*</td><td>that will not provoke a fight;</td></tr>
<tr><td>*trobar papillos rellenos*</td><td>sing stuffed chicken necks, a treat</td></tr>
<tr><td>*en los viernes en la noche:*</td><td>that you consume on Friday night.</td></tr>
<tr><td>*trobar en sangre coger*</td><td>Sing of catching in a bowl</td></tr>
<tr><td>*de lo que aueys degollado;*</td><td>the blood of slaughtered lamb or kid;</td></tr>
<tr><td>*trobar en nunca comer*</td><td>sing of how you never did</td></tr>
<tr><td>*lo del Raui deuedado,*</td><td>eat foods that the rabbis forbid,</td></tr>
<tr><td>*sino manjar trasnochado.*</td><td>but rather Sabbath casseroles.[19]</td></tr>
</table>

Though Montoro was undoubtedly a Judaizing *converso,* he died in 1477, several years before the Inquisition began to operate. His widow, Teresa Rodríguez, was burned as a heretic sometime prior to 1487.[20]

A late fifteenth-century satiric poem by Román against the converso *poet Antón de Montoro lists among the foods considered indicative of his Judaizing* **"radishes and stuffed crop."**[17]

Radishes and Stuffed Crop

Serves 2

2 chicken necks

Stuffing

¾ cup bread crumbs

2 tablespoons diced onion

1 clove garlic, diced

2 tablespoons minced fresh green herbs
   (parsley, oregano, thyme)

2 eggs, beaten

3–4 teaspoons coarsely diced chicken
   fat

Chicken broth

4 radishes, thickly sliced

1. With a very sharp knife, cut around the inside of the chicken necks to remove the neck bones and meat. Be careful not to cut the necks.

2. Wash the neck skins and pat dry.

3. Sew shut one end of the necks.

4. Combine all of the stuffing ingredients and mix to a smooth texture.

5. With a small spoon, stuff the necks, but not too full: the stuffing will expand during cooking.

6. Sew shut the other neck ends.

7. Place the necks into a simmering stew or broth and simmer gently 30 minutes or longer.

8. To serve, take the necks out of the broth. Lay them on a plate and surround them with the sliced radishes.

NOTES

Chicken necks with their skins are sometimes difficult to find. You may have to ask the butcher to save them for you.

This recipe can be easily doubled or tripled.

A Drizzle
of Honey

120

The thirteenth-century *Al-Andalus* cookbook contains four chicken recipes explicitly labeled "Jewish dishes." These recipes give much more detail about cooking procedures than the Inquisition references. The numbers and variety of spices in a single dish reflect culinary traditions in the Islamic world, and they also indicate that those Jews living in Islamic Iberia had adopted the same culinary traditions.

We have translated the four recipes here. Like many medieval recipes, the directions in the *Al-Andalus* cookbook exhibit gaps, inconsistencies, dangling clauses, and illogical connectives. Our translation into English is from Huici Miranda's Spanish version of the Arabic manuscript, with bracketed additions from Perry's English translation.[21] We have maintained Huici's punctuation.

Jewish Chicken Dish

Clean the chicken and remove the innards, separate the thighs and the breasts and neck; salt the chicken and let it sit; take its extremities, neck and innards and put them in a pot with selected spices and all the flavorings: cilantro and onion juices, whole pine nuts, a little vinegar and a little almorí, good oil, citron leaves and two sprigs of fennel. Place it over medium heat and when it is done and most of the sauce is gone, thicken it with three eggs and bread crumbs and fine flour, mash the liver, stir it into the mix and cook it little by little, until the liver and mix are cooked and stick together; then take the chicken and fry it slowly and beat it with two eggs, oil and almorí, and don't cease basting the chicken with these inside and out until it is fried and golden; then take a second pan and in it put two tablespoons of oil, and a half of almorí, another half of vinegar and two of rose water, onion juice, spices and flavorings; put it over the fire until it cooks slowly and when it has cooked, leave it until it has absorbed the juices; then pour it onto a second platter [and pour the rest of the sauce on it, and cut up an egg and sprinkle with spices, and ladle the preceding almonds into another dish], and garnish it also with egg yolks; sprinkle spices over it and present the two plates, if God wills.[22]

Obviously this recipe for chicken describes three processes, but it is not precisely clear how the three are to be combined. Given the order of the directions, we have made some guesses about which sauce coats the chicken when baking, and which one later tops it.

Jewish Chicken

Serves 4

8 pieces chicken	salt

Sauce # 1

Cilantro Juice
    1 cup chopped fresh cilantro   5 tablespoons water

Onion Juice
    ½ onion, diced   1½ tablespoons water

Almorí Sauce
    2 tablespoons almorí (Pennyroyal   1 tablespoon vinegar
        or Simple [page 21])   1 tablespoon water

Sauce # 2

1 tablespoon oil   1 tablespoon vinegar
2 tablespoons almorí (Pennyroyal   2 tablespoons rose water
    or Simple [page 21])   ¼ cup very finely chopped onion

Liver Coating Sauce

Innards and neck pieces of 1 chicken   1 tablespoon fennel seeds, ground
¼ pound chicken livers   2 stalks fresh fennel or fresh dill
Sauce #1 (see above)   ½ cup water
½ cup pine nuts   2 eggs, beaten
3 tablespoons olive oil   1 tablespoon finely ground bread
3 tablespoons vinegar   crumbs
6 thin slices lemon, cut in half

2 eggs, beaten
2 tablespoons almorí (Pennyroyal or
    Simple [page 21])
2 tablespoons olive oil, plus 4
    tablespoons for frying

A Drizzle of Honey

122

Garnish

2 hard-boiled eggs, sliced or quartered   1½ teaspoons cinnamon for sprinkling
¼ cup slivered almonds   2 teaspoons sugar for sprinkling

1. Wash the chicken pieces and pat them dry. Salt them and put them in the refrigerator.

Make sauce # 1:

2. Make the cilantro juice: Puree the chopped cilantro with the water in a blender or food processor. Put the puree in a small bowl and set it aside.

3. Make the onion juice: Puree the diced onion with the water in a blender or food processor. Pour it into the cilantro juice and mix the two.

4. Make the *almorí* sauce: Combine the *almorí,* vinegar, and water in a medium nonreactive bowl.

5. Add the cilantro and onion juice to the *almorí* mixture and stir to combine.

Make sauce # 2:

6. Place the oil, *almorí,* vinegar, rose water, and onion in a small pan and heat over low heat just until the ingredients combine well.

7. Remove from the heat and set aside.

Make the liver coating sauce:

8. In a medium stew pot, place the fowl innards, neck pieces, and livers, sauce #1, and the next seven ingredients (pine nuts, olive oil, vinegar, lemon, fennel seeds, fresh fennel, and water). Combine well. Cover and gently simmer over medium heat for about 30 minutes, stirring often.

9. Take the livers from the pot and puree them. Remove the other chicken parts (the neck, innards) and set them aside. Return the liver puree to the pot.

10. Combine the two beaten eggs and bread crumbs. Add to the pot and continue to simmer the mixture until it forms into one mass and thickens, about another 15 minutes. Stir often so that it does not stick or burn. Remove the pan from the heat and set aside.

Cook the chicken:

11. Combine the two beaten eggs, *almorí,* and the 2 tablespoons olive oil. Let sit a few minutes.

12. Baste the chicken with the egg and *almori* mixture.

13. Heat the remaining 4 tablespoons olive oil in a skillet large enough to hold all of the chicken pieces. If you must, use two skillets. Add the coated pieces and fry over medium heat for 15 minutes, turning the pieces often, until they are golden brown.

14. Spread the liver coating sauce over them. Continue to cook, turning the pieces carefully, another 8–10 minutes, or until the chicken is cooked through.

Serve:

15. Place the chicken in a heated large casserole or other heatproof serving dish.

16. Pour sauce #2 over it.

17. Garnish with sliced hard-boiled eggs and slivered almonds. Sprinkle the chicken with cinnamon and sugar. Serve it immediately.

This recipe is not atypical in its random specification of quantities of ingredients. In this case, the liquids have precise quantities stipulated, but the dry ingredients, including herbs, nuts, and the bread crumb thickener, are left to the cook's imagination and past experience.

Jewish Chicken Dish

Clean the chicken and mash its innards with almonds, bread crumbs, a little flour, salt, chopped fennel and cilantro; beat it with six eggs and with the amount of four pounds of water; then put the chicken a little while on the fire and put it in a clean pan with five tablespoons of sweet oil and do not stop stirring it in the oil on the fire until it turns lightly golden; then coat it with the prepared stuffing and leave it until it sets and gets firm; turn it out and put the dressing around it and adorn it with chopped fennel and rue, sprigs of mint and chopped almonds and present it, if God wills.[23]

Jewish Chicken Dish

Serves 4

2 large boneless, skinless chicken
    breasts

Coating

4 chicken livers

½ cup almonds

4 eggs

10 teaspoons bread crumbs

4 teaspoons flour

1½ teaspoons salt

6 tablespoons dried fennel

⅔ cup chopped fresh cilantro

6 tablespoons olive oil

4 tablespoons chopped fresh mint

½ cup fresh lime juice

1. Wash the chicken breasts and pat them dry. Cut them in half lengthwise.

2. Place the four breast pieces in a medium pot. Cover them with water. Bring to a boil; then turn the heat down and simmer very gently for 8 minutes. Remove the pieces and drain them. Cut each piece in half lengthwise again to make eight pieces.

3. Meanwhile, mix the coating: In a food chopper, blend the livers until they are liquid. Add the almonds and mix. Add the eggs, bread crumbs, flour, and salt. Mix again. Add the fennel and cilantro. Mix until all ingredients are well combined.

4. Preheat the oven to 350°. In a large ovenproof skillet or pan, heat the oil over medium-low heat. Lightly brown the chicken breast pieces on both sides, about 5 minutes.

5. Coat the chicken pieces all over with the almond-liver-herb mix.

6. Bake 7–10 minutes. Turn the chicken pieces over with a spatula and cook another 5–7 minutes or until golden brown on both sides.

7. Remove the pan from the oven. Garnish the fowl with fresh mint. Sprinkle about 2 teaspoons of the fresh lime juice over it. Reserve the rest to pass at the table.

A Drizzle of Honey

NOTE

The elegant, brown crusty coating keeps the chicken breasts tender and juicy.

126

This recipe calls for two different kinds of cinnamon. Chinese cinnamon is a cinnamon-like bark called cassia. In many medieval cookbooks the terms seem to have been used interchangeably, and the fifteenth-century Italian *La pratica della mercatura* documents show that the two types were imported roughly the same number of times.[24] However, the *Al-Andalus* cookbook is careful to distinguish between the two. It is interesting to note that both types of cinnamon are called for in this recipe and in another recipe ascribed to Jewish cuisine, "Jewish Eggplant." In both instances they are combined with lavender.[25]

Jewish Partridge

Clean the partridge and season it with salt; then beat its innards with almond and pine nuts and add to this the almorí, *oil, a little cilantro juice, pepper, cinnamon, Chinese cinnamon, lavender, five eggs and enough salt; boil two eggs and fill the partridge cavity with the stuffing; cover it with the boiled eggs and put the filling between the skin and the meat and some of it in the partridge's cavity; then take another pot and put in it four tablespoons of oil, a half of* almorí *and two of salt. Put the partridge in it and put it over the fire, after having reinforced its cover with dough and shake it continuously until it is equally covered, and when the sauce has dried, take off the top and add half a tablespoon of vinegar, citron sprigs and mint and break over it two or three eggs; then put over it a clay pot or one of copper, filled with glowing coals, until it is golden, and then turn it around, until the other side is golden, and everything is fried; then put it on a platter and around it put the filling and garnish it with the yolks with which you have garnished the pot [or with roast pistachios, almonds and pine nuts] and sprinkle it with pepper and cinnamon, then with sugar, and present it, if God wills.*[26]

Jewish Partridge

Serves 2

2 partridges, including innards
(see Notes)

Cilantro Juice

1 cup chopped fresh cilantro, stems
and leaves

5 tablespoons water

Stuffing

Partridge livers, gizzards, and hearts

3 eggs, beaten

1 tablespoon almorí (Pennyroyal or
Simple [page 21])

1 tablespoon olive oil

½ teaspoon pepper

1½ teaspoons cassia (see Notes)

1½ teaspoons cinnamon

1 teaspoon lavender

Cilantro juice (see above)

2 hard-boiled eggs, diced

1 tablespoon pine nuts

2 tablespoon blanched slivered almonds

2 tablespoons olive oil

½ tablespoon almorí (Pennyroyal or
Simple [page 21])

½ teaspoon salt

½ cup loosely packed chopped fresh
mint

2 tablespoons cider vinegar

4 slices lemon, cut in half

Garnish

1 tablespoon chopped pistachios

1 tablespoon chopped almonds

1 tablespoon chopped pine nuts

1 teaspoon cinnamon-sugar

½ teaspoon pepper

Prepare the birds:

1. Remove and save the innards. Wash the birds and pat them dry.

2. Carefully sever the membrane between the breast meat and the skin,
   without cutting the skin.

3. Sprinkle the birds all over with salt. Set them aside.

Make the cilantro juice:

4. Puree the chopped cilantro with the water in a blender or food processor. Set it aside.

Make the stuffing:

5. In a processor, put the livers, gizzards, and hearts and process until nearly liquefied. Add the three eggs. Mix until combined.

6. Add the *almorí,* oil, pepper, cassia, cinnamon, and lavender and process for about 20 seconds, or until all the ingredients are well combined.

7. Pour into a bowl. Stir in the cilantro juice. Add the diced hard-boiled eggs, pine nuts, and almonds.

Stuff the birds:

8. Open the birds' cavities. Spoon the stuffing into the cavities until they are about two-thirds filled. Carefully separate the breast meat and the skin and with a teaspoon insert more stuffing, trying to omit the diced egg pieces. You should have about one third of the stuffing mixture left.

First cooking:

9. Heat the olive oil in a large ovenproof skillet.

10. Mix the *almorí* and salt. Add the mixture to the skillet, stirring briefly.

11. Carefully place the birds in the skillet, breast up. Cover tightly. Fry over medium-low heat for 10 minutes, shaking the pan once or twice to make sure the birds do not stick to the pan.

12. With a large spatula, turn the birds over. Cover again and fry another 10 minutes until they are golden.

Second cooking:

13. Preheat the oven to 350°. Remove the skillet from the heat. Uncover.

14. Place the chopped mint on top of the birds. Pour the vinegar evenly over the birds.

15. Ladle about half the leftover stuffing mixture over each bird. Top with the lemon slices.

16. Cover the pan and bake in the oven for 30 minutes until the stuffing mix is firm and brown.

Serve:

17. Remove the skillet from the oven. Let it sit about 5 minutes.

18. Then ladle the birds onto a warmed serving platter.

19. Combine the garnish ingredients and sprinkle them over the birds.

NOTES

Cornish hens or other small game birds may be substituted for the partridges.

For the cassia in the stuffing, you may substitute 1½ teaspoons ground cinnamon.

There is a lot of salt in this recipe. You may omit the salt added to the frying pan in step **10.**

The adornment of this dish gives it color, texture, aroma, and subtly varied flavors. The color comes from the contrast of the yellow hard-boiled egg yolks and the green mint pieces. The aroma and additional flavor are supplied by the rose water. The two different nuts add texture and flavors to the stewed fowl. Pistachios were known at least by authors on the Iberian Peninsula by Isidoro's time in the sixth century. Though they are rarely mentioned in northern cookbooks, they are an integral part of Arabic cooking and often serve as a topping for stewed dishes, perhaps because they were thought to be "good for the stomach."[27]

Jewish Partridge Dish

Clean, quarter and place [a partridge] into the stew pot with all of the spices and flavorings, fresh cilantro juice, onion water, almorí, *half a tablespoon of vinegar, three of oil and just enough water, mint sprigs, citrons and whole pine nuts; when it has cooked and the major part of the sauce has evaporated, chop the gizzards and liver until soft and beat them with three eggs and paste; add it to the stew pot and stir until it thickens; cover with egg yolks and then pour it out and adorn it with egg yolks and mint sprigs, chopped pine nuts and pistachios, and sprinkle it with rose water and present it, if God wills.*[28]

Jewish Mint Pistachio Partridge

Serves 4–6

Cilantro Juice

1½ cups chopped fresh cilantro

5 tablespoons water

Onion Juice

1 medium onion, chopped

3 tablespoons water

Spice Mixture

2 tablespoons almorí (*Pennyroyal or Simple [page 21]*)

2 teaspoons cinnamon

1 tablespoon dried rosemary

1 teaspoon pepper

2 teaspoons dried thyme

3 tablespoons balsamic vinegar

½ cup water

1 tablespoon olive oil

8 pieces skinless partridge (see Notes)

5 tablespoons chopped fresh mint

4 slices lemon

¼ cup pine nuts

Thickener

2 chicken livers

3 eggs, beaten

Garnish

¼ cup pine nuts

3 tablespoons chopped pistachios

2 tablespoons chopped fresh mint

2 hard-boiled eggs, sliced (optional)

1 tablespoon rose water

Make the spice mixture:

1. Make the cilantro juice: Puree the chopped cilantro with the water in a blender or food processor. Put the puree in a medium bowl and set it aside.

2. Make the onion juice: Puree the chopped onion with the water in a blender or food processor. Add it to the cilantro mixture.

3. In another nonreactive bowl, combine the *almorí,* cinnamon, rosemary, pepper, and thyme. Stir in the vinegar, water, and oil.

4. Add the spice mixture to the cilantro and onion juice, and combine well.

Maria and Martin Garcia's Bird at Hand Stewed with Rosemary and Capers

Serves 2

6–8 pieces poultry (see Notes and Variations)
1½ teaspoons garlic powder
3–5 tablespoons olive oil
2 broth cubes (see Variations)
2 cups water (see Variations)

2 sprigs of fresh rosemary
1 teaspoon salt
½ teaspoon pepper
2 tablespoons capers
2 cups fresh green peas (see Variations)

1. Wash the poultry pieces and pat them dry. Sprinkle with the garlic powder.

2. In a large stew pot, heat the olive oil over medium heat. Add the poultry pieces and fry them on both sides until the skin is golden. Remove from the skillet with a slotted spoon. Pour out the oil.

3. Place the poultry pieces, broth cubes, water, rosemary, salt, and pepper in the stew pot. Cover. Bring the liquid to a boil, then turn down the heat and simmer slowly for 20 minutes. Stir occasionally.

4. Add the capers and peas. Simmer another 10 minutes uncovered, until the peas are tender.

5. Remove the poultry pieces, peas, and capers to a warmed platter and keep warm. Turn the heat under the stew pot to high and boil the re-maining liquid until it reduces by about half. Add salt and pepper to taste. Drizzle half of the broth over the poultry pieces on the platter. Pass the other half at the table as a sauce.

NOTES

The cut-up pieces should total 1½–2 pounds.

The stewed poultry is good served over rice or couscous.

VARIATIONS

Any edible fowl will do: partridge, Cornish hen, quail, dove, and so forth.

Substitute 2 cups of chicken or vegetable stock for the broth cubes and water.

Choose whatever Old World green vegetable is in season: cabbage, chard, mus-tard greens, asparagus, etc.

One other green herb, such as chives, can also be added in step 4.

Fowl

María and Martín García's Bird at Hand with Dried Fruits

Serves 2

8 dried figs, sliced in half (see
  Variations)
8 dried apricots, sliced in half (see
  Variations)

1 cup hot chicken broth
2 chicken breasts, split in half, or 4
  chicken legs

Spice Mixture

2 tablespoon almorí (Pennyroyal or
  Simple [page 21])
5 tablespoons flour

5 tablespoons whole wheat flour
1 teaspoon ground anise

1 cup chopped fresh cilantro
5–6 tablespoons olive oil

⅓ cup lemon juice

1. Soak the dried figs and apricot pieces in hot chicken broth for 30 minutes. Drain and reserve the broth.

2. Soak the fowl in cool water for 10 minutes. Drain. Do not pat dry.

3. Make the spice mixture: Combine the *almorí*, the two types of flour, and the anise in a small bowl. Place the mixture in a flat pan.

4. In a food processor puree the chopped cilantro in ¼ cup of the reserved chicken broth (from step 1).

5. Dredge the chicken in the spice mixture.

6. Heat the olive oil in a large skillet over medium heat. Fry the chicken slowly, until it is browned on all sides, about 12 minutes.

7. Add the apricots and figs. Add the cilantro juice-broth mixture. Simmer, covered, over low heat for 10 minutes. Stir occasionally.

8. Take the lid off the skillet. Add the lemon juice and continue to simmer another 10 minutes until the liquid has nearly evaporated. Turn the meat pieces occasionally to ensure that they are coated on all sides. Serve hot.

*A Drizzle
of Honey*

136

VARIATIONS

You may substitute any Old World dried fruit for the figs and apricots, such as raisins, apples, or pears, but not mangoes or pineapple.

Any edible fowl will do: partridge, Cornish hen, quail, dove, etc.

Ansarón Asado

Geese in the barnyard are more assertive than guard dogs. Geese on the table speak louder than chicken or turkey. In medieval and Renaissance times geese were often found on the holiday tables of the nobility. Residents in Seville in the fifteenth century even called their men at the court "goosers" (*ganseros*) because the food was identified with the court and the nobles had large flocks of geese.[33] Fifteenth-century confraternity menus in Valladolid show a preference for fowl for their banquets, and geese figure prominently in the list. Although they cost somewhat more than chickens or hens, their price was not exorbitant.[34] Occasionally, recipes for goose appear in English, French, and Iberian medieval cookbooks. Generally the recipes concentrate on sauces for the fowl, usually with modest amounts of milder spices. Recipes for goose have all but disappeared from Sephardic cookbooks in the twentieth century. Only Roden's *Book of Jewish Food* offers some Ashkenazi recipes.[35] The spices for our roast are culled from two recipes for geese found in the *Al-Andalus* cookbook.

Unfortunately, geese are one of the fattiest of fowl, and they can be messy to clean and messy to cook. They are generally roasted slowly so that the fat has ample time to percolate out through the cuts in their skin. Cooking time for a medium-size goose is about five hours.

Geese *were commonly* **roasted** *by crypto-Jews for special occasions.*[31] *A satire against Antón de Montoro also identifies as a Jewish dish a "fat* **goose** *for curing with* **spices.**"[32]

Roast Goose

Serves 6–8

1 (10–13 pound) whole goose, fresh or completely thawed, including   innards (see Notes)

Spice Mixture

1 tablespoon cassia (see Notes)   2 teaspoons dried rosemary
1 tablespoon dried thyme leaves   1 teaspoon cumin

12–15 slivers fresh ginger   1 apple, cored and quartered
1 onion, quartered   Slivered almonds (optional)

The day before serving:

1. Remove the innards from the goose cavity and wrap and store for future use. Wash the bird inside and out. Place the bird on a rack in the kitchen sink. Pour one large teakettle of boiling water over all of the bird, inside and out, to reduce the amount of fat. Let the goose drain in the sink for 2–3 minutes.

2. Meanwhile, combine the spice mixture ingredients in a grinder and crush to a fine powder.

3. Place the bird, breast side down, on a rack on a large roasting pan. With a sharp, long-bladed knife, loosen the skin from the meat. With fingers or a spatula, spread one third of the spice mixture along the back meat, under the skin.

4. With a sharp knife, pierce the bird in several places on the back. Place one third of the ginger slivers in half of the slits. Leave the other slits empty (this allows the fat to exit the body more easily).

5. Turn the bird over. Repeat steps **3** and **4** for the goose breast, using two thirds of the remaining spice mixture and half of the remaining ginger slivers. Spread the remaining spice mixture over the goose legs.

6. Place the onion and cored apple pieces and the rest of the ginger in the large cavity.

7. Cover the bird with plastic wrap and then put the bird—still in the pan—in a plastic bag that can be sealed well. Place the bird in the refrigerator until ready to cook the next day.

Cook the bird:

8. Preheat the oven to 450°. Take the plastic wrappings off the goose. Let the goose sit while the oven is preheating. Sprinkle the almonds over the top of the breast, if you are using them.

9. Cook the bird at 450° for 1 hour. Then turn down the oven to 325° and continue to cook, calculating approximately 22 minutes per pound. At least twice during the baking, remove the goose from the oven and siphon off the accumulating grease. The goose is done when you prick the thigh with a knife or fork and the juice runs clear.

10. Remove the goose from oven and let sit 10 minutes before slicing. Discard the apple and onion in the cavity.

NOTES

Geese are greasy fowl. Use kitchen gloves as you move the bird around.

Cinnamon may be substituted for the cassia.

Cover the wings partway through the baking to keep them from burning.

Save the uncooked goose innards and some of the roast drippings for making Goose Stew (page 142) or for Pedro Núñez Franco's Lamb and Liver Stew (page 201).

Adafina de Ansarón

Os haré comer de boda,	For the wedding, I shall serve you
. . . adafina de ansarón,	. . . **goose stew**
que coció la noche toda,	that cooked all night,
sin tocino.	without salt pork.[36]

By the fifteenth century it was fashionable for the Castilian royal courts to be entertained after dinner by court fools, musicians, and jugglers. Unlike their northern European counterparts, Castilian court fools seemed to have relied less on physical humor and more on their poetic wit. The line between court fool and courtier was very imprecisely drawn, for nobles of all ranks seem to have ventured into the lists to joust with the professional and semi-professional merrymakers. The humor was by turns bawdy and intellectual, *ad hominem* (or *ad feminam*) and generic, directed at a particular occasion ("today they made me hunt boar") or at human foibles in general. Moreover, in the courts of Juan II (1406–54), Enrique IV (1454–74), and Isabel (1474–1504), a substantial number of the poetic jousters were *conversos*.

The result was that many of the surviving poems, assiduously collected by the royal anthologizers, deal with the fifteenth-century clash of cultures. In the days before the Inquisition, the unassimilated, Judaizing *conversos* were thought funny, at least among the old-Christian elements at court, and there are dozens of poems that allude to the *conversos*' "peculiar" customs. As we might expect, both Sabbath stews and Jewish holiday foods attracted their share of attention. For the cultural anthropologist these poems provide—among many other things—clues to what foods in that milieu were routinely considered to be Jewish.

Here by way of example is the fourth stanza from a poem by the old-Christian Count Paredes lampooning the *converso* Juan Poeta. The poem asserts that every Christian cult item that Juan touches takes on Jewish characteristics:

No dexemos la patena	Let us not forget the paten
a que la boca llegastes,	and the Host that tongues extol,
que luego que la besastes,	for the moment that you kissed it
se dize que la tornastes	there are rumors that it twisted
caçuela con berengena.	into eggplant casserole.
El ara qu'es consagrada,	And the consecrated altar

y de piedra dura y fina,	of fine marble, hard and new,
de vuestra mano tocada,	at your touch gave up its matter
en un punto fue tornada	and became a great round platter
atayfor con adafina.	loaded up with Sabbath stew.[37]

That at least some of these stews were made from goose can be seen in the snippet of verse from which this recipe is derived.

We take the leftover roast goose to prepare a goose stew, building on the spices of the already cooked meat. It was not unusual in medieval Iberian cooking to double-cook main dish ingredients, and given the substantial amount of fat in geese, using already-roasted goose meat as a base for the stew is a good way to keep down the amount of fat in the stew. Our recipe is loosely inspired by a sauce which is called "Saracen Sauce" in medieval English cookbooks, another indication of how the importance of color was often attributed to Islamic influence. This sauce imparts a rosy red hue, a subtle flavor, and a crunchy texture to the final product. Since this goose stew was served at a wedding, we have added some elegant touches for its presentation.

Goose Stew

Serves 4–6

Innards from 1 goose
1 bay leaf
1 onion, quartered
6 cups coarsely chopped leftover roast
 goose (see Variations)
½ cup roast goose drippings
¾ cup red wine

⅓ cup rose hips, pounded
1 tablespoon cassia or cinnamon
1½ teaspoons shredded fresh ginger
1 teaspoon pepper
Seeds of 1 pomegranate
¼ cup honey

Garnish

½–¾ cup loosely packed fresh rose
 petals
½ cup coarsely chopped pine nuts

½ cup loosely packed chopped mint
 leaves

1. Place the uncooked innards, bay leaf, and quartered onion in a large stew pot. Barely cover with water. Cover and simmer for 30 minutes. Skim off any fat or residue.

2. Add the chopped already-roasted goose meat, drippings, wine, rose hips, cinnamon, ginger, pepper, and half the pomegranate seeds. Cover and gently simmer for 30 minutes.

3. Add the remaining pomegranate seeds and the honey and continue to simmer for 30 minutes.

4. Take the lid off and let the stew simmer and the liquid nearly evaporate, about 10 minutes more.

5. To serve: Discard the bay leaf. Pour the stew onto a warmed platter. Decorate with the garnishes.

NOTE

This stew is very good when served with couscous.

VARIATIONS

If you do not wish to use the innards, start the stew at step **2,** adding barely enough water to the wine to just cover the meat.

If you wish, make the stew from an unroasted goose.

1. With the goose in the kitchen sink, pour boiling water all over it, inside and out to remove some of the fat.

2. Hack the goose into 4 to 6 big pieces. Place the pieces and the innards in a large heavy pot and cover with water. Simmer for an hour. Remove the goose from the pot with a slotted spoon. Discard the water and fat. Return the goose to the pot, add the bay leaf and quartered onion, add water to barely cover, and simmer another hour. Skim off the fat. Continue from step **2** above.

Use a combination of red wine and vinegar.

Clara Fernandes's Carne Fria com Azeite

One of Manoel
Fernandes's
daughters reported
that her stepmother,
Clara Fernandes,
was in the habit of
*eating **"cold sliced***
chicken or beef
dressed with olive
***oil."*[38]*

Crypto-Judaism was so strong in the late sixteenth century in the sugar communities of northeast Brazil that the Portuguese Inquisition sent several investigative teams to the region to ferret out Judaizers and to return them to Portugal for trial. The reports of these teams make fascinating reading, for they detail not only crypto-Jewish customs but also the folk religions of the region's large black community, brought to Brazil as slaves to work the sugar fields. In addition, the investigators seem to have been particularly concerned with homosexuality, which they viewed as a religious abomination, and their reports are unusually explicit about both male and female practices.

Clara Fernandes, the widow of the old-Christian jailer Manoel Fernandes, was denounced in the late 1590s by the family's *mulatta* serving girl Isabel Ramos. Apparently Manoel had some children with another woman as well, for one of the illegitimate daughters told Isabel that her stepmother Clara used to clean her house on Sundays and that she often whipped a little silver crucifix.

Isabel reported that Manoel had complained to her that his wife "ought to be burned because she was a bad Jew who ate cold meat with olive oil." Eating food cold, or at room temperature, on Saturday was one way of complying with regulations that prohibited cooking on the Sabbath. Quick-witted *conversos* devised alternate explanations for the custom. For example, when Joana Libiana of Barcelona was asked why she ate cold partridges on Saturdays, she responded that the meat tasted better cold.[39]

Clara Fernandes's Cold Meat with Oil

2 teaspoons fresh tarragon or 1
  teaspoon dried
Salt and pepper to taste

2 tablespoons olive oil
1 pound sliced cooked chicken or beef

1. Combine the tarragon, salt, pepper, and olive oil in a small container and cover tightly. Shake. Let sit for 5 minutes or so to allow flavors to meld.

2. Lay the sliced meat on the platter or in serving bowls. Shake the dressing container well and sprinkle the dressing over the meat. Serve.

VARIATION

This cold meat dish obviously can be served with any number of herbs and spices and other condiments. In keeping within the Iberian medieval palate, fresh cilantro, onion, or capers would have been common. Brazilian new-Christians might have added a pinch of allspice or red chile powder.

Fowl

Beef

The astounding number of Inquisition references to meat lead us to two conclusions. The first is that, compared to most of the rest of Europe, Spaniards—Jews and *conversos* among them—ate a lot of meat. Cattle ranching was particularly important in the south of Spain, where the fifteenth-century final reconquest of Islamic lands had opened up high, dry grasslands for cattle grazing. Municipalities, too, dedicated some of their common land to pasturage. To avoid confusion about ownership of the cattle, registers of cattle brands were kept in the town halls. In every region, an annual fair marketed beef and hides. In fact meat, both beef and lamb, was such an important part of the Iberian diet that to raise money for the Reconquest War, at one point the papacy granted contributors an exemption from the rules prohibiting eating meat on Friday or during Lent.[1] So much beef was available that it was not considered a high-prestige food. In the 1438–69 accounts of a confraternity in Valladolid, beef appears on 80 percent of the menus, and was generally reserved for the poor. The same accounts indicate that at 70 percent of the banquets for officials chicken was served.[2] About the same time in the Toledo hospice for the poor, the indigent were served beef, generally boiled, while veal was reserved for the administrators.[3]

The second conclusion is that several customs associated with the preparation and consumption of meat were good indicators of Judaizing and thus drew a lot of attention from the inquisitors and their networks of informants. The key indicators were of three sorts: customs related to the slaughtering and preparation of meat; meat recipes specifically identified as Jewish, or as prevalent among Jews; and meat dishes prepared on Fridays for the Sabbath, or on the eve of certain holidays, or on days prohibited by the Christian calendar.

Prior to the expulsions from Spain and Portugal, meat was generally slaughtered in the ritual fashion by a kosher butcher; after the expulsions crypto-Jews had to slaughter at home. Either way, the animal was quickly dispatched by bending back its head and drawing a specially sharpened knife across its throat in a single stroke. The carcass was hung and the blood drained out and discarded, and the stained earth covered with dirt or with ashes. To make certain that every trace of blood had been removed from the meat, some crypto-Jewish housewives soaked the meat several times in salted water, and then hung it to drain in a wicker basket.[4] These customs persisted for an extraordinary length of time: as late as 1720 a trial identified some twenty families whose principal Judaizing custom was to soak and drain their meat.[5]

In addition to removing the blood, when crypto-Jews dressed their meat they tried to remove all excess fat.[6] A checklist of Judaic customs prepared for inquisitors in the 1480s explains the custom in some detail: "Removing the fat from meat and abstaining from eating it recalls how the people of Israel used to make a sacrifice to God of the fat, throwing a piece of fat the size of a walnut into the fire; and these pieces of fat were commonly taken from the loin and haunch of the beef before putting it in the cooking pot."[7] As late as 1603 in Mexico City a soldier told inquisitors how he had gone "to light the brazier and warm the room in Violante Rodríguez's house and he had found a pile of pieces of fat she had removed from the meat, and he went back to Miguel Gil's room crossing himself and saying, 'This Duarte Rodríguez is a real devil.'"[8]

Lastly, most crypto-Jews also removed the sciatic vein from their joints of meat. The reason, as the Inquisition checklist of Judaic customs put it, was "in remembrance of when the Angel fought with Jacob and he was left lame; and because of this the children of Israel do not eat the nerve in the leg nor the fat which is connected to it . . . as is written at the end of Genesis."[9] Later generations of crypto-Jews quite naturally forgot the reasons for the customs. In Brazilian Bahía in the 1590s several women said that they removed the vein because that made the meat taste better. María Lopes confessed that she even porged the vein from pork before she roasted it.[10]

The injunction against work on the Sabbath means that Saturday's dinner has to be prepared on Friday. Medieval Jewish cooks favored one-dish meals that either could be prepared on Friday and then eaten at room temperature on Saturday or started in an iron or ceramic pot Friday afternoon and kept warm in a banked fire until the family sat down to dine on Saturday after prayer. The Inquisition memorandum calls the Sabbath casserole *ani*:

> Ani, *which means hot food, was usually made with fat meat, chickpeas, faba beans, green beans, hard-boiled eggs, and any other vegetable. It was cooked all night on Friday, because on Saturday the Jews could not cook food. And that dish was kept hot on its warming oven until mealtime on Saturday. And thus this* ani *was a principal way of keeping the Sabbath.*[11]

As the memorandum states, the dish could be made of just about anything. Often the base was stewing beef, or—depending on the region and what was available—goat or lamb. Fish casseroles were especially popular on the coasts, but the widespread availability in Iberia of river and ocean fish, fresh as well as dried and salted, meant that fish casseroles were common everywhere. Eggs were also a common protein source in the Sabbath stews.[12] For poorer families, or during those times of the year such as the forty days of Lent when eating meat was forbidden to Christians and *conversos* had to be particularly circumspect about what they ate, vegetables might form the base of the Sabbath stew. Again, these varied by region, by time of year, and by what vegetables were growing outside the particular cook's door.

Because the Sabbath casserole was so common, it was known by many different names in addition to *ani*. *Hamín,* derived from the Hebrew word for "warm," appears in a 1484 trial in Teruel.[13] *Conversos* in Segovia in the 1480s used the Spanish term for the same concept: *caliente.*[14] *Trasnochado,* Spanish for "kept overnight," is the name cited in a late fifteenth-century anti-*converso* poem.[15] Around Granada in the 1580s the dish seems to have been called *boronia,*[16] a term which may come from the *Al-Andalus* cookbook's recipe for a baked casserole of eggplant and mutton combined with beaten eggs and seasonings called *buraniya.*[17] But by far the most common name was *adafina,* derived from the Arabic term for "hidden," since the pot's cover, which helped retain the heat, hid the contents from view. This term was so widely used that it has lodged in the language to this day, where the expression *ir de adafina* was used well into the 1960s in parts of Castilla-León to indicate the cold meal carried along on a journey.[18]

Diego Enríquez's Carne con Yerbabuena

In modern elegant dining, presentation is important: texture and arrangement offer a visual feast before the first fork is lifted. A pleasing aesthetic whets the appetite, and both sight and scent promote hunger. A touch of color may highlight the presentation: a sprig of parsley alongside a slice of beef, a swirl of raspberry syrup on crème caramel, a black olive punctuating a bowl of rice.

Medieval diners were as sensitive to the importance of the visual aspect of dining as we credit ourselves to be, perhaps more so. In medieval meal planning color was often one of the primary concerns. It is to Islamic cuisine where we can look for the inspiration of medieval cooks.[20] Already in tenth-century Baghdad's court, food color was extolled in verse: "Here capers grace a sauce vermilion."[21] A tenth-century Iraqi cookbook emphasizes colorful garnishes which include combinations of ingredients, such as rue and a diced boiled egg or egg yolks and pomegranate seeds.[22] The thirteenth-century *Al-Andalus* cookbook contains numerous references to color as part of its instructions and recipe titles.[23]

Perhaps imitating Arabic models, medieval Christian cooks favored certain ingredients or combinations of ingredients to achieve certain colors for their dishes. The most-mentioned colors are green, yellow, and white, but red is also evident in the choice of spices and coloring agents.[24] The primary colors were not the only desired hues, and recipes sometimes distinguish subtle shadings, as between tints of green. Some titles of medieval recipes even highlight their color, such as in "Blue Jelly" and "Golden Soup."[25] Furthermore, written directions often indicate how a specific preparation is to look when finished: "This pot wants to be yellow," says Nola, as he instructs adding saffron to the recipe for leg of lamb.[26] Other times he enjoins the cook not to let a sauce boil, so it won't lose its green color.[27]

Green apparently was the most commonly stressed color in Christian, Jewish, and Muslim kitchens. The addition of combinations of mint, parsley, cilantro, and spinach—all easily cultivated in the back-door garden—made this color relatively easy, and cheap, to attain. Several recipes from Arabic cookbooks require cilantro juice, which adds flavor as well as color. Elsewhere, mint served much in the same way. Most of the green sauces have names which include the word "green," but others simply use the main ingredient to designate a dish whose color all cooks would instantly recognize.

In Toledo in 1580 Ana López used to spy on the converso *Diego Enríquez family through the cat hole in their door. She saw them make an* adafina *of* **"meat with parsley, onions, cabbage, and mint."**[19]

Beef

149

One of the sauces in Nola, entitled simply *Perexilada* ("Parsleyed"), is the common medieval "green sauce" that has variations in England, France, and Germany.[28]

Yellow, too, was especially popular. Nola offers a "yellow plate" and prescribes that another dish "be yellow and very bright."[29] One way to emphasize the yellow color was to add egg yolks—lots of them.[30] But spices were the most usual agents of color, and saffron was the most prized spice. While in other parts of Europe turmeric also may have been used, Iberian cooking almost always preferred saffron, despite its cost. Saffron (Latin: *crocus;* Spanish: *azafrán*), mentioned once in the Bible (Song of Solomon 4:13), was extremely important in Mediterranean lands. It was used by both Egyptians and Romans. By the tenth century the Muslims had brought it to the Iberian Peninsula. Its northern journey to France, Germany, and England took two or three centuries longer.[31] Medieval recipe titles for yellow dishes also used terms like *dorada* (golden), from the word for gold, *oro,* and *ginestada* (yellow) from the Spanish name for the yellow flowers of the broom plant.[32]

Red was also desirable for its stunning contrast to the food's original natural color.[33] Red can be created with onion skins, as when boiling eggs,[34] or with the red root of alkanet borage, or even with parts of roses. The fourteenth-century English cookbook, the *Forme of Cury,* has a sauce recipe calling for pounded rose hips with almonds, red wine, and spices. Its name is *Sawse Sarzyne,* or "Saracen Sauce," a clear allusion to Arabic influence. Medieval recipes from elsewhere in Europe sometimes called for red sandalwood, a spice from an East Indian tree. We have not found references to this spice in the Iberian Peninsula's Christian cookbooks, but that does not ensure that it wasn't used, especially since there is one recipe calling for its use in the *Al-Andalus* cookbook.[35] It seems that the pomegranate's seeds and juice may have been preferred on the Peninsula.

The final touches in meal presentation often featured bright color combinations. Garnishes of violets, rose petals, snips of green herbs such as parsley or cilantro, pistachios or almonds, and diced hard-boiled eggs, were not only tasty but pleased the eye as well. Sometimes the garnishes were of two or more colors for a checkerboard effect.[36] More costly banquets might even present the dishes garnished with peacocks' feathers and garlands of flowers for added visual display.

The Sabbath stews, because they simmer for long periods of time, tend toward the brown end of the palette. Adding spices such as cumin, as is sometimes specified, serves to make them browner. Given the medieval predilection for color, we suspect that the occasional bright garnish, added as the dish was put on the table, would not have been deemed to violate the Sabbath's strictures against work.

Diego Enríquez's Beef Mint Stew

Serves 4

3 tablespoons olive oil, plus more if
  needed
3 cloves garlic, coarsely chopped
2 onions, quartered
1½ pounds beef, cut into 1–1½-inch
  cubes
Beef or Vegetable Broth (page 24)
  and/or water

1 tablespoon salt
1½ cups loosely packed chopped fresh
  mint
2½ cups loosely packed chopped fresh
  parsley
4–5 cups chopped cabbage

1. In a large ovenproof stew pot, heat the olive oil. Fry the garlic until golden, on medium-high heat. Add the onions and sauté until golden, stirring so that they will not burn, about 5–6 minutes. Remove the garlic and onions and set aside.

2. Sauté the meat on medium-high heat until lightly browned on all sides, adding more oil if needed to keep it from sticking. Return the garlic and onion mixture to the pot. Add just enough broth and/or water to barely reach the top of the meat. Cover and simmer for 2½ hours, stirring occasionally.

3. Add the salt, mint, parsley, and cabbage to the pot. Stir once. Cover the pot. Turn the heat up and bring the stew to a bubbling boil. Turn the heat down and simmer, covered, for 20 minutes.

4. Preheat the oven to 250°. Put the covered stew pot into the center of the oven and continue cooking until ready to serve, at least 2 hours, but as long as all night. The stew will resemble a thick brown soup.

NOTES

Serve in bowls. This is a good stew to serve with *cuez* bread. See recipe page 251.

This stew emits an enticing mint aroma while it is cooking. The mint and parsley flavors are subtle, and for that reason there are no spices other than salt in this stew.

Rita Besante's Carne con Garbanzos y Berzas

Rita Besante was the wife of Jaime Martínez de Santángel. They had both been converted to Christianity around 1412 as a result of the preaching campaigns of the Dominican friar Vicente Ferrer. Rita testified before inquisitors in the Aragonese city of Teruel in January of 1486 in the trials of her two daughters, Brianda and Alba de Santángel. Rita confessed that when her daughters were very young she had not dared to reveal her Judaism to them, but that when they were older she taught them how to cook and insisted that they prepare food in the Jewish fashion.

On Sukkot the two girls frequently visited the booths of their Jewish friends, where they were given treats of peaches and candy. They also liked to watch the bulls being run through the streets of Teruel's Jewish quarter. Despite the Santángel family's commitment to their Jewish heritage, when the two girls reached puberty, they opted to abandon their Judaizing in order to assimilate into the Christian mainstream. With emotions which we can only surmise, their mother permitted them to break off their crypto-Jewish life two years before their marriage, since their prospective husbands were old-Christians. In fact Brianda's husband, the soldier Juan Garcés de Marcilla, was in charge of carrying out the Inquisition's sentences in Teruel.

The inquisitors concluded that because the two girls' Judaizing activities were their mother's fault, and because they had willingly abjured from their former practices, they were to be absolved of guilt and reconciled with the Catholic Church without penalty.

Brianda de Santángel reported that her mother, Rita Besante, had her maids cook a Sabbath stew of **"meat, chickpeas, and cabbage."**[37]

Beef

Rita Besante's Meat, Chickpeas, and Cabbage Stew

Serves 6

3 tablespoons olive oil, plus more if
needed

2 cloves garlic, diced

1 large bay leaf, fresh if possible

1 large onion, cut into large pieces

1½ pounds boneless stewing beef, cut
into 1–1½-inch cubes

¾ cup broth or water

Spice Mixture

1 tablespoon sugar

4 teaspoons ground anise

1 teaspoon salt

1 teaspoon pepper

2 (15-ounce) cans chickpeas, drained

1 small cabbage (about 2 pounds)

1. Heat the olive oil in a large ovenproof pot or Dutch oven. Add the garlic and bay leaf and sauté over medium heat until brown. Remove the bay leaf and garlic to a plate.

2. Add the onion and sauté until lightly browned (about 5 minutes), stirring occasionally. Remove to a plate.

3. Add the stewing beef to the pot and fry gently until browned on all sides, adding more oil if needed to keep it from sticking.

4. Return the onions, garlic, and bay leaf to the pan.

5. Pour the broth (or water) over the mixture and bring it to a boil. Turn the heat down to simmer. Cover and cook for 1½ hours.

6. Preheat the oven to 300°.

7. In a small bowl, mix the spices. Stir the spice mixture into the meat. Add the drained chickpeas.

8. Pull the cabbage apart leaf by leaf. Lay the whole leaves on top so that they cover the chickpea/meat mixture. Cover the pot and bake for 1 hour.

9. To serve, ladle the stew carefully on plates or into bowls so that the cabbage covering remains intact. Discard the bay leaf when serving.

NOTE

This stew may be kept warm overnight at your oven's lowest setting.

Blanca Ramírez's Olla de Garbanzos y Habas

Blanca Ramírez's 1523 trial in Toledo makes reference to events fifty years earlier, before the expulsion and before the Inquisition was established in that city. It makes clear how thoroughly intermingled the Jewish and *converso* communities were in those bygone days. Blanca's maid, Ana Díaz, reported how the *converso* Ramírez family used to dress up on Friday nights before going to the synagogue, where they washed their hands at the door and lit candles. They contributed money for the Jewish poor. The Ramírez family kept as kosher a kitchen as possible, instructing their maids to "remove the fat and the vein from the leg of lamb, and to soak it three times in salt water." When Blanca baked she always threw a few bits of dough into the fire, telling her maid that "the smoke that rose from those pieces ascended to heaven."[39] On the day before Yom Kippur, Blanca washed herself in the *mikvah* with the Jewish women, and then gathered with her family for a meal of olives and unleavened bread, followed by meat. On Sukkot, the *conversa* women put on their finest clothes and went to visit the booths of the Jews.

A servant named María, who worked for Blanca's mother-in-law, contributed this extraordinarily detailed recipe for Sabbath stew, which continues with these cooking instructions:

> . . . and the aforesaid stew began to cook at sundown until the next day at noon. And when they wanted to cover it up the night before they would put into the stew pot **Swiss chard** that had been sliced and chopped and pounded; and if there was no Swiss chard they put in **radish leaves.**

*Blanca Ramírez's Sabbath meal was "**chickpeas** and **beans,** the fattest available **meat** or **udder,** put in a pot with **eggplant,** if it was in season, with dried **coriander** and **caraway and cumin and pepper and onion.** And they called those spices and onion güesmo."[38]*

Beef

Blanca Ramírez's Chickpeas and Bean Stew

Serves 6

1 cup dry chickpeas, rinsed

1 cup dry white beans, rinsed

2 medium onions, sliced

2–3 tablespoons olive oil

2 pounds boneless beef or lamb, cut into 1-inch cubes

1–1½ cups broth or water

1 medium-large eggplant (about 2½ pounds)

Spice Mixture

1½ teaspoons coriander seeds

1½ teaspoons cumin seeds

1 teaspoon caraway seeds

2 teaspoons salt

1 teaspoon peppercorns

50 Swiss chard leaves, washed

1. In separate pots, bring the beans and the chickpeas to a boil in water to cover. Boil for 2 minutes. Remove them from the heat and let cool 30 minutes. Drain and rinse them.

2. In a large stew pot, fry the onions in the olive oil over medium heat until translucent, about 5 minutes. Remove and set aside.

3. Sauté the meat over medium heat in the pot until browned on all sides.

4. Return the onions to the pot. Add broth or water to barely cover the meat. Simmer, covered, for 1 hour.

5. Meanwhile, peel the eggplant and cut it into 1-inch cubes. Sprinkle them with salt and let them sit for about 30 minutes. Rinse and pat dry.

6. Add the beans, chickpeas, and eggplant to the simmering meat. Cook covered 1 hour more.

7. Grind the spices together and add them to the pot. Continue to simmer, 1–1½ hours more, until the meat is tender.

8. Remove the stems from the chard. Chop the leaves. Pound the larger chard stems until soft. Add the chard to the pot.

9. Simmer, covered, 30 minutes, stirring occasionally.

NOTE

Serve with rice or couscous.

Hamín de Toledo

One of the many women of the region of La Mancha who were accused of preparing and eating Sabbath *adafina* was Catalina Alfonso, the wife of the physician Gómez de Ayllón, of Huete, who was tried in 1493. Typical of the Judaizing converts of the expulsion generation, Catalina and Gómez felt a deep attachment to their former religion. Witnesses described how at night, prior to 1492, the couple used to sneak off to the local synagogue, where their hearts would overflow with emotion to see the niche where the Torah was kept. Moreover they demonstrated their commitment to the Jewish community by donating oil for the synagogue lamps every Friday. Like her Jewish neighbors, Catalina koshered her meat by soaking and salting it; and like them she abstained from eating prohibited foods such as pork, rabbit, or scaleless fish. On Saturdays Catalina kept a hank of wool by her side so that if anyone came in she could pretend to be working. The doctor must have died about the time of the expulsion, for his widow was overheard saying how she lamented not having been able to bury him in Jerusalem and how sad she was that she, too, would have to be buried in Spain.

In one of the garbled prayers that Catalina recited for inquisitors in 1493 we can already see signs of Christian influence, as it defines a God who is Jewish by being explicitly not Christian:

> *There is none but You alone, God, who is glorified in the council of angels, blessed be our God, blessed be our God, blessed be our creator, in you there is no start nor finish, nor an end in life rather than death, for you were not killed or buried.*[41]

This variant of the basic Toledo *adafina* recipe differs from the previous one in its flavorings.

*In Toledo Sabbath stew was often **chickpeas and white beans with meat**.*[40]

Sabbath Stew, Toledo Style

Serves 4

½ cup dry white beans
½ cup dry chickpeas
2 medium onions
1½ pounds meat (beef or lamb), cut
    into 1-inch cubes

2 cloves garlic
1 teaspoon saffron threads
½–1 cup water

Spice Mixture

½ teaspoon cloves
½ teaspoon pepper

1 tablespoon finely chopped fresh
    ginger

2–3 tablespoons olive oil

2 teaspoons cinnamon (optional)

1. Cover the beans and chickpeas with cold water and soak 4 hours. Drain.

2. Quarter one onion. Put the meat, garlic, quartered onion, and just enough water to cover in a medium to large stew pot. Simmer covered 1 hour.

3. Add the beans, chickpeas, saffron, and water (only enough to reach the top of the mixture). Continue to simmer covered 3 hours.

4. In a small bowl, combine the spice mixture.

5. Thickly slice one onion. Heat the oil in a medium fry pan over medium heat. Lightly fry the spice mixture for 2 minutes. Add the sliced onion and fry until it is translucent, about 4 minutes more.

6. Add the fried spices and onion to the stewing meat and legumes and stir to combine. Continue to simmer gently covered 1½–8 hours more, stirring occasionally to ensure that the stew does not stick to the bottom of the pan. The meat will shred apart and the stew will be golden brown.

7. If desired, sprinkle with the cinnamon when serving.

NOTE

You may reconstitute the dried legumes more quickly, as directed on page 15. This dish can be simmered in the oven at the lowest setting overnight, or placed in the refrigerator and reheated the next day.

María Alvarez's Olla de Carne

*The Sabbath stew of María Alvarez, the wife of Master Bernal the physician, of Almazán, consisted of **beef, chickpeas, onions, and spices,** "cooked until the meat fell apart and shredded."[42]*

In the opening years of the sixteenth century the Bernal family lived in Almazán's formerly Jewish neighborhood next door to the building which had been the synagogue prior to 1492. Master Bernal's medical library, according to one witness, included books written in Arabic script. Once, when their neighbor, Juan Gutiérrez, brought Master Bernal a urine sample to examine, he found him in bed, groaning in pain, and his wife exclaiming in the fashion of the Jews, "Oh, woe is me!" Gutiérrez added that he had never heard María call for help to Jesus or the Virgin Mary or to any other of the Church's saints.

Like many of the *conversa* housewives in Almazán, and for that matter everywhere else in *converso* Spain, María took care to kosher the family's meat before having it cooked. She used to stand over her servant Francisca while she picked out the vein and trimmed off all the fat with her thumbnail (if she did not remove it all, María beat her, Francisca reported). Then she had her "soak the meat in water five or six times until it was white and dead looking."[43] This method of preparing meat seemed so odd to the *conversos'* old-Christian servants that it is described in hundreds of testimonies. In the trial of one of María's *converso* neighbors, a servant reported her horror at seeing how the meat had been koshered: "What devil has been at this meat? I gave it to you in one piece and laced with fat and you bring it back all full of holes, as if some chickens or mice had been picking at it!"[44] Another old-Christian kitchen maid in the neighborhood complained to her mistress: "Why did you do that? You've spoiled the meat. How can I cook this for dinner when you've trimmed off all the fat?"[45]

The trimming, soaking, and salting was so routine to *conversa* housewives that it may well have been retained without necessarily having any religious significance. María Alvarez herself made this point when she alleged that she salted meat mainly to keep it from going bad: "during the summer we used to bring meat from the field house, and so that it would not spoil we washed it and salted it several times while it was hanging free in the air or in a basket."[46] The conversation that the laborer Juan de Cubo claimed to have had in Almazán around 1494 with Leonor, the wife of Pedro de Fonseca, made a similar point. Leonor "had a joint of lamb across her knees, on her skirt, cut open in the middle, and with a knife she was cleaning out the fat." Juan allegedly remarked, "That's what you used to do when you were Jews; it belongs back when you were Jews." To which Leonor

Beef

replied, "What? You mean we can't do this anymore?" When he told her she couldn't, she fell silent, got up, and went inside.[47]

For this stew, we have adapted a recipe for a spice mixture that Nola calls *polvo de duque,* "duke's powder."[48] The combination calls for three times the amount of sugar that we have found pleasing to the modern palate. We reduced the amount of sugar, which balances the pungent flavors of the other spices.

Maria Alvarez's Beef Stew

1 pound stewing beef, cut into 1-inch
    chunks

8 tablespoons salt
1 cup dried chickpeas

Spice Mixture (see Variations)

2 teaspoons ginger
¼ teaspoon galingale
⅛ teaspoon cloves
1 teaspoon cinnamon

1 teaspoon pepper
1 teaspoon nutmeg
1 teaspoon grains of paradise
3 tablespoons white sugar

3 tablespoons olive oil
2 cloves garlic, diced

2 onions, sliced into eighths
1 cup water (see Variations)

1. Early in the day, soak the beef in saltwater (water to cover plus 2 table-spoons salt) for 3 hours, changing the saltwater three times. Then drain the meat.

2. At least 2 hours before assembling the dish, prepare the chickpeas: Wash them and place them in a pan. Cover with water and bring them to a boil. Boil 1 minute. Remove them from the heat and set aside for 1–1½ hours. Drain the chickpeas.

3. Make the spice mixture: Grind and mix all the spices and the sugar together and set aside.

4. In a medium ovenproof stew pot, heat the olive oil over medium heat. Add the garlic; stir-fry for about 2 minutes. Add the onion and continue to fry until the onion begins to brown, about 6–7 minutes, stirring to separate the onion pieces. Remove the onion and garlic from the pot and set aside. Add the beef and stir-fry over medium heat until the beef browns lightly, about 7 minutes. Return the onion and garlic to the pot and combine.

5. Add the drained chickpeas and the spice mixture. Combine thoroughly. Add enough water to just barely reach the top of the ingredients.

6. Over medium heat, bring the stew to a gentle boil. Turn down to low, cover the pot, and simmer, stirring occasionally, for 2 hours. If you must, add more water or broth only just to cover the meat and chickpeas.

Beef

161

7. Preheat the oven to 300°. Place the covered pot in the center of the oven. Cook for 2 hours. Turn the heat down to 250° and continue to cook until ready to serve, a minimum of 7 hours. The longer you cook the stew, the more the meat will shred apart.

VARIATIONS

Use Vegetable Broth (page 24) or beef broth instead of the water.

Instead of the spice mixture above, add 4 tablespoons of baked Nigella *Almorí* mixture for a subtle flavor (see page 22).

If you are not making this dish as a Sabbath stew, try adding ½ pound fresh chopped spinach or chard 20 minutes before serving.

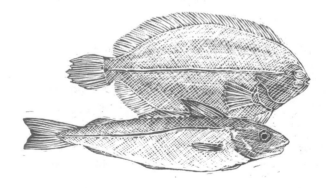

Juana Núñez's Olla de Carne y Berenjenas

If there was one single custom that defined crypto-Jews to their old-Christian tormentors it was the Jewish avoidance of pork. *Tocino*—meaning both salt pork and bacon—was the most commonly used flavoring for meat dishes in Iberian Christian cooking. Cured pork sausages kept well and were likely to be eaten by Christians all winter long. Pork was so common, so cheap, so versatile, and so tasty, that its avoidance by converted Jews (and Muslims) prompted both incomprehension and derision.

For crypto-Jews, too, abstinence from pork came to have deep symbolic meaning. "I have never eaten pork and I will never eat it. I am not a pig to eat pig meat as the old-Christians do," Grácia Dias Correia told inquisitors in Evora around 1570.[50] "People who eat pork turn into pigs," asserted João Carvalho in Goa, India, in 1627.[51] "Judaizers can't eat pork," Isabel de Rivera told the Mexican Inquisition around 1646, "because pigs are men who have been cursed by God, and until pigs rejoin the blessed, one cannot eat them."[52]

Such strong feelings made for good humor. From the 1450s and for the next two hundred years, the savagely pointed racial jokes that so delighted the upper classes made much ado about pork. Good examples are found in the works of the satirist Francisco de Quevedo, who, in the first third of the seventeenth century, was particularly annoyed by newly rich upstart *conversos* trying to masquerade as old-Christians. "They so exaggerate the cleanliness of their lineage," he wrote, ". . . they keep it clean by refusing to eat pork."[53] The great Baroque *converso* poet Luis de Góngora was one of Quevedo's favorite targets: "I will rub my works with *tocino* so that you won't be able to bite them, little Góngora."[54]

The persistence of this *tocinophobic* humor can be seen in the many proverbs about Jews and pork still current in the Hispanic culture:

"Pork in a Jew's house? Hypocrisy."

"Don't invite a Jew to mass or to bacon."

"'Don't tremble, bacon,' said the Jew, 'for no one here will bother you.'"[55]

"Mari Gómez, you eat pork?!" "Woe is me, don't make me choke!"[56]

So common was the alleged *converso* aversion to pork, that to avoid the sort of situation that led Lucía Fernández in 1511 to denounce Juana Núñez (and give us this recipe), would-be assimilators had to be certain to eat pork frequently, and in public where their neighbors would see them.

*In Ciudad Real in 1511 the serving girl Lucía Fernández said that "when her mistress Juana Núñez had **eggplants,** she made [Lucía] cook them and fry them in oil and throw them in a pot **with meat,** without salt pork."*[49]

The dilemma (to avoid pork and be faithful to *kashruth,* or to eat pork and pass for a true Christian) was felt by every crypto-Jew. Antón de Montoro, a *converso* poet of late fifteenth century, highlighted this dilemma poignantly in two satirical poems. The first was directed to a nobleman who invited him to hunt boar:

Por vuestros mandos y ruegos	At your urging and command
presumi de muy montero,	a pretend hunter I became,
y, por Dios, buen caballero,	so by God, it's by your hand
que me veo entre dos huegos:	I find myself between two flames:
si le huyo, pensareys	if I flee, you'll watch me squirm
que so couarde mendigo,	and say I acted cowardly;
y, si le mato, direys	but if I kill him, you'll affirm
que mate a mi enemigo.	that I dispatched my enemy.[57]

The second, much more bitter in its complaints about the difficulties of assimilating, Montoro directed to none other than Queen Isabel herself. This is its opening stanza:

¡Oh ropero amargo, triste,	Oh, Ropero, sad and bitter,
que no sientes tu dolor!	would your pain would go away!
¡Setenta años que naciste	You are seventy today,
y en todos siempre dixiste	and you never ceased to say
inviolata permansiste	"Virgin was our *Sancta Mater.*"
y nunca juré al Criador!	I swore not to the Creator;
Hice el Credo y adorar,	I communed and said the Creed.
ollas de tocino grueso,	On fat bacon I did feed,
torreznos a medio asar,	half-cooked pork roast I did chew.
oír misas y rezar,	I heard mass and prayed my beads
santiguar y persignar,	crossed myself with industry,
y nunca pude matar	yet I never could succeed
este rastro de confeso.	in shaking off the name of "Jew."[58]

A Drizzle of Honey

164

Juana Núñez's Meat and Eggplant Stew

1 small to medium eggplant (about
   1½ pounds)
4 teaspoons Pennyroyal Almorí
   (page 21)
4 teaspoons balsamic vinegar
¾ cup red wine
½ cup water

3 tablespoons olive oil
2 cloves garlic, diced
1 onion, sliced
1 pound stewing beef, cut into
   ½–1-inch cubes
3 tablespoons olive oil

1. Prepare the eggplant: Cut 10 thick slices (each about ½–¾ inch thick).
   Gently simmer 8 minutes in water to cover. Drain. Set them aside.

2. In a small bowl, mix the *almorí* with the vinegar. Pour the wine and
   water into the mixture and stir. Set aside.

3. Heat the oil in a large pot over medium heat. Fry the garlic for about 2
   minutes. Add the onion and continue to fry until the onion is golden,
   about 6 minutes. Remove the garlic and onion.

4. Turn the heat to high. Place the beef in the pot and quickly stir-fry
   until just barely pink, about 3 minutes. Stir in the onion and garlic. Add
   the *almorí*-water-wine mixture and stir again. There should be enough
   liquid to just barely cover the meat. Cover and bring to a boil, then turn
   down the heat and simmer very slowly for about 1 hour, or until the
   meat is tender.

5. Meanwhile, in a large frying pan, heat the 3 tablespoons olive oil over
   medium heat. Add the drained eggplant slices and fry until lightly
   golden, about 15 minutes, turning once or twice. You may have to do
   this in batches.

6. Add the eggplant slices to the stewing beef. Simmer another 15–20
   minutes, uncovered, stirring occasionally, until most of the liquid has
   evaporated.

Leonor Méndes's Olla de Tripas de Carnero

*"They took **lamb**
or beef tripe and
lamb and beef
hooves . . . and
cooked them in a
pot for Saturday . . .
and they threw in
turnips when they
had them. . . ."*[59]

Leonor Méndes used to have her maid, María de Xódar, prepare this Sabbath stew for the family. Leonor's neighbor, María Alvarez, was observed preparing the same dish.[60]

The Méndes family lived in a new-Christian neighborhood in Almazán in the heart of what had formerly been the Jewish quarter, on the New Street (*Calle Nueva*), today called Nuns' Street (*Calle de las Monjas*). Leonor's husband, Pedro Méndes, was a jeweler who also sold hats in his shop, which was just down the street from their home. Once, when Ximeno de Luna, another resident of Almazán who was also a Judaizing new-Christian, complained about the quality of one of the hats, Pedro reputedly cried, "By God, you'll never find nicer hats than these!" He used the Judeo-Spanish term for God, *el Dió,* rather than the Christian term *Dios,* since *conversos* believed that the "s" indicated the plural Christian deity.

According to María de Xódar's 1505 testimony in the Sorian town of Almazán, Leonor was extremely fastidious about the meat the family consumed, having her maid remove the veins, scrape out the abdominal cavity, and remove any trace of fat. One of the Luna family servants reported that the Lunas were equally fastidious. When the family's maid, Catalina, prepared meat for stewing, whatever she scraped off she used to throw to the family cats.[61]

Leonor Méndes's Sabbath Tripe Stew

Serves 4

¾ pound tripe (see Notes)

Herb Mixture (see Variations)

2 sprigs of fresh thyme
2 sprigs of fresh sage (about 20 leaves)
1 long sprig of fresh rosemary
1½ teaspoons pepper (see Variations)

3 tablespoons grated or thinly sliced
  fresh ginger (see Variations)

2–3 tablespoons olive oil
2 cloves garlic, chopped
1½ cups chopped onions
2 bay leaves, fresh if possible

2 cups water or to cover
1 pound beef, cut into 1½-inch cubes
1 turnip (about ⅔ pound) (see
  Variations)

On Thursday:

1. Cook the tripe, covered, in a small nonreactive pan in salted water to cover over very, very low heat, for 2½ hours. Rinse with cold water. Rinse again. Store in the refrigerator overnight in a nonreactive container in new water to cover.

On Friday:

2. Drain the tripe. Cut it into 1-inch squares. Set it aside.

3. Make the herb mixture: Wash the thyme, sage, and rosemary and de-stem them. Chop or cut the sage into small pieces. Place the herbs in a small bowl. Add the pepper and ginger. Stir to combine. Divide the herb mixture into two equal portions.

4. In a large ovenproof stew pot, heat the olive oil over medium heat and fry the garlic in it for 2 minutes. Add the onions and stir-fry just until they are translucent, about 4 minutes. Add the bay leaves and fry another minute.

5. Add one-half of the herb mixture to the stew pot and continue to stir-fry 2 minutes more.

6. Turn the heat to low. Stir in 1 cup water. Add the tripe pieces to the pot and just enough water to cover. Cover the pot. Cook over very, very low heat for 1 hour.

Beef

167

7. Add the beef to the pot. Continue to cook, covered, for about 3 hours, or until the beef and tripe are nearly tender.

8. Meanwhile, peel and dice the turnip. Parboil it in water for 20 minutes. Drain.

9. When the meat is nearly tender, add the turnip and the other half of the herb mixture to the pot. Cook, covered, 1 hour longer.

Before sundown:

10. Preheat the oven to 225°. Place the pot in the oven and cook until ready to serve on Saturday. Remove the bay leaf before serving.

NOTES

Honeycomb tripe is best.

This stew can also be made for serving on the same day as prepared. At step **9:** Cook 2 hours, covered, or until the meat, tripe, and turnips are tender. Take the lid off for the last 10 minutes of cooking.

VARIATIONS

If you use the purple-topped turnips, do not add pepper to the stew.

Instead of turnips, use 20 Swiss chard leaves, chopped into 2-inch pieces.

You may substitute 1½ teaspoons fennel seeds for the ginger for a less pungent stew.

You may substitute dried spices for the fresh ones:

1 teaspoon dried thyme
1 teaspoon dried sage
1 teaspoon rosemary

Brazilian Olla Amarella

From the 1550s on, Branca Dias lived with her husband, Diogo Fernandes, and their several daughters in the sugar factory town of Camarigibi near Olinda, in the Brazilian state of Pernambuco. It was rumored that the family had fled to Brazil because of Inquisition pressure in Portugal. The family was wealthy enough to be able to accept five- to eight-year-old girls into service in their house and to instruct them in the arts of cleaning, sewing, and cooking.

When the Portuguese Inquisition's board of inquiry came to Pernambuco in 1593–95, Branca and Diogo were both dead, but many of their descendants fell under suspicion. About a dozen of their former serving girls, now middle-aged, testified in great detail that Branca's and Diogo's major Judaizing activity was to observe the Sabbath: having the servants scrub the walls and floors, putting on their best clothes, and gathering all their daughters to eat with them, things which they did not do on other days of the week.[63] Other witnesses alleged that on Saturdays Branca used to place a small statue of a bull's head on her bed as a kind of saint, and also that she habitually beat a crucifix and in church spoke disparagingly of the consecrated host.[64]

This yellow stew was enormously popular among Brazilian *cristãos-novos* of the late sixteenth century. The Bahian new-Christian Clara Fernandes made a similar dish, according to Isabel Ramos, one of their *mulatta* servants: "With the meat she mixed grains and crushed them and added seasonings without covering them . . . and they said that that was the Jewish way."[65] Another Brazilian servant denounced the new-Christian Beatriz Antunes, who around 1575 lived on the plantation of Bastiam de Faria in Mathoim, and who "took beef and fried it in oil with onion and added grains."[66] For some of these dishes the onions were braised in a frying pan with olive oil before adding the meat. In Bahia, Joana Fernandes was denounced by a servant for "frying onions with oil and then throwing them into a pan with meat for everybody to eat." She had also seen Joana prepare food this way in the 1560s in Lisbon.[67]

*On the Sabbath, the Brazilian Fernandes family ate a special "**yellow-colored dish** . . . made from **grains, meat, oil, onions, and spices.**"*[62]

Beef

169

Brazilian Yellow Stew

Serves 6

2 dried red chile peppers (see Notes)
3–6 tablespoons olive oil
6 cloves garlic, chopped
2 bay leaves

2 onions, sliced
2 pounds beef, cut into 1-inch cubes
2 large mangoes, peeled and sliced

Spice Mixture

1½ teaspoons saffron threads
1½ teaspoons ground allspice

2 teaspoons salt
1 teaspoon pepper

½ cup bulgar

Garnish

½ large avocado, peeled and sliced
1 mango, peeled and sliced

⅓ cup cashew pieces, chopped

1. Open the chile peppers. Discard the seeds. Cut the peppers into small pieces.

2. In a large pot, heat 3 tablespoons of the oil over medium heat. Fry the garlic, bay leaves, and chile peppers for 3 minutes. Add the onion slices and fry until translucent, about 5 more minutes. Remove to a plate.

3. Add oil if necessary. Fry the meat until lightly browned on all sides, about 6 minutes. Stir in the onion mixture.

4. Add just enough water to barely cover the meat. Bring to a boil. Turn down the heat. Cover and simmer 1½ hours. Stir occasionally.

5. Stir in 1 sliced mango. Combine the four spice mixture ingredients in a small bowl. Stir the spice mixture into the stew. Stir in the bulgar. Continue simmering the stew, covered, another 45–60 minutes, until the meat is very tender. Remove the lid during the last 15 minutes of cooking.

6. Remove the bay leaves. Add the second sliced mango. Stir just to mix in. Then thicken the stew broth (see Notes).

7. Serve in a large bowl with the garnish.

NOTES

Use plastic gloves when working with the chiles.

See page 16 for suggestions about thickeners for the broth.

The Fernández's Olla de Vaca, Carnero, y Puerco

Guiomar and her husband, Zulema aben Ahin, left Spain in 1492 and went to Elves, Portugal. The two of them joined the bulk of Portuguese Jews in conversion in 1497, when Zulema took the name Luis Alvarez. After their baptism, Guiomar and her husband returned to Guadalajara, leaving in Elves a sister named Violante and two brothers who owned small shops, one of sewing supplies and the other of clothing and jewelry. Back in Spain, Luis served the Duque del Infantado as an accountant, and also helped administer the property of doña Brianda de Mendoza, in whose household Guiomar also served.

Guiomar was arrested as a Judaizer in 1520. She protested to her inquisitors that she had been a faithful Christian ever since her baptism twenty-three years earlier, but that her mistress had made her keep the Sabbath and observe other Jewish customs. Because of a tumor on her throat Guiomar was not put to the full range of tortures, but merely the rack. Even under duress she steadfastly maintained her commitment to Christianity. In 1523 she was sentenced: she had to pay a twenty-ducat fine to the Inquisition; she was required make a pilgrimage to a local shrine; and she was ordered to fast and recite fifteen "Hail Marys" and "Our Fathers" every Friday for a year.[69]

Although many other recipes, especially Catalán recipes, call for salted meat, this is one of only two crypto-Jewish recipes that we have found that unashamedly contain pork. The second reference, from Mexico ca. 1603, is to Ysabel Rodríguez bringing turkey stuffed with eggs and salt pork to Ruy Díaz Nieto in prison. Much more common are allusions to eating pork under duress or from fear. For example, Leonor de Cáceres said in Mexico in 1600 that salt pork was added to her father's stew "in order to comply [with the Christian law] . . . and he ate it, but that she gave the salt pork to one of their little house dogs."[70]

Guiomar Fernández testified in 1517 that her mistress, doña Brianda de Mendoza, sometimes ordered her to make a stew of **"beef, lamb, and pork vertebrae and onion and chickpeas and spices,** and sometimes she mixed in with the beef and lamb **chopped cabbage and onion . . . with saffron and pepper and salt,** and sometimes she put in **salt pork** and other times she didn't."[68]

Beef

171

The Fernández's Beef, Lamb, and Pork Stew*

Serves 6

Meat Mixture

5 tablespoons olive oil

2 medium onions, chopped into large pieces

¾ pound stewing beef, cut into 1–1½-inch cubes

¾ pound stewing lamb, cut into 1–1½-inch cubes, bones reserved

8 ounces salt pork, sliced

½ cup water

1½ tablespoons olive oil

2 tablespoons thinly sliced fresh ginger

2 tablespoons juniper berries, lightly crushed

2 teaspoons ground cloves

½ tablespoon salt

½ tablespoon pepper

4–6 cups diced cabbage

Chickpeas

2 tablespoons olive oil

1 teaspoon crushed saffron threads

2 onions, coarsely chopped

½ cup very hot water

1 (29-ounce) can chickpeas, drained

Prepare the meat stew:

1. Heat 4 tablespoons olive oil in a large pot over high heat. Stir-fry the 2 chopped onions until they begin to brown, about 6 minutes.

2. Remove the onions from the pot with a slotted spoon. Place them in a large bowl.

3. Add the remaining tablespoon olive oil to the pot. Add the beef. Stir-fry over high heat until lightly browned, about 3 minutes. Remove the meat with a slotted spoon and put it with the onions.

4. Add the lamb and its bones to the pot. Stir-fry over high heat until lightly browned, about 3 minutes. Remove all with a slotted spoon and put it with the onions and beef.

5. Add the pork. Stir-fry over high heat until lightly browned, about 6 minutes. Remove it with a slotted spoon and put it with the onion-meat mixture.

6. Drain the remaining grease from the stew pot.

7. Put the onion-meat mixture back into the pot. Add ½ cup water. Cover, and simmer the mixture over medium-low heat.

A Drizzle of Honey

*This recipe is not kosher.

8. In a medium frying pan, heat 1½ tablespoons olive oil over medium-high heat. Add the ginger, juniper berries, and cloves and fry 2 minutes. The mixture will absorb the oil. Scrape the mixture into the simmering meat pot. Add the salt and pepper.

9. Simmer the meat 2 hours, until it is nearly tender.

10. Add the diced cabbage and continue to simmer 1 hour more. Remove the lid from the stew pot and simmer another 30 minutes. The cabbage will not retain its green or crunchy nature. About half of the juices will be absorbed. If you like, thicken the sauce (see Notes).

Prepare the chickpeas:

11. In the skillet used to fry the meat spices, heat 2 tablespoons olive oil. Add ¾ teaspoon of the saffron and fry over medium heat for 30 seconds. Add the 2 coarsely chopped onions and fry until they are translucent and the saffron oil is absorbed, about 4 minutes. Place the saffroned onions in a bowl.

12. In ½ cup very hot water, place the remaining ¼ teaspoon crushed saffron and steep for 3 minutes. Pour the water mixture into the frying pan and scrape all of the liquid from the pan into the bowl of onions.

13. Pour the drained chickpeas in with the saffron-onions. Set aside.

14. About 15 minutes before serving, place the chickpea mixture into a medium pot and heat it slowly over medium-low heat to a boil. Turn the heat down and simmer for 10 minutes.

15. Serve the meat mixture in one warmed bowl and the chickpea mixture in another.

NOTES

See pages 16–17 for suggestions about thickeners.

Although this was a Sabbath stew, which traditionally would have been prepared in one pot and served after having sat all night next to the coals, for variety we have elected to prepare this stew as a two-dish meal, somewhat akin to the modern Spanish *cocido*. To more closely approximate what Guiomar would have done, prepare the chickpea mixture at the same time as you prepare the meat. When you add the cabbage also add the chickpea mixture.

If you prefer the cabbage crunchy and green, add it during the last 10 minutes of cooking.

Beef

Blanca Ramírez's Olla de Pelotas

Here is a second recipe from testimony in the Blanca Ramírez trial in Toledo in 1523:

*"Friday night they cooked **meatballs and another stew pot of Swiss chard with its spices and chickpeas,** and when they were going to bed they covered the stew pot with an iron pot with burning coals in it, and the next day they uncovered the stew pot and ate from it."*[71]

A Drizzle of Honey

174

Meatballs, like sausages, take time to prepare and require lots of chopping. In our day they can be made ahead in bulk to be stored in the kitchen freezer and taken out when needed. Meatballs are extremely versatile. They can be eaten alone or can be added to innumerable dishes. They can be sweet or sour or bland or tangy, depending on the spices used for the meatball itself or the sauce or stew in which they are cooked. They can range from the size of an olive to the size of an orange. They are made from any chopped meat, or combination of meats, or combination of meats and vegetables, or for that matter from chopped fish. Meatballs were a feature of ancient Roman cuisine as well. Apicius gives directions for making balls of chopped meat and both braising and stewing them.[72]

But the Spanish word for meatball, *albóndiga*, confirms that by medieval times in Iberia they were thought of as typically Arab food. The word probably stems from the Arabic *al-bundaq*, meaning "round."[73] A glance at early and medieval Arabic cookbooks confirms the importance of meatballs in the Islamic diet. Both the thirteenth-century *Baghdad Cookery-Book* and the *Al-Andalus* cookbook give recipes for the meatball as a stand-alone food, sometimes with a whole almond in its center. More often meatballs are thrown into a pot of stewing meat as a sort of decoration: one recipe's direction is to "adorn" the dish with meatballs. There are fish *albóndigas* in the medieval Arabic cookbooks as well. On the Iberian Peninsula, there is a recipe for meatballs in the Portuguese cookbook that forms the chopped meat around an already hard-boiled egg, and Granado's cookbook has several recipes for them, including those made out of fish.

Together with the Sabbath stew, *adafina*, meatballs were—at least in old-Christian eyes—one of the defining characteristics of Ibero-Jewish cooking. Frequently in the trials the two dishes are linked, as when in 1523 in Guadalajara Guiomar Fernández was accused of "having practiced Jewish rites, preparing *adafina* and *albóndigas* in the Jewish fashion, and keeping the Sabbath."[74] A mid-sixteenth-century Spanish traveler to Bethlehem wrote about the number of Andalusian Jews he found there, and how they sighed "for the *albondeguillas* and *adafinas* that they used to make in Seville."[75]

It is no wonder that the expelled Iberian Jews took their meatball recipes with them to North Africa, Italy, Turkey, and later to the Low Countries as well. On its journey the *albóndiga* was transformed into the Turkish or North African *kefte* (and forms like *koofteh, kjoftes, kiofles*), the French *boulette,* the Syrian *kibbe,* the Syrian *kartee,* and other forms and words.[76] In modern Sephardic cuisine it has a thousand variants: the meatball, or fish croquette, gets combined with vegetables like spinach or leeks; it can have a surprise in the center; it is fried in oil or stewed in a sauce; it adorns other meat dishes, or stands alone as a tasty reminder of the *albóndigas* that their Sephardic ancestors used to savor in Iberia.

This meatball stew has several steps and is best made a day or two before serving to allow the flavors to meld. We have based the ingredients and the instructions on a meatball recipe found in the *Al-Andalus* thirteenth-century cookbook.

Blanca Ramírez's Meatball Stew

Serves 6

Spice Mixture for the Meatballs

1 tablespoon Pennyroyal Almorí
(page 21)
1 scant tablespoon white vinegar

2 teaspoons coriander seeds
1 teaspoon cumin seeds
½ teaspoon dried thyme

1 pound lean ground beef
½ onion, very finely diced
1 egg

1 tablespoon matza meal or finely
ground bread crumbs

To Fry the Meatballs

6 tablespoons olive oil
3 cloves garlic, diced

1 tablespoon Almorí (Pennyroyal or
Simple [page 21])
1½ tablespoons white vinegar

2 cups water

Stew Ingredients

2 tablespoons Pennyroyal Almorí
(page 21)
2 tablespoons white vinegar

2 cups reserved broth
6 cups chopped ruby red chard
1 (15-ounce) can chickpeas, drained

Make the meatballs:

1. Mix the *almorí* and the vinegar together. Set aside.

2. Grind the spices together. Set aside.

3. In a medium bowl, mix the meat, onion, and egg. Mix in the matza meal (or bread crumbs). Add the spices and the *almorí* mixture.

4. Form into 1-inch round balls (see Notes). You can refrigerate the un-cooked meatballs for a day, allowing the spices to meld.

Fry the meatballs:

5. Heat the 6 tablespoons oil in a medium skillet. Over medium heat, fry the garlic for about 2 minutes.

6. Stir in the *almorí* and the vinegar. Add the meatballs (approximately ten at a time) and fry for about 5 minutes, gently moving the pan so they

won't stick. They need not be completely cooked through, but they will be browned and hold together firmly.

7. Remove the meatballs from the pan and drain them on a paper towel.

8. After you have fried all of the meatballs, turn the heat off under the skillet. Add 2 cups of water and stir with a spatula to remove the drippings. Place the resulting broth in a container to use when making the stew.

Prepare the stew:

9. In a large pot, combine the *almori,* vinegar, and the reserved broth. Add the chard and chickpeas. Bring to a boil; turn down the heat, cover the pot, and simmer for 15–20 minutes. The broth will reduce by about a third.

10. Add the number of meatballs desired: about four per person. Continue cooking, covered, for another 15 minutes.

11. Thicken the sauce if you wish (see Notes). Serve hot.

NOTES

Dipping hands in cold water helps keep the meat from sticking to them.

This makes about 30 medium meatballs. The meatballs can be made ahead and refrigerated or frozen. Bring them to room temperature before placing them in the stew.

See pages 16–17 for suggestions about thickening the stew.

For extra tang, sprinkle the finished stew with a tablespoon of vinegar.

For a stew more like the Sabbath stew of Blanca Ramírez, add the cooked meatballs to the chard and chickpeas mixture and keep the stew warm until you are ready to eat it. The meatballs may lose their form.

Beatriz de Díaz Laínez's Albondequexos

The conversa
Beatriz de Díaz
Laínez reputedly
*"chopped up **raw***
***meat** and threw it in*
*a mortar with **spices***
***and some eggs** and*
blended it, and
when it was blended
they formed it into
round balls and they
fried them in a pan
with oil or in a
pot and they called
*them **albonde-***
***quexos.** "*[77]

Beatriz was married to Ruy Díaz Laínez of Navarre. A neighbor woman, Juana de Fuente Albilla, said that the family cooked a separate stew, with salt pork, for their servants. Beatriz stirred the family pot with a wooden spoon and the servants' pot with an iron one, which she said she could not put in her mouth because of her bad teeth.[78]

In cooking two separate meals, Beatriz was evidently following the common practice of Judaizing *conversa* housewives of her generation. Her neighbor, Catalina Laínez, did the same thing: she had salt pork put into the stew for the serving boy, and cooked a separate stew for her family. "She ordered that one pot be stirred with a wooden spoon and the other with an iron spoon, and she did not allow the spoon from one pot to be used in the other."[79] In Ciudad Real in 1511 a scullery maid in the de la Sierra family complained similarly that her mistress "did not let her wash the family's plates and pans with the scrub rag they used to wash the servants' dishes."[80] Their neighbors, the González sisters, also "kept their pots and spoons and pans separate."[81]

Ana Gómez, who worked as a kitchen maid in Beatriz's house in Almazán from 1499 to 1501, included in her report to the Inquisition on the family's Judaizing this recipe and another for a meat pie made of lamb.[82] The spices in this recipe are typical of combinations from medieval cookbooks from northeast Iberia.[83]

Beatriz de Díaz Laínez's Meatballs

Serves 4

1 pound lean ground beef

1 egg, beaten

Spice Mixture

½ teaspoon cloves

¾ teaspoon cinnamon

1 teaspoon ground ginger

½ teaspoon ground cardamom

½–1 teaspoon salt

¼ teaspoon pepper

¼ cup chopped fresh cilantro

2 tablespoons flour

⅓ cup olive oil

1. In a large bowl, mix the meat and egg together.

2. In a small bowl, mix the spice mixture ingredients together and add them to the meat mixture. Add the cilantro and mix thoroughly.

3. Form meatballs 1 inch in diameter (see Notes).

4. Roll the meatballs in the flour.

5. Heat the olive oil in a large skillet. Fry the meatballs over medium heat until they are brown, turning them frequently with a slotted spoon or by shaking the skillet. You may have to fry the meatballs in two batches. About 6 minutes of frying per batch will leave the meatballs slightly pink in the center and very juicy. For well-done meatballs, fry 2 minutes longer.

NOTES

Dipping hands in cold water helps keep the meat from sticking to them.

This recipe makes about 20 meatballs.

These meatballs may be eaten as a main course or added to soups or stews.

VARIATIONS

Add one or more of these combinations to the spice mixture:

2 tablespoons currants and 2 tablespoons crushed walnuts

1½ teaspoons minced fresh parsley with 1 teaspoon vinegar

2 tablespoons ground pine nuts and 2 teaspoons honey

Clara de Puxmija's Carne Picada con Huevos

Clara de Puxmija

(d. 1455) of Teruel

used to make a Sabbath

dish as follows: "She

*broke some **eggs** into*

a . . . skillet and after

they were cooked she

*sprinkled on **chopped***

***meat** that had been*

*braised with **onion**.*

And simultaneously she

*beat other **eggs** and*

poured them on top.

And she took another

*pan with **broth** and put*

it on top, and you could

smell all the odors

mixed together."[84]

Clara and her husband, Belenguer Acho, were typical of the completely unassimilated converts of the second quarter of the fifteenth century. Though they and their children converted in the wake of the Dominican preaching campaigns of circa 1413, they continued to behave as if they were still Jews. When the Inquisition began in Teruel, Clara and Belenguer had been dead for nearly thirty years. Even so, in 1486 a maid who had served in their house in the early 1450s was so frightened by the Inquisition's call to come forth and testify, that she detailed to the Holy Office the activities of the deceased Clara and Belenguer, and a half dozen of their living children. Among her accusations were these:

In addition to ignoring the Christian liturgical calendar, the family rigorously kept the Jewish Sabbath, Rosh Hashanah, and Passover. They observed *kashruth*. The women visited the local *mikvah*. They blessed their children in the Jewish fashion, and to make sure that they, too, received a good Jewish education they contracted with a rabbi from nearby Albarracín to come to their house and give the children private lessons in reading Hebrew. The superstitious practices of the Jews in the region also continued to hold sway over them. For example, when anyone in the family got sick, they sprinkled drops of water into a hot frying pan and from the spatter pattern predicted the person's chances of recovery. When the children sneezed the parents chorused *"Shaday!"* When a family member died, they followed all the Jewish mourning customs, and—according to the maid—secretly buried the person in the Jewish cemetery, and sent a coffin weighted with a log to be buried in the church.

The outcome? The family were declared heretics. The estate was confiscated. The bodies were exhumed and burned. The descendants were disqualified from ever holding public office.

Clara's recipe resembles one of the several that the thirteenth-century *Al-Andalus* cookbook specifically calls Jewish recipes.[85] Our translation from the Spanish does not attempt to simplify the instructions:

Jewish Dish with Hidden Stuffing

Slice the meat, chop it fine taking care that it not have any bones, put it in the
pot and mix in all of the spices except the cumin, four spoonsful of olive oil,

strong rose-water, a little onion juice, and a little salt and cover it with a thick cloth; carefully cook it over a medium fire, mash up the meat, like one does for meatballs, add aromas and form it into little meatballs and cook them in the pot until they are done, and when all this is done, beat five eggs, salt, pepper and cinnamon; make a thin pancake in a frying pan and with another five eggs do the same to make another pancake; then take a new pot and put a spoonful of olive oil in it and boil it a little; in the bottom put one of the two pancakes, pour the meat onto it and cover it with the second pancake; then beat three eggs with a little white flour, pepper, cinnamon and a little rose-water with the rest of the chopped meat and throw it on top of the pot; then cover it with some hot coals until it browns and take care that it does not burn; then break open the pot and put the whole dish on a platter and cover it with sprigs of mint, pistachios and pine nuts and sprinkle on it scented condiments; on top of this dish put all that we have said except the rose-water for which you substitute a spoonful of cilantro juice mixed with onion and a half a spoonful of moistened almorí; *with all this you do what you did with the first dish, if God wills.*

Don't panic: it is not as involved as it sounds. The recipe is accomplished in six steps. You may complete step 1 ahead of time and refrigerate the meat. It may even be better to do so, in order for the flavors to meld. The final *almorí* sauce (step 4) can be prepared ahead of time as well. In actual time the recipe takes about 1½–2 hours to make, and the final result is well worth it.

Clara de Puxmija's Chopped Meat in Egg Pancakes

Serves 4

Step 1: Meat Mixture

1½ pounds ground beef or lamb

1 onion, finely minced

1½ tablespoons grated fresh ginger

¾ teaspoon ground cloves

1½ teaspoons pepper

1½ teaspoons salt

3 tablespoons olive oil

4 tablespoons rose water

3 tablespoons chopped fresh mint

1 teaspoon chopped fresh rosemary

1 teaspoon chopped fresh basil

Step 2: Egg Pancakes

8 eggs

1 teaspoon pepper

1 teaspoon salt

1½ teaspoons cinnamon

3 tablespoons olive oil

Step 3: Assembly and Cooking

2 tablespoons olive oil

3 eggs

1½ tablespoons flour

¼ teaspoon pepper

½ teaspoon cinnamon

1½ tablespoons rose water

Step 4: Almorí Sauce

2 teaspoons Pennyroyal Almorí (page 21)

4 teaspoons finely diced onion

½ cup packed finely chopped fresh cilantro

2 tablespoons balsamic vinegar

Step 5: Garnish

¼ cup coarsely chopped pistachios

¼ cup pine nuts

¼ cup torn fresh mint leaves

3 tablespoons coarsely chopped crystallized ginger, rose petals, violet petals, and/or dates

Step 1: Make the meat mixture.

1. In a large frying pan, over medium heat, brown the meat, onion, and spices in the olive oil. Stir frequently to separate the meat. When the pink color of the meat is fading, stir in the rose water. Remove from heat.

2. Stir the mint, rosemary, and basil into the meat mixture. Refrigerate 1 hour or overnight. About 1 hour before serving, remove the meat from the refrigerator.

Step 2: Make the egg pancakes.

3. Beat the eggs, pepper, salt, and cinnamon together in a bowl.

4. Heat the oil in a 10-inch skillet over medium-high heat. When the oil is hot, turn the heat to medium-low. Pour in half of the egg mixture and fry gently. Do not stir or scramble, but let it sit. When the edges of the egg pancake start to make a crust, use a spatula to loosen the egg from the side of the fry pan. Shake the pan gently over the heat to move the uncooked liquid to the underside of the pancake.

5. When the pancake is firm on top, slip the pancake onto a large plate, cooked side down.

6. Make the second pancake with the other half of the egg mixture, and slide it onto a second plate.

Step 3: Assemble and cook.

7. In a large (12 inches wide or more), deep ovenproof casserole, heat 2 tablespoons olive oil over medium heat. Remove from the heat. Slide one egg pancake, cooked side down, into the casserole.

8. Cover it with half of the meat mixture from step 1.

9. Cover the meat mixture with the second egg pancake, cooked side up.

10. Preheat the oven to 350°.

11. In a medium bowl, beat 3 eggs.

12. In a small bowl, stir together the flour, pepper, and cinnamon. Add the rose water and combine well, making sure the flour does not cake. Add a little of the beaten eggs and mix well.

13. Pour the rose water and flour-spice mixture into the beaten eggs. Stir.

14. Add the remaining meat mixture from step 1. Stir well.

15. Pour this mixture on top of the second pancake in the casserole. Cover the casserole.

16. Bake for 30 minutes.

Step 4: Make the *almorí* sauce.

17. While the casserole is baking, in a small bowl, mix the *almorí,* onion, and cilantro with the vinegar.

Step 5: Prepare the garnish.

18. While the casserole is baking, in another small bowl, combine the nuts, mint, and flavorings for the garnish.

Step 6: Serve.

19. Remove the casserole from the oven. Uncover.

20. Sprinkle the casserole with the nut and mint garnish. Dot it with the *almorí* sauce.

21. Serve hot from the casserole dish.

Violante Vaz's Hígado de Vaca

Violante Vaz was tried in the Portuguese city of Coimbra in 1571. In addition to eating meat during Lent, she was accused of keeping the Sabbath and of koshering meat by removing the vein. The Coimbra Inquisition judged these crimes to be minor, and merely sentenced her to march in procession to an *Auto de fe* with a lighted candle in her hand, and there publicly abjure her Judaizing.

All the edible parts of animals were served throughout the Middle Ages, and extant recipe books contain directions for how to serve tripe, livers, kidneys, lungs, spleen, and other innards. Our version of this liver dish is based on one found in the Catalán cookbook by Roberto de Nola.[87] It emphasizes a sweet-sour tartness which is typical of medieval meat recipes, using vinegar and warm spices combined with cinnamon for fragrance.

*During Lent, Violante Vaz used to eat "**meat** and **beef liver** . . . on Saturdays [when she was] healthy."*[86]

Violante Vaz's Beef Liver

Serves 4

½ cup unseasoned dried bread crumbs

6 tablespoons white vinegar

6 tablespoons sweet sherry or other
   sweet wine

2 onions, thinly sliced

1–2 tablespoons olive oil

1½ pounds beef or calf's liver, sliced
   into 1½-inch cubes

1 tablespoon cinnamon

½ cup water

Salt and pepper to taste

1. In a nonreactive bowl, combine the bread crumbs and white vinegar. Stir and mash. The liquid will all be absorbed. Let sit for about 15 minutes. Add the sherry or wine.

2. In a large skillet, fry the onions in the olive oil for 6–7 minutes over medium heat, until they are translucent.

3. Add the liver cubes all at once. Brown on all sides.

4. Mix in the bread-vinegar-wine mixture.

5. Add the cinnamon and water, stirring continuously. Cook another 3–4 minutes, or until the flavors have time to combine. The mixture will thicken fairly quickly. Serve hot.

Lamb and Goat

The only mammals that the laws of *kashruth* permit to be eaten are cloven-hoofed ruminants, which in the Iberian context limits the field to cows, goats, and sheep. In medieval times, most country people kept a cow for milk and slaughtered the occasional calf for meat. The regions with good mountain pastures sustained a small cattle industry for both cheese and meat. Where the pasturage was poorer, goats were exploited for milk and cheese. Goat meat was relatively high prestige, at least in comparison with lamb or mutton, probably because Iberia sustained so many more sheep than goats.[1]

But to an extraordinary extent, in the Middle Ages Spain's wealth derived from sheep. The production of wool, meat, and cheese had been a feature of the Iberian Peninsula from at least Roman times. In the thirteenth and fourteenth centuries the industry boomed. Rapid Christian advances in the Reconquest War opened vast new territories for the herds. The population of Europe overall was on the increase, and new bodies meant new needs for clothing. The insatiable textile factories of Italy and the Low Countries demanded larger supplies of wool just at the time when the Hundred Years War between England and France cut off their traditional British suppliers. Black-faced merino sheep were introduced into Iberia from North Africa, and the crossbreeding with native varieties produced abundant, high-quality wool. An idea of the relative importance of sheep and cattle ranching can be seen in the Islamic historian Ibn Idhari's description of a raiding party in the region of Avila which brought back to Andalucía two thousand cows and fifty thousand sheep.[2] The annual wool fairs in cities like Medina del Campo and Sahagún attracted merchants from all over Western Europe and created jobs for money changers, money lenders, and linguists, many of them Jews. The national sheep ranchers' guild, the *Mesta,* was chartered by Castile's King Alfonso the Wise in 1273. By the end of that century it was the wealthiest and most powerful economic force in Iberia, building and maintaining a network of highways—some of them three hundred fifty miles long—to conduct the herds between their summer and winter pastures.

No wonder so many Iberian Sephardic recipes feature these ruminants. The wool may have fed the looms of Flanders, but the mutton filled the stew pots of Iberia and made Sabbath dinners that were simply ovine! Lamb was eaten all year long, and it was especially associated with Passover (Exodus 12, Numbers 9–11, Deuteronomy 16:2–4). In 1570 in Evora, the physician Cristovão Lopes said that his family would roast an unblemished white lamb for Passover.[3] In 1589, Diego Mora, of Quintana de la Orden, said that the Passover lamb must be eaten while standing,[4] a custom confirmed by Juan de León in Mexico in 1642.[5]

Juan de Teva's Carnero Asado

The draper Juan de Teva was at least a third-generation crypto-Jew. His grandfather, Alonso Martínez, had been born a Jew. His father, Fernando, who had served the Ciudad Real *converso* community as rabbi, had gone to the stake on February 23, 1484. When the Inquisition again turned its attention to the family in 1513, Juan fled to Portugal, leaving behind his wife, Juana Núñez.[7] Because they were well known as crypto-Jews, allegations against the Teva family occur in dozens of Ciudad Real trials of the period. Before Juan's escape the Tevas had always celebrated the Sabbath with rigor, putting on clean clothes, blessing the lighting of their candles, and dining on special foods. They kept the major Jewish fasts. Teva and his brother could always be counted on to make the *minyan* of ten men required for Sabbath services.[8]

It was their old-Christian serving girl, Lucía Fernández, wife of the shepherd Francisco de Lillo, who reported that when Juan de Teva brought home a leg of lamb from the butcher he used to slit it lengthwise and take out the sciatic vein. Curiously, and despite ample testimony to the contrary in the region, the defense attorney assigned to the Teva case argued that this was unlikely, since "removing the fat and deveining the leg was women's work, not men's."[9]

According to Lucía, Juan de Teva generally held all things Christian in scorn. She reported, for example, that one Monday she had heard him say, "The day I don't deceive some Christian is like a day I don't eat breakfast, and I'm out of sorts."[10] María Ruiz added that she used to keep her eyes on Juan de Teva in church, and that whenever the priest mentioned the name of Jesus he used to spit on the floor.[11] He also used to sleep late on days when he was supposed to get up and attend mass.[12]

Juan was condemned in absentia and burned in effigy on September 7, 1513.

We have no information about which of the many possible ways the Teva family preferred to roast their leg of lamb. In both Christian and Muslim medieval traditions, lambs were frequently roasted whole and stuffed with a variety of flavorful ingredients. The following recipe uses seasonings for lamb found in *Al-Andalus* and Granado, and applies them as a coating rather than as a stuffing.

*The Teva family used to devein a **leg of lamb** and roast it for Sabbath.[6]*

Lamb and Goat

189

Juan de Teva's Roast Lamb

Serves 6–8

1 boneless leg of lamb (about 4 pounds)

Coating

3 cups fresh cilantro, including stems
1 cup chopped fresh mint
1 tablespoon water
1 egg, beaten

2 teaspoons pepper
2 tablespoons fresh marjoram
1½ teaspoons salt

Sauce

½ cup frozen orange juice concentrate
½ cup water
3 tablespoons red wine vinegar

¼ teaspoon ground cloves
½ teaspoon cinnamon

The day before serving:

1. Place the lamb, free of any net or packaging, in a nonreactive roasting pan.

2. Wash and pat dry the cilantro (including the stems) and the fresh mint.

3. Put all the coating ingredients in a food processor; chop the mixture very finely.

4. With a spatula or flat wooden spoon, press the coating into the slit where the bone has been removed, and then onto the meat.

5. Cover the coated meat with plastic wrap. Refrigerate it for at least 8 hours; overnight is better.

The day of serving:

6. Preheat the oven to 450°.

7. Remove the lamb from the refrigerator and take off the plastic wrap.

8. Bake the lamb for 30 minutes.

9. Meanwhile, in a small pan, combine the sauce ingredients. Over medium-low heat, heat them until hot, not boiling.

10. After 30 minutes, remove the lamb from the oven. Reduce the heat to 350°.

11. Slowly pour the sauce mixture over the lamb. Return it to the oven. Roast another 12 minutes per pound for medium-rare.

12. Remove the lamb from the oven and let it sit for 10 minutes. Slice and serve.

NOTE

Modern sweet oranges were unknown in medieval Iberia. We have substituted undiluted frozen orange juice for the typical medieval combination of Seville orange and sugar.

Olla de Cataluña

In Cataluña in the late fifteenth century, Isabel, the wife of Francesca Pallarès, testified that in September she and her husband kept the "fast of 'Equipur.'" She cooked a special dish for her husband into which she put "spinach, chickpeas, mutton, salt meat, and eggs," which she knew was a Jewish dish.[13]

Spain was just in the process of coalescing into a single, unified country at the time these cooks and their neighbors and servants were testifying before the Inquisition. During the eight hundred years of the Reconquest War, as Iberian Christians gradually pushed their frontier into the Muslim south, a number of individual kingdoms and principalities emerged. From west to east across the north these were Galicia, Asturias, Leon, Castile, the Basque Provinces, Navarre, Aragon, and Cataluña. After centuries of internecine wars, marriages, alliances, and treacheries, two giant kingdoms subsumed all the others: Castile (including Galicia, Asturias, Leon, and the Basque lands), and Aragon (with sway over Cataluña, Valencia, the Balearic Islands of Majorca and Menorca, and Naples and Sicily). Even after Castile and Aragon were yoked in 1469 by the marriage of Ferdinand and Isabel, tiny Navarre held out as a separate kingdom until 1512, when Ferdinand's armies incorporated it by force. By then it, too, had expelled its Jews.

Cataluña, where this recipe comes from, comprises the extreme northeast corner of the Iberian Peninsula. It was both part of the kingdom of Aragon, and culturally quite separate. Catalonians speak Catalán, which is a dialect of Occitaine, the tongue of the Languedoc region of southern France, with which it has always maintained close cultural and economic ties. While the Jews of Castilian Toledo, and even those of Aragonese Zaragoza, felt part of the cultural orbit of Seville, Córdoba, and the Maghreb, Catalán Jews tended to be much closer to Jews in Perpignan and Toulouse. Although Cataluña and Aragon had always had far fewer Jews than the Castilian territories—Andrés Bernáldez, Ferdinand and Isabel's official chronicler, estimated the ratio at ten to one—[14] in the Middle Ages Cataluña's three largest cities, Barcelona, Girona, and Lleida, all housed large and distinguished Jewish communities. There were Jews in a host of smaller towns as well.

The conversionist pressures began earlier in Cataluña than in Castile. In the 1230s Raymond de Peñafort spearheaded from Barcelona the conversionist campaigns of the Dominican friars. As early as 1263, King Jaime I required the great Nahmanides (Rabbi Moses ben Nahman of Girona) to publicly debate the truth of the Talmud with the convert Pablo Christiani in the first of the great Iberian disputations which were staged to prove to the Jews the superiority of Christianity. In 1391 the anti-Jewish riots spread from Andalucía up the Mediterranean coast into Cataluña. Many Jews were killed and many converted, while others fled into southern France. The most famous disputation of all, held in 1413 in Tortosa, just south of the city of Barcelona, produced many more conversions. As a result, the number of openly practicing Jews left in Aragon in 1491 may have been as low as ten thousand.

There are several reasons why there tended to be many fewer Judaizing *conversos* in Aragonese Cataluña than in Castile. The proximity of European havens meant that people whose Jewish allegiance was the most important aspect of their lives could emigrate to where they could practice Judaism openly. The Catalán disputations were early compared with those in Castile, and the conversions that followed in their wakes tended to be somewhat voluntary. This meant that the new-Christians there were more likely to try to assimilate than to retain their Jewish customs.

All this helps explain why our research has turned up many fewer Catalán crypto-Jewish culinary references than it has Castilian. Additionally, those we have found so far do not tend to differ from the those of their Castilian neighbors in any significant way. A variant on the current recipe, apparently without mutton, was the Saturday stew of Gabriel Comte's wife Aldonça, who lived in Girona.[15] It is almost identical to another associated with Mayor González of Ciudad Real, who, in 1512, was accused of eating a Sabbath stew containing "eggs and spices and lamb."[16]

Lamb and
Goat

193

Catalán Stew*

Serves 4

3 tablespoons olive oil
1 medium onion, chopped
2 cloves garlic, chopped
1½ pounds lamb, cut in 1-inch cubes

5 ounces beef jerky, chopped (see
  Notes)
½–1 cup Vegetable Broth (page 24),
  meat broth, or water

Spice Mixture

1 teaspoon dried rosemary or 2
  teaspoons fresh chopped
1 teaspoon dried thyme or 2 teaspoons
  fresh chopped

2½ teaspoons caraway seeds
½ teaspoon pepper

1 (15-ounce) can chickpeas, drained
½ pound spinach leaves, washed and
  coarsely chopped

2–3 hard-boiled eggs, chopped

1. Heat the olive oil in a medium stew pot over medium heat. Fry the garlic and onion in the olive oil until they begin to brown, about 7 minutes. Remove them and set aside. Sauté the lamb until it begins to brown, about 8 minutes. Put the onion and garlic back in. Add the beef jerky and just enough broth to cover the mixture. Simmer, covered, for 2 hours.

2. Grind the spice mixture ingredients together and add them to the stew pot, with the drained chickpeas. Simmer another hour, covered.

3. Uncover the pot. Stir in the spinach leaves and chopped hard-boiled eggs. Simmer, uncovered, 15 minutes more, until the spinach leaves are cooked through.

NOTES

In keeping with the Old World flavor, the beef jerky should not have chiles, tomatoes, or corn products in it.

Serve hot in bowls.

If you make the dish the day before serving, complete steps **1** and **2**. Refrigerate it overnight. The next day skim off the fat. Over medium heat, bring the pot to near boil and then continue with step **3**.

For a Sabbath stew use an ovenproof pot. Complete steps **1**, **2**, and **3**. Then place the pot in an oven at 200° until ready to eat.

*For some Jewish groups, this recipe is not strictly kosher.

Cristóbal Cubero's Olla de Carnero y Garbanzos

Cristóbal Cubero was one of many new-Christians whose Judaizing habits were denounced in 1502 to the Inquisition in Aranda. As a young man he had served the famous fifteenth-century nobleman and poet Iñigo López de Mendoza, Marqués de Santillana, as a sort of assistant groom, whose chief responsibility was to help the marqués on with his spurs. Later, when he was of age, he left noble service to make barrels, and like many artisans at the beginning of the Spanish Renaissance, took a last name that indicated his profession: barrel maker.

Juan de Salcedo, Cubero's brother-in-law, told the inquisitors what little respect Cubero had for things Christian. He reported that one day somebody in Aranda came around collecting money for oil for the Virgin Mary's lamp in Aranda's church and Cubero allegedly quipped, "You and she should both dress in mourning, and you're as blind as she is; those drunkards will drink the money all up to the detriment of Our Lady."[19]

Cubero was particularly fond of this recipe, which either he or his sister would prepare on Friday afternoon for eating on the Sabbath, or sometimes on Saturday night for his Sunday breakfast. The witness Juan de Salcedo reported that once he asked Cubero whether he had confessed the practice, or whether he had some special permission to make a Sabbath stew. Cubero allegedly replied, "Don't you worry about my soul, for as my father used to say when they were getting ready to go to Portugal, 'El Dió barohú' will save it." Cubero combined the Judeo-Spanish word for God, *el Dió*, with the Hebrew for "Blessed be he."

Salcedo had no problem with these Hebrew terms, for before his conversion he had been a Hebrew teacher, a *melammed,* who after his conversion continued to teach Hebrew to the children of Jewish families in Aranda.[20] In fact, he was engaged in this activity at Passover in 1492 when the pot maker Fernando de Guernica burst in to interrupt the Hebrew lesson with news of the impending expulsion, screaming:

> What are you doing? Misfortune come to you. You are wasting time. Reading, reading! . . . You would do better, holiday or not, [to spend your time] thinking how you are going to liquidate your property, and how you are going to leave. Some people say that you should become Christian, but may God punish [me] if I advise it. The reason is once you have become Christian, then they will find a way to put your face in the fire. . . .[21]

*In Soria in 1502, Cristóbal Cubero ate a Sabbath stew that included **lamb shanks, chickpeas, and eggs.**[17] A similar recipe was ascribed to Beatriz Núñez and her husband, who allegedly used to prepare for the Sabbath "a **stew of lamb stomach and feet** with chickpeas."[18]*

Lamb and Goat

195

Cristóbal Cubero's Lamb Stew

Serves 6

1 anise or fennel plant, stalk with
    leaves
4–6 tablespoons olive oil
4 cloves garlic, diced
1 large onion, sliced
2 pounds lamb shank or stew meat,
    including bones

2 tablespoons chopped fresh rosemary
1–2 teaspoons salt
2 cups water
2 (15-ounce) cans chickpeas, drained
6 hard-boiled eggs, cut into eighths

1. Wash the anise or fennel and dice the stem. Set the leaves aside for later use.

2. In a large pot, heat the olive oil over medium heat. Fry the garlic 2 minutes and add the onion. Stir-fry until the onion slices begin to turn brown, about 7 minutes. Remove.

3. Cut the lamb into 1-inch cubes. Add the lamb to the pot and stir-fry over medium heat until it loses its pink color, about 10 minutes. Add the diced anise or fennel stem and fry 2 minutes more. Return the onion and garlic to the pot.

4. Add the rosemary and salt and enough water to just reach the top layer of meat in the pot. Stir to combine and cover. Bring the mixture to a gentle boil and turn the heat to low. Simmer 2 hours.

5. Add the chickpeas and hard-boiled eggs. Cook an additional 2–3 hours. The meat should be dropping off the bones.

6. Uncover the pot. Chop the anise or fennel greens and stir them into the stew. Simmer 10 minutes.

Mayor González's Cazuela de Carnero

The reference to the *white* color of this casserole reminds us how medieval cooks and diners were cognizant of color in their meals.[23] Foods yellow, red, green, blue, and every hue in-between glimmered from their plates and trenchers like pigments on an artist's palette. But the most esteemed color seems to have been white. Even the white flour we take for granted was in the Middle Ages a luxury product, more tan or gray than white, since it was ground whole kernel and then not bleached but only sifted many times to "whiten" it. When a medieval someone mentioned that a bread she ate was "white," we know that it was a special bread.[24]

Writers took note when any dish was white. Medieval cookbooks contain recipes for dishes like *"Tafaya blanca,"*[25] *"White Porray,"*[26] and *"Salsa blanca"* (white sauce).[27] Generally, these dishes have in common almonds and what we might term beige or at least lightly tinted foods. Occasionally there are other white ingredients. *"Faludaya blanca"* is a recipe for a white sweet, made with milk and white sugar.[28] A white honey dish is confected from egg whites, as well as chopped almonds. The directions clearly say to cook the mixture over a fire until it turns white.[29] In other recipes, directions sometimes call for the white variety of specific ingredients, especially sugar, flour, cheese, wine, and even bread.

Mayor González's casserole most likely incorporated a version of the famous *blancmange* (from the French, literally "white eating") which was so popular in the Middle Ages.[30] There are recipes for it in English, French, Portuguese, and Catalán cookbooks. These all have elements in common, such as the ever-popular almond milk, sugar, and chicken broth. Most *blancmange* recipes use chicken as a base. The meat would be boiled to make the broth, and then shredded and mixed with the sauce to make a sort of chicken casserole.

Nola's Catalán cookbook offers a white sauce which approximates *blancmange* in its main ingredients, but differs in that it requires rose water and ginger, and specifically states that the ginger flavor should be dominant. For this lamb casserole we have adapted this *blancmange* sauce, which uses rice as well as almond milk.

Mayor González, the wife of Pedro Núñez Franco of Ciudad Real, had Juana González, her kitchen maid, prepare for the Sabbath a **"casserole of lamb** . . . *which was* **white** . . . *and [Pedro Núñez] shared slices of it with all the [members of his family], and it was cold when they ate it."*[22]

Lamb and Goat

Mayor González's Cold White Lamb Casserole

Serves 4

4 teaspoons thinly sliced fresh ginger
¼ cup rose water
2 pounds boneless lamb
½ cup rice
¾ cup water

1 (¾-inch) stick cinnamon
4–5 whole cloves
1¾ cups Almond Milk (page 19)
2 tablespoons olive oil
2 teaspoons sugar

1. In a small bowl, combine the ginger and rose water and let the mixture sit at least 30 minutes.

2. Slice the lamb into 1 × 2-inch cubes.

3. In a small saucepan, combine the rice, ¾ cup water, cinnamon, and cloves. Take 2 teaspoons of the ginger from the rose water. Reserve the rose water but discard the remaining ginger. Cover the saucepan. Bring the mixture to a boil, turn the heat to a low simmer, and cook 10 minutes. Remove the pan from the heat.

4. In a blender, puree the rice with 1–1¼ cups of the almond milk. It will be a little soupy. Place the mixture in a large pot. Set it aside.

5. In a large frying pan, heat the olive oil. Quickly stir-fry the lamb over high heat until it is barely pink, about 5 minutes. You may have to do this in several batches.

6. Pour the lamb into the rice mixture. Add 2 teaspoons sugar, 1 tablespoon of the reserved rose water, and enough of the remaining almond milk to make a thick sauce. Cook over low heat an additional 5 minutes to allow the flavors to meld, stirring so that it does not stick. Refrigerate. Serve cold.

NOTE

This stew is also delicious when reheated and served hot.

Pedro Núñez Franco's
Carnero con Menudo de Ansarón

The Ciudad Real textile merchant Pedro Núñez Franco was described by one of the family servants in 1511 as a man who knew "everything there was to know about woolen cloth manufacture, and was always visiting the shearers and carders and dyers and the officials in charge of making cloth, and at home he used to take out his books and accounts and ink and would spread out his papers all over the table."[32]

Núñez and his wife, Mayor González,[33] who had already confessed to Judaizing in the early days of the Ciudad Real trials in 1483, were re-arrested in 1513 and charged with being relapsed heretics. Although his file is no longer extant, and although his wife's trial contains some obviously perjured testimony, we can be reasonably certain of some aspects of his family's Judaizing. A family maid testified that she used to see little Alvaro kiss his father's hand after the Sabbath meal, and that Pedro would then place his hand on his son's head, but would never make the sign of the cross. The maid also said that first thing in the morning she used to hear Pedro, who slept with his wife and son in a little room over the kitchen, singing prayers in a low voice, and that "they could not have been Christian songs because they were sung deep in the throat as if he was choking."[34]

In the confession offered in her own defense, Mayor González tried to shift the blame from her husband to herself and to describe her own Judaizing more as residual customs from her childhood than as a guide to her current beliefs. "Even after I married," she reported, "I continued with the habits and my husband often reprehended me. . . . Occasionally, actually only a very few times, I cooked something on Friday afternoon for the Sabbath, and my husband did not like it and scolded me for it." But with further questioning she admitted that her husband only scolded her sometimes, and other times he celebrated along with her.[35]

One of the maids reported that while the Núñez children also used to join their parents in abstaining from work on the Sabbath when they were little, as they grew older they dropped the custom.[36] This ambivalence suggests that had the Inquisition not intervened, probably within a generation the Núñez family would have completely assimilated to Christianity.

In a curious footnote to the Núñez family case, the defense moved to discount for reasons of animus any testimony by the wife of Miguel the

*Pedro Núñez Franco "killed a **goose**, and the next day, a Saturday, they ate **the innards with a piece of lamb.**"[31]*

Lamb and Goat

butcher, "because back when she was a whore she slept with Pedro Núñez Franco and gave him the pox." When asked why she had poxed Núñez and Mayor González, she stated before witnesses that "she would like to pile faggots on the fire that burned him in Toledo."[37]

We don't know whether she personally got her wish, but Pedro Núñez Franco perished at the stake in an *Auto de fe* in 1516.

Our recipe for the mixed meat stew is based on one we found in the thirteenth-century *Al-Andalus* cookbook. Blending two different meats in one stew was not unusual in Iberian medieval cooking. The combination of spices and cilantro and citrus juices is typical of Andalusian stews. The Arabic cookbook calls for rue as the green to be used with the meat, but as rue is now considered unsafe for culinary use, we have substituted other greens.

Pedro Núñez Franco's Lamb and Liver Stew

5 tablespoons olive oil

2 large onions, thickly sliced

3 pounds lamb, cut into 1–1½-inch cubes

1½ pounds goose or chicken innards (livers, hearts, gizzards), trimmed and cut into 1-inch pieces

Cilantro Juice

1 cup tightly packed fresh chopped cilantro

5 tablespoons water

4 tablespoons balsamic vinegar

2 lemons, cut into ¼-inch-thick slices

About ⅔ cup broth or water

Spice Mixture

4 teaspoons ground coriander

1 tablespoon cumin seeds

4 teaspoons pepper

1½ teaspoons ground cloves

3 tablespoons sugar

½ cup sliced almonds

½ cup pine nuts

12–15 mustard green leaves, coarsely chopped (see Notes)

Garnish

½ cup chopped fresh cilantro

¼–⅓ cup chopped almonds

2–4 tablespoons cinnamon-sugar

Lemon slices, cut in half

1. In a large pot, heat 3 tablespoons of the olive oil over high heat. Fry the onions in the olive oil until they are nearly brown, about 7 minutes. Remove the onions and set aside. Add the remaining 2 tablespoons olive oil to the pot. Fry the lamb over high heat until it begins to brown, about 8 minutes.

2. Put the onions back in the pot. Add the goose innards. Turn the heat to medium-low. Simmer, covered, while you make the cilantro juice.

3. Make the cilantro juice: Mix the cilantro and water in a blender until the mixture is a watery paste.

Lamb and Goat

4. To the cooking meat, add the cilantro juice, vinegar, half of the lemon slices, and just enough water or broth to barely reach the top of the meat, about ⅔ cup. Bring the mixture to a slow boil. Cover, turn the heat down, and simmer for 2 hours.

5. Combine the spice mixture ingredients and grind them together to a fine consistency.

6. Add the spice mixture, the nuts, and the greens. Add four more lemon slices. Cover and continue to simmer 1 hour more. The meat should be fork tender and the sauce thickening. If the sauce is very watery, remove the lid during the last 30 minutes.

7. Put the stew in a large serving bowl. Garnish with the cilantro, almonds, remaining lemon slices, and cinnamon-sugar, and serve.

NOTES

Mustard greens have a spicy flavor. You may use any other green or combination that you prefer. We suggest lovage, turnip greens, or kale.

You may thicken the broth. See pages 16–17 for suggestions.

This dish is good with rice or couscous.

Another of the several dishes that the thirteenth-century *Al-Andalus* cookbook labels as "Jewish" is this **eggplant,** which is stuffed with spiced meat from a **leg of lamb**. This recipe is a good example of the importance of aroma as well as visual presentation of a dish at an Arabic table. The cook is advised to add "scents" (*aromas*) three times and specifically rose water twice more. The author of the *Baghdad Cookery-Book* declared food and scent to be two of the six pleasures of life.[38] It is clear here how scent is perceived as an integral part of sustenance.

Jewish Dish of Eggplants Stuffed with Meat

Blanch the eggplants, scoop out their seeds but leave them whole; take meat from a leg of lamb, chop it finely with salt, pepper, cinnamon, Chinese cinnamon,[39] and lavender, beat into it eight egg whites, reserving six egg yolks; with this stuffing stuff the eggplants; then take three cooking pots, and in one of them put four tablespoons of olive oil, onion juice, spices, scents, and a tablespoon of scented rose water, pine nuts, a sprig of citron, another of mint, and sufficient salt and water; simmer it lightly and place in it half the stuffed eggplants and in the second pot place a tablespoon of vinegar, diced onion, spices and scents, a sprig of thyme, another of heather, a citron leaf, two sprigs of fennel, a tablespoon of olive oil, almonds, soaked chickpeas, and approximately a half dirhem[40] of ground saffron and three diced garlics; cover with enough water and boil several times and place in it the rest of the stuffed eggplants and in the third pot place a tablespoon and a half of strong vinegar, crushed onion, almonds, pine nuts, a sprig of heather and citron leaves; sprinkle it with rose water and dust it with scents and decorate the second with the egg yolks, chopped heather, and sprinkle it with scents; cut into the third an egg boiled with heather, dust it with pepper, and serve.[41]

This recipe is not as hard to make as first appears. As with other recipes from this cookbook, the directions are lengthy and specify several separate preparations, in this case seven different processes each with several steps. This dish requires four different mixtures and pots. Although there is no indication of just how the third sauce is related to the two pots for cooking the eggplants, we believe that it is to be presented at the table as a condiment. The presentation of the cooked eggplants is stunning and is most impressive when they are cut at the table.

Eggplants Stuffed with Lamb

Serves 4

2 medium eggplants (about 2 pounds each)

Lamb Filling

4 eggs, separated

4 teaspoons salt

2 teaspoons pepper

4 teaspoons cinnamon or 2 teaspoons
each cinnamon and cassia

2 teaspoons crushed lavender flowers

1½ pounds ground lamb

Pot 1

6 tablespoons chopped onion

2 tablespoons water, plus 2 cups

2 teaspoons ground coriander seeds

2 tablespoons rose water

2 tablespoons pine nuts

1½ cups loosely packed fresh mint
leaves

2 bay leaves

4 teaspoons olive oil

1 teaspoon salt

½ teaspoon cloves

1 teaspoon pepper

Pot 2

2 tablespoons red wine vinegar

4 tablespoons chopped onion

1 teaspoon ground coriander seeds

2 teaspoons chopped fresh thyme or 4
teaspoons dried

1 bay leaf

2 sprigs of fresh fennel or 4 teaspoons
dried

2 teaspoons olive oil

2 tablespoons slivered almonds

1 teaspoon saffron threads

½ teaspoon ground cardamom

½ teaspoon fresh sliced ginger

4 cloves garlic, cut in half

2 cups water

1 (30-ounce) can chickpeas, drained

3 egg yolks (from the eggs for the lamb
stuffing)

Pot 3 (Condiment Sauce)

4 tablespoons balsamic vinegar

2 tablespoons diced red onion

2 tablespoons lightly crushed slivered
almonds

2 tablespoons lightly crushed pine nuts

4 teaspoons rose water

4 teaspoons chopped fresh mint

2 lemon slices, peel removed and diced

Garnish

2 lemons, sliced

Prepare the eggplants:

1. In a pot large enough for the whole eggplants, boil enough water to cover them.

2. Plunge the unpeeled eggplants in the boiling water for 4 minutes.

3. Turn occasionally to scald them on all sides.

4. Remove them and set them aside to cool.

Mix the lamb filling:

5. Beat the four egg whites until frothy. Reserve three egg yolks for pot 2. Discard the remaining yolk.

6. Combine the lamb filling spices and add them to the egg whites, stirring until they are well mixed.

7. Add the lamb and mix thoroughly.

Stuff the eggplants:

8. With a sharp knife, cut the stem from each eggplant. Using a spoon, scoop out the eggplant seeds and pulp, leaving about a ½–¾-inch exterior layer of the eggplant. Leave the eggplants whole.

9. With a teaspoon, stuff the lamb filling into the cavity of each eggplant. Be sure to stuff the entire cavity. Set the eggplants aside.

Make both stewing mixtures before beginning to cook the eggplants:

10. Pot 1: In a food processor, puree the chopped onion in 2 tablespoons of the water. In a pot large enough to fit one eggplant, combine all of the pot 1 ingredients, including the pureed onion and the remaining water.

11. Pot 2: In another pot large enough to fit an eggplant, mix all the pot 2 ingredients, except the egg yolks.

Stew the eggplants:

12. Place each pot over medium heat. Stir and bring the stewing mixtures to a slow boil. Turn heat down to simmer.

13. Put one eggplant in each pot. There should be about 1–1½ inches of liquid in the bottom of each pot. If not, add water. Simmer slowly in

covered pots for 50 minutes, turning occasionally. If the eggplants begin to stick, add a little more olive oil.

14. Beat the three egg yolks and stir them into pot 2. Stir the liquid for about 3 minutes or until the yolks have started to cook. Cover the pot and simmer for 7 minutes.

Make the pot 3 condiment sauce:

15. Mix together all of the ingredients for the condiment sauce in a non-reactive bowl. Set aside to serve at the table.

Serve:

16. Take the eggplants out of the pots. Drain. Place each one on a platter. Ladle the chickpeas from pot 2 into a bowl. Discard what remains in the two pots.

17. At the table, slice each eggplant into 1-inch slices and lay one slice of each eggplant on each plate.

18. Ladle the chickpeas around and on top of the eggplant slice from pot 2.

19. Spoon a little of the condiment sauce on each eggplant slice. Garnish with a lemon slice.

NOTES

If there is leftover meat filling, make meatballs to serve with the eggplant: Add matza meal and chopped onion to the ground lamb. Form into golf-ball-size balls. To cook: Place between two layers of paper towels on a microwave-safe baking pan and microwave for 7 minutes at the roast/bake setting, or in a heavy frying pan simmer for 10 minutes in 3 tablespoons of olive oil. They are done when brown all the way through.

Save the scooped-out eggplant pulp for mixing into another casserole.

Olla de Cabrito de las Islas Canarias

The off-shore African islands (the Canaries, the Azores, and Madeira) were explored by Spanish and Portuguese mariners early in the fifteenth century. By the end of the century small colonies of farmers had settled in, while merchants and provisioners to the South Atlantic trade established commercial centers. With the exploitation of America, the Atlantic galleons found the islands a convenient stopover point.

Communities of *conversos,* among them many crypto-Jews, took root early in the islands. By 1502 Judaizers from the Canaries were appearing in the Seville and Córdoba courts. Inquisition business was so brisk that a Tribunal was founded in Las Palmas in 1505, with the first island *Auto de fe* five years later. A trial in 1520 mentions a clandestine synagogue in Las Palmas, and the presence of a kosher butcher. All in all, some twenty-seven Canarios were tried in three rounds of investigations: ca. 1530, 1600, and 1660. A number of these people were tried in absentia, meaning that they had successfully escaped the islands before they could be arrested. The statues of eleven convicted Judaizers were burned in *Autos de fe*.[43]

In addition to attempting to control Judaizing, the island Tribunal feared the Protestant influence brought by north European sailors. That, and the sporadic Iberian wars against England, whose high point (or low point, depending on your political allegiance) was the expedition of the Invincible Armada in 1588, made it especially risky for British sailors to go ashore in the Canaries. Fourteen of them were paraded in an *Auto de fe* in 1587, and one, George Gaspar, was executed.[44]

The rocky, dry terrain of the islands is well-suited for raising goats, so it is not surprising that these animals figure in *converso* cuisine.

*In the Canary Islands Sabbath stew was **goat meat stewed with lots of onion and olive oil,** accompanied by unsalted barley cakes.*[42]

Lamb and Goat

Canary Islands Goat Stew

Serves 6

4 cloves garlic, chopped

4 tablespoons olive oil

4 large onions, sliced

3 pounds goat, cut into 1-inch cubes

½ cup water

Spice Mixture

1 cup almonds

4 teaspoons galingale

1 tablespoon fenugreek

2 teaspoons nutmeg

2 teaspoons salt

1. In a large, heavy pot over medium heat, sauté the garlic in hot olive oil. Add the onions and sauté them until they are translucent, 5–7 minutes. Remove the onions and garlic.

2. Turn the heat to high, and sauté the goat until brown on all sides, about 10 minutes. You may have to do this in several batches. Return the onion and garlic to the pan.

3. Add the water, bring the mixture to a boil, and turn the heat down to a simmer. Cook, covered, for 1 hour.

4. Grind the spice mixture ingredients together and stir them into the stew pot. Simmer, uncovered, for another hour, or until the meat is tender.

VARIATIONS

Substitute lamb for goat.

This stew is also very good with the addition of fruit, which sweetens the flavors. In step **4** add 2 Bartlett pears, cut into eighths, with the spices.

If you wish, thicken the stew. See pages 16–17 for suggestions.

Sausages

"Every pig has its St. Martin's day" goes the old Spanish proverb.[1] November 12, the saint's feast day, was until recently set aside in Spanish villages for Christians to slaughter their pigs and to make sausages. It was a festive occasion as families gathered in the streets in front of their houses to eviscerate the slaughtered animals, drain the blood, chop and grind the meat, measure the spices, wash the intestines, and then stuff and tie off the new-made sausages, called in modern Spanish, among other terms, *chorizo, longaniza, morcilla,* or *salchicha,* depending on the locale and the specific ingredients.

Sausages were ubiquitous from ancient times on. Apicius's several recipes for minced meats in intestines indicate the Roman taste for sausages. In the East, the thirteenth-century *Baghdad Cookery-Book* contains one recipe with detailed directions on how to clean the tripe and how to sew the individual sausages with cotton thread.[2] At the other end of the Muslim world, sausages are included in the *Al-Andalus* cookbook. In fact the cookbook's first recipe is for *mirkas,* sausages made from cooked minced meat mixed with *almorí,*[3] pepper, coriander, lavender, and cinnamon, which the author asserts are just as nutritious as are meatballs and as easy to digest.[4] This cookbook's lamb sausages are called *tafaya*.[5]

The popularity of sausage is easy to understand. Sausages were an efficient use for what are sometimes today euphemistically called "variety meats": the ears, snout, feet, kidneys, spleen, lungs, tongue, and other bits not always suitable for a main course, morsels which Enrique de Villena in his 1423 *The Art of Carving* called "those parts which are not, because of their flavor and cleanliness, of the sort which should be given to people of quality or of delicate nature."[6] The finished products could be hung and smoked or cured, and thus preserved for a long time, an important consideration in cultures lacking refrigeration. Sausage links were portable and, most important of all, delicious.

Sausages, as Apicius's recipes show, could be either strong or sweet; they could be cured or eaten fresh; they could be boiled or fried or—in the case of cured sausage—sliced and eaten cold. In medieval Christian Europe they are documented everywhere. In the north they are found in English, French, and German cookbooks.[7] Despite their being a staple of common folk, they were not exclusively poor men's fare. *Goodman of Paris* includes them in his banquet lists, generally as part of one of the earlier courses.[8] Late medieval Catalán cookbooks also feature sausages. In *Sent soví* there are several made of goat, lamb, and even fowl. Granado gives a recipe for a "summer sausage" of veal.[9] The upper-class Spanish *Manual de mugeres'* pork sausage recipe calls for white wine among its ingredients. Its recipe for *morcilla,* a term which in modern Spanish generally refers to blood sausage, is instead a dessert-like, meatless concoction of almonds, pine nuts, cloves, cinnamon, egg yolks, and sugared scented water, bound together with pork grease.[10] Nearly the same recipe is found in the Portuguese cookbook.[11]

Although Judaizing *conversos* of the expulsion generation rigorously avoided pork and the blood of any animal, these strictures dropped from some *conversos'* consciousness as time passed. One 1621 report from Toledo describes how a *converso* manufactured *morcilla*—clandestinely, because it was during Lent—using both blood and salt pork:

> . . . *just before the start of Lent they had gone to the slaughterhouse and had brought two baskets of tripe and blood, and one of the first Sundays in Lent they chopped up a lot of salt pork and blood and spices and made* morcillas *and they let them dry for two days and then put them in their stews. . . . And the Sunday when they made the* morcillas *they did not go to mass.*[12]

The wide variety of flavors and appearances of sausages are due to the near-infinite combinations of ingredients. Chopped meat is combined with other minceables such as hard-boiled eggs, leeks, onions, greens like lovage or parsley, nuts, and bits of fat. However, the real stars of a sausage are its flavorings. For strong flavors, garlic, oregano, pepper, mustard, cumin, juniper berries, sage; for a sweeter sausage, raisins, dill, thyme, ginger, cinnamon, sugar.

Among Christians, the preferred sausage meat was almost always pork, and in fact the thirteenth-century Parisian Cooks' Guild's by-laws stipulate that "Sausages may be made only from pork and only from healthy meat . . ."[13] Muslims and Jews, to whom pork was forbidden, made their sausage of beef, lamb, goat, and fowl. Converts had to be especially careful. Since pork was a definitional ingredient of Christian sausage, sausages which avoided pork would have had to be made and consumed clandestincly. San Martín was clearly not a neighborhood feast for Iberian *conversos*.

Sausages are still popular among Levantine Sephardis. Both Marks and Stavroulakis give recipes for beef and lamb sausages. Marks's recipe is from Asian Georgia where, he says, Jews still hang the sausages on long poles for curing and drying.[14]

General Directions for Making Sausages

Making sausages is not all that hard, but it does take some time and patience. In fact, *Goodman of Paris* suggests to his wife that she have the pastry cook cut up the ingredients.[15] You will need sausage casings, a sausage stuffer, which is a metal tool shaped like a funnel, and an instrument to push the stuffing mixture through the funnel. Sausage casings, preserved frozen in salt, are sold in many supermarkets and butcher shops. The stuffer can be purchased at almost any kitchen store. We have found that the old wood pushers are readily available at antique stores. You will also need white string and scissors at your side while you make the sausages.

Here are some general guidelines that should be read before making sausage:

The Intestine Casing:
1. Soak and rinse the intestines in cool water for an hour, changing the water twice. Place them in a bowl of fresh cool water to soak a third time.
2. When ready to use an intestine, place it in a small bowl of clean, cool water.

Threading the Casing:

Intestine is fairly sturdy material, so don't be afraid to push and pull it. Take the soaking intestine and work one end of it gently with your fingers to begin to stretch it open. Once the end is open and able to be stretched, slip it over the opening onto the sausage stuffer's end. Work on both sides and push the entire casing length onto the sausage stuffer. It helps to wet the intestine occasionally. You can reasonably thread 36 inches of intestine onto the stuffer. The process may take about 15 minutes.

Stuffing the Casing:

1. It is a good idea to have a plate under the sausages as you work so that you can rest the completed sausages on the plate.

2. Tie a string tightly around the end of the sausage casing. With a spoon, fill the wide end of the funnel with the mixture. Using the pushing tool, push the mixture into the casing, making sure that you do not leave large air pockets in the sausage.

3. Stuff the casing so that each sausage has about a ¾-inch diameter or a little less. Do not stuff it too tightly because the sausages will swell when they are cooked.

4. When you have a stuffed length of about 3 inches, take white string and tie off the sausage tightly. Snip the string and push the stuffer another ½ inch and tie the casing again. (This double tie allows the sausage links to be cut apart.) Then push more stuffing through the funnel to make the second sausage to the same diameter and length. Tie off the sausage, remembering to push more of the casing off to make a second tying before starting on the third sausage. Repeat until either casing or stuffing is used up.

Storing the Sausages:

All of the sausages in this book are "fresh" sausages that should be eaten within a few days of their making. In the interim, it is best to let them sit a day or two in the refrigerator to allow the flavors to meld. Either place them on a plate (covered loosely with plastic wrap), or hang them, with a plastic bag loosely wrapped around them.

Cabaheas de Almazán

Cabaheas seems to be a local name for Jewish sausages from Almazán, for the word appears frequently in the 1505 Inquisition testimony there and is not found elsewhere in the literature of that period. It evidently was a preferred Sabbath dish in the region. Here are some variants:

- According to her maid, María Sánchez, who testified in 1505, the Almazán *conversa* Angelina de León used to make her *cabaheas* in this way: "On Sunday nights she set the heads of steers and goats to stew; and after they were cooked . . . [she] chopped them finely and stuffed them into goat tripe and smoked them; and later she ate them."[17] María said that each year the León family would slaughter an ox and four goats, and then Angelina would order María to prepare this sausage, which no one but the husband and wife were allowed to eat.[18]

- Pero Vélez used to bring home "some intestines from the meat store and innards and meat and gave them to . . . Leonor, his daughter, who made them like *torteruelos,* all tied on a string, just like the Jews used to do and they ate them on meat days."[19]

- The *converso* Master Bernal and his wife prepared their *cabaheas* of "cow head and internal organs with garlic and spices which they ate on Saturdays."[20]

- Ruy Díaz de Alvez's family "killed two cows and then cooked the innards and the heads and after it was cooked they threw in cut-up garlic and then stuffed the cow intestines and smoked them."[21]

- Ruy and Beatriz Díaz "killed three cows and made cooked sausage out of them . . . which they cooked in three pots . . . and this witness saw them hanging."[22]

- Catalina Laínez made "sausages out of beef head and heart and innards, and cooked it and mixed it with cilantro."[23]

- Leonor Méndez made them "out of ox heads, cooked and mixed with spices."[24]

- The tavern keepers Grauiel and Graçiana, whose last names were not reported, made theirs out of goat: "[he] ordered some goat innards

*María and Fernando Vélez "took an **ox head** . . . and cooked it one night and in the morning . . . chopped it up and added **chopped garlic** and **dry cilantro** and took the **ox tripe** and stuffed it with the mixture, like **sausages.***"[16]

and cooked them along with a little of the goat's meat. After it was cooked, he minced it and added dried cilantro and salt and garlic and put it in lamb intestines he had brought. . . . This they did one Sunday morning and they cooked it, and ate it that afternoon."[25]

While there is some variance in the lists of ingredients given for the dish, *cabaheas* appear to have been sausages made from the head and internal organs of cattle, lamb, or goats.[26]

Almazán Sausages

1 pound stewing beef, without bones
   (see Notes)
1 onion, quartered
2 cloves garlic

1 bay leaf
1 small beef kidney (about ¾ pound)
1 quart water
1 tablespoon white vinegar

Spice Mixture

6 large cloves garlic, chopped
2 teaspoons salt
2 tablespoons ground coriander seeds

1½ teaspoons pepper
2 tablespoons chopped fresh ginger

5 tablespoons wine vinegar
⅓–½ cup chopped fresh lovage
2 tablespoons melted shortening (see
   Notes)

2 pieces intestine, about 48 inches long
   total

For Cooking

2 tablespoons olive oil
2 tablespoons water

1–2 tablespoons vinegar (optional)

Prepare the ingredients (see the general directions, page 211):

1. Simmer the stewing beef with the quartered onion, garlic, and bay leaf
   in just enough water to cover until the beef is tender (about 2½ hours).

2. Wash the kidney. In a small pot, put the water, vinegar, and kidney.
   Bring to a boil over medium heat and gently simmer the kidney 20 minutes, uncovered. Remove it from the heat and plunge it in cold water.
   Let it sit until it is cool enough to handle. Then drain the water and
   chop the kidney, removing the membrane and fat.

3. Grind the kidney and stewing beef together, using a meat grinder. Place
   the meat in a medium nonreactive bowl.

4. Combine the spice mixture ingredients and grind them finely using a
   food processor. You may add the vinegar if it will help grind the spices
   finely.

5. To the meat, add the spice mixture, lovage, melted shortening, and
   vinegar (if you did not use it in step 4 above). Mix well. Set aside.

Make the sausages:

6. Prepare the intestines for stuffing.

7. Stuff the sausages about ¾ inch in diameter and 3 inches long. Do not cut the individual sausages apart.

8. Hang them in the refrigerator until time for frying, from overnight to 3 days.

Cook the sausages:

9. Place the olive oil and water and the vinegar, if you are using it, in a large frying pan and heat over medium heat. Add the sausages and simmer, covered, for 5 minutes, turning occasionally. Take off the cover and continue to fry for another 3–4 minutes, or until the sausages are browned on all sides. Serve hot.

NOTES

If there is beef fat on the meat, cut it off and set it aside to render later and use in place of shortening.

If you wish, you may refrigerate the meat and spice mixture for a day after step **5.**

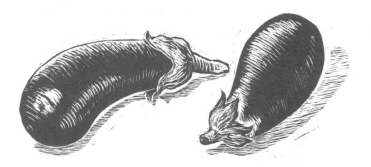

Teresa's Alvillos Rellenos

In 1502, Diego and Teresa—whose last names are not recorded in the document—feared for their lives when Diego's brother, who lived in Peñaranda, wrote that the Inquisition was looking into their affairs. His letter is an eloquent reminder of the sense of panic that such news would bring to a *converso* family:

> You must watch out, for Juan de Salcedo[28] has condemned and burned many people in this city. After you read the letter, burn it so that no one will find it, because great danger could result from that, and don't let anyone find out. I don't know whether or not the priests' bailiff has an arrest order for you. If he doesn't, get out of this city, pack up your belongings, and go to Navarre, where there is no Inquisition.[29]

Beyond the usual patterns of Judaizing activity, the depositions include two curious bits of information about Master Diego. Once he reportedly advised a friend not to marry a woman who had been twice widowed, because "the Old Law prohibited a man from marrying a woman who had buried two or more husbands."[30] He also advised a patient not to waste money on masses for the dead, because God knows their merits and will release them from Purgatory when he pleases.[31]

We don't know what happened to Diego and Teresa.

In nearby Almazán two years later, Beatriz de Díaz Laínez was reported to have made sausages in a similar "Jewish" fashion. She would "take lamb tripe and chopped spleen, stuff in hard-boiled eggs with the whites chopped and the yolks whole . . . which they put on to cook, and they ate them on Saturdays and other days when meat was permitted."[32]

*In 1501, a servant girl said that the physician Diego and his wife Teresa, conversos of Soria, had meat brought on Thursday night for cooking that night or Friday morning. Teresa "chopped the **meat** . . . with **spices** and took the **intestines of a lamb** . . . and filled them with that chopped meat and tied them with string when they were plump and **fried them in beef fat**."[27]*

Sausages

217

Teresa's Lamb Sausages

Makes 9 sausages

1 pound ground lamb   2 eggs, beaten

Spice Mixture

1 teaspoon grains of paradise   ½ teaspoon fenugreek
1 teaspoon caraway seeds   1 teaspoon salt

1 clove garlic   2–3 teaspoons chopped fresh rosemary
3–4 teaspoons chopped fresh oregano   2 tablespoons pine nuts

1 piece intestine, about 36 inches long

For Cooking

1–2 tablespoons oil

Prepare the ingredients (see the general directions, page 211):

1. Place the lamb in a medium bowl. Add the beaten eggs and mix well.

2. Grind all of the spice mixture ingredients together in a grinder or mortar. Add them to the lamb and mix thoroughly.

3. Press the garlic clove through a press, or dice it very finely. Add it, the herbs, and pine nuts to the lamb mixture. Combine well. Refrigerate the mixture for 2 hours to allow the flavors to meld.

Make the sausages:

4. Prepare the intestine for stuffing.

5. Stuff the sausages about ¾ inch in diameter and 2½ inches long. Do not cut the individual sausages apart.

6. Cure them by hanging them in the refrigerator from overnight to 3 days.

Cook the sausages:

7. Heat the oil in a medium skillet.

8. Cut the sausages apart.

9. Over medium-low heat, fry the sausages for 10–15 minutes, turning them occasionally for even browning. Serve hot.

Beatriz Núñez's Tripa con Higado y Yemas

Beatriz and her husband Fernán González Escribano, of the village of Cañamero, which is in Extremadura near Guadalupe, were tried by the Inquisition in 1485. Among the witnesses who testified to their Judaizing activities was Catalina Sánchez Serrano, who had lived with them for three or four years. Catalina complained that her mistress made her work on Sundays, that the family did not go to mass, that they kept the Sabbath, and that once a month when her period came Beatriz took a complete bath. Catalina also noted that when they prepared their Sabbath meals, they made a separate dish containing salt pork for the servants. Beatriz herself confessed to not eating pork or scaleless fish, to slaughtering in the kosher fashion, and to a host of other Jewish practices.

The Guadalupe Inquisition found Beatriz guilty of being an unrepentant heretic, and burned her alive in 1485.

*Beatriz Núñez and her husband made a Sabbath dish by "stuffing a **sheep's intestine** with ground-up **liver and egg yolks and spices.**"[33]*

Beatriz Núñez's Liver and Egg Sausage

Makes 8 sausages

1 pound livers (chicken, lamb, or veal)

Spice Mixture

2 large cloves garlic, finely diced   1 teaspoon pepper
¼ cup chopped fresh thyme   1 tablespoon chopped fresh green sage
1 teaspoon cumin seeds, ground

2½ tablespoons olive oil   3 hard-boiled eggs
½ cup finely diced onion

1 piece intestine, about 36 inches long

For Cooking

1–2 tablespoons olive oil   ¼–⅓ cup lime juice (see Variations)

Prepare the ingredients (see the general directions, page 211):

1. Clean the livers. Cut them in half. Parboil them in boiling water to cover for 1 minute. Remove them from the water and drain. Set them aside to cool in a medium nonreactive mixing bowl. When cooled, chop them into tiny pieces.

2. In a food chopper, combine and chop the spice mixture ingredients.

3. In a medium skillet, heat 2½ tablespoons olive oil over medium heat. Add the onion and stir-fry until it is barely translucent, about 2 minutes. Add the spice mixture and continue to stir-fry, about 3 minutes longer. Remove from the heat.

4. Dice the yolks of the hard-boiled eggs. Discard the whites or refrigerate them for another use. Add the yolks and the cooled onion and spice mixture to the liver. Mix thoroughly.

Make the sausages:

5. Prepare the intestine for stuffing.

6. Stuff the casings, making sausages about 2½ to 3 inches in length and ¾ inch in diameter.

7. Cut the sausages apart after the casings have been completely stuffed.

A Drizzle
of Honey

Cook the sausages:

8. Heat 1 tablespoon olive oil in a medium skillet. Fry the sausages over medium-low heat for about 8 minutes, browning evenly on all sides. Add more oil if needed.

9. Add the lime juice. Cover the pan and turn the heat to low. Simmer, turning occasionally, for another 6–8 minutes, until the lime juice has been absorbed.

NOTE

These fresh sausages are best when made and served the same day. They can be refrigerated for 2 days at most.

VARIATIONS

For a crunchy, flavorful addition to the stuffing ingredients, add ½ cup chopped pine nuts.

Instead of the lime juice for simmering the sausages, try red wine or a combination of red wine and red wine vinegar.

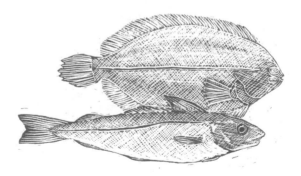

Meat and Fish Pies

In medieval Europe everyone, including Iberian Jews and *conversos,* loved *empanadas,* which are pies or pastries filled with meat, vegetables, or fish. *Empanadas* were universally popular because they were so versatile. The bulky dough provided a tasty way of turning the meager protein of the filling into a satisfying meal. They could be served for breakfast, lunch, or dinner; hot, cold, or tepid; as an appetizer, a main course, or a dessert. The tightly sealed envelope of dough made a convenient pressure cooker for a tasty sauce. They were probably the world's first take-out food, self-contained and portable. Though they could be made at home, most houses did not have ovens, so *empanadas* were often manufactured and sold commercially in bake shops and on the street, as Simple Simon happily discovered when he met the pie man on the way to the fair. During the *Auto de fe* celebrated in Madrid's Plaza Mayor on July 4, 1632, during which seven people perished at the stake, King Philip IV and his party consumed twenty little breads (most likely *empanadas*), which they washed down with wine and finished off with flavored shaved ice.[1] *Empanadas* are equally versatile for the modern kitchen, since they can be half-cooked and frozen, and then baked just before serving. As a bonus, they microwave well.

In the Middle Ages almost every country had a turnover, or pie, or pasty, or *panada* in several variations, depending on the type of dough and size of the finished product. Some were baked deep-dish in crusts like modern pies. Some were stuffed into an unleavened batter and fried. Some were wrapped in bread dough and baked. Some cooks folded them over, sealed and baked them like our modern calzone or *runzas*. Some cultures rolled them like enchiladas. The sauces could be bland, tangy, or sweet. The fillings could be anything at hand: fish, meat, vegetables, fruit, or cheese.

The pastry crust of a pie was more than a simple lid of dough that held in the sauces and steamed the main ingredients. It was also a stage on which to play out special effects for special occasions. Depending on the degree of ostentation, the crust could be decorated with colors, coatings, or even gold leaf. If not the stage itself, the crust could act as a stage curtain, cut aside to reveal a dramatic surprise inside, such as the familiar nursery rhyme's "four and twenty blackbirds." When the lid (sometimes called the "coffin" in medieval English) was lifted, the live birds would fly away. Presumably such pies were more for the looking at than for eating.

Empanadas could also hide less pleasant surprises. Their very nature abets concealment, for the outside crust gives no clue as to the nature of the minced odds and ends of the filling. Whatever was too ugly to be sold straight out might well find a buyer when wrapped in tasty dough. British abuses led to this 1379 London ordinance: "Because that the Pastelers . . . have heretofore baked in pasties rabbits, geese, and garbage, not befitting, and sometimes stinking . . . it is ordered that . . . no one of the said trade shall buy . . . at the hostels of the great lords, of the cooks of such lords, any garbage from capons, hens, or geese, to bake in a pasty, and sell."[2] In seventeenth-century Madrid, the satiric poet Quevedo skewered a notorious baker this way: "In his time there were no dead dogs, no rickety horses, monkeys, cats, flies, or animal skins that did not find a home in his pies."[3] Even in our days Spaniards use a proverb derived from these abuses: "Don't let them give you cat for rabbit" ("*No te dejes dar gato por liebre*").

Medieval cookbook writers—most of whom seemed fond of pies— categorized *empanadas* not by their shapes, or sizes, or types of dough, but by their fillings. In this the Iberian cookbooks mirror those of their European neighbors. The Iberian Christian cookbooks ordered their recipes by whether they contained meat or fish, with the latter recipes listed with the

Meat and Fish Pies

223

foods for Lent. While the *empanada* recipes in these books are roughly similar, each writer seems to stress some particular culinary effect. For example, the Portuguese cookbook offers recipes for eight kinds of *pasteis,* almost all topped with cinnamon and sugar. The *Manual de mugeres* contains a recipe for quince *empanada* that adds honey to the cinnamon–sugar. A similar recipe for quince pies in the Portuguese cookbook incorporates beef marrow, probably to help gel the main ingredient while the pie was baking. The *Al-Andalus* cookbook contains several recipes for *empanadas* for both fish and meat, sometimes directing that the pastry dough be coated with eggs before cooking. Villena, whose *Arte cisoria* focused on carving, remarks that slicing an *empanada* requires special attention.

Among Sephardis today, meat pies go by several names. In the Levant they are called *borekas* (from the Turkish *böreklar*).[4] One of the United States' cookbooks categorizes them as *borekas, boyos,* or *bulemas,* based on the kind of dough.[5] A version made with lamb innards, called *pastele* or *komotin,* is common among modern Greek Sephardis.[6]

The informants who provided the recipes that follow, like the formal writers of cookbooks, tended to focus on the filling. However, we have tried to give equal emphasis to the dough. Although each of the recipes in this chapter suggests a particular dough and mode of preparation for a particular filling, to a large extent these are interchangeable, and you should feel free to experiment without jeopardizing the medieval character of the dish.

Carne Picada com Massa do Brasil

From its discovery in 1500, the Portuguese colony of Brazil was a magnet for new-Christians, some of whom, in the semirelaxed atmosphere of the vast new land, continued to adhere to their Jewish practices. Some came for economic reasons. A *cristão-novo* consortium was granted a concession to exploit Brazil wood as early as 1502, and many later settlers were drawn by the burgeoning sugar business. In addition, the Portuguese Inquisition frequently exiled minor offenders to the colonies for a specified period, viewing the rigors of the colonies as a kind of purgatory that would encourage sinners to return to a decent life. By the late sixteenth century, the ten thousand European-descended inhabitants of Brazil may have included some two thousand new-Christians,[8] many of them employed in the sugar-mill towns known as *engenhos,* several as chief administrators or even owners. As such they formed part of the colony's elite, dealing as equals with the cream of old-Christian society, owning slaves, and building sumptuous mansions.

The Church found it scandalous that some of these people Judaized openly, even maintaining semiclandestine synagogues in some of the *engenhos*. Old-Christian members of the growing middle class of storekeepers and professionals resented the fact that new-Christians were also heavily represented in this group. The year 1570 saw the beginning of a number of anti-*cristão-novo* measures that culminated around the turn of the century when the Portuguese Inquisition sent several investigatory teams to look into alleged Jewish and other heretical practices in Bahia, Pernambuco, Olinda, and Salvador. As a result of these investigations, some two hundred seven people were indicted for Judaizing and returned to Portugal for trial; forty were convicted.[9] The detailed testimony included in these trial dossiers, and in several subsequent investigations, gives a vivid picture of Brazilian crypto-Jewish practices.

The few unfortunate Judaizers who were shipped back to Portugal were clearly only a minor part of Brazil's crypto-Jewish community. When the more tolerant Dutch captured Recife in 1630, they followed the custom of Amsterdam and permitted limited freedom of worship in the now-Dutch colony. Many secret Judaizers began to practice openly. During the twenty-four-year Dutch occupation, these were joined by many more European Jews who came seeking their fortunes in the New World. The Jewish communities of Recife and Maurícia even imported rabbis from Amsterdam.

*In the 1590s the Fernandes family of Bahia made for the Sabbath a kind of meat pie, "putting **ground meat into the dough with olive oil and onion and grains and spices** and other things, sealing it tight with dough around it and putting it into the oven until it was cooked."*[7]

During the Dutch occupation, many of the newly uncloseted Portuguese crypto-Jews moved much closer to normative orthodox Judaism. When the Portuguese regained control in 1654, some of the fugitive Jews returned to Europe, while others strengthened communities in the remaining Dutch American colonies: Curaçao and New Amsterdam. A few attempted to remain in Brazil as secret Jews, and scattered groups persisted until the mid-eighteenth century, which saw the last wave of Inquisition trials.

Brazilian Meat Pies

Makes 8 pies

Dough

1 package dry yeast
2 teaspoons sugar
½ cup warm water
1½ cups whole wheat flour

1½ cups white flour
1 teaspoon salt
1 tablespoon olive oil

Filling

1 tablespoon olive oil
1 clove garlic, finely diced
1 medium onion, finely diced (about
   ½ cup)

1 pound ground beef

Spice Mixture

1½ teaspoons sugar
½ teaspoon ground allspice
½–1 teaspoon paprika (see Notes)

¾ teaspoon salt
¼ teaspoon pepper

½ cup wheat bran

1 green pepper, thinly sliced

Make the dough:

1. Combine the yeast, sugar, and warm water. Let sit 5 minutes.

2. In a medium bowl, sift the two flours and salt. Add the yeast liquid and oil. Knead 3 minutes on a board lightly dusted with flour. If the dough is sticky, sprinkle a little more white flour on it.

3. Let the dough rise on the board in a warm place, covered with a damp towel, for 30 minutes.

Make the filling:

4. Place the olive oil in a large frying pan. Over medium heat, fry the garlic for 2 minutes. Add the onion and continue to fry until the onion is translucent, about 3 minutes more. Add the ground beef and fry, stirring to make it crumbly, until the pink is nearly gone, about 8 minutes more.

*Meat and
Fish Pies*

227

5. Mix the ingredients for the spice mixture together. Add them to the meat. Stir and simmer over low heat for 3–4 minutes. The meat will be uniformly brown.

6. Remove the filling mixture from the heat. Stir in the wheat bran. Allow the mixture to sit for 5–10 minutes for the flavors to meld.

Assemble the pies:

7. Preheat the oven to 350°. Lightly grease a cookie sheet.

8. Knead the bubbles out of the dough. Take egg-size pieces and roll each flat into a rectangular shape, about ⅛ inch thick.

9. Place 2 tablespoons of the meat mixture in the center of the rectangle. Place a thin strip of green pepper on the middle of the filling. Fold over the long sides and ends of the dough. Pinch to seal.

10. Bake in a 350° oven 10 minutes or until lightly browned.

NOTES

You may substitute a grain cereal (like Grape-Nuts) for the wheat bran.

For a spicier meat pie, add more paprika.

A Drizzle of Honey

Hernando de Soria's Empanadas de Carnero

In Soria *conversos* made special *empanadas* called *haravehuelas* from the "cow's **spleen and spices.**"[11] Nine years after Hernando de Soria was accused, Luis Vélez was reported to make his *empanadas* from "chopped meat fried in oil, and sheep's heads."[12]

Hernando de Soria was one of many Castilian Jews who in 1492 chose to brave the rigors of exile and the emotional trauma of separation from his ancestral homeland rather than to give up his Judaism. He and his family, along with several Jewish neighbors from Sigüenza, fled to Portugal during the summer of the expulsion. But evidently, as the years went on, the call of his native village grew stronger and stronger until, early in the 1500s, Hernando and his family nominally converted to Catholicism and returned to Sigüenza, where he repurchased the house he had sold in 1492.

Despite his conversion, Hernando and his family remained firmly committed to Judaism. His household became a favorite gathering place for Judaizing *conversos* of that region. His wife, who was the daughter of a *mohel*, even circumcised all of their male children. This recipe for one of the family's favorite Sabbath dishes appears in Hernando de Soria's posthumous trial.

Recipes such as this one, which combines cheese and lamb, are one of three types of evidence that Iberian Jews and *conversos* largely ignored the dietary prohibition against mixing milk and meat. The second is that the Inquisition checklists of telltale customs indicative of Judaizing make no mention of the milk-meat prohibition, though they are minutely attentive to other kosher customs. The third is that the thousands of confessions by *conversa* housewives, and the thousands of depositions of witnesses against them, rarely make mention of the custom.[13]

*Shortly after 1492 Hernando de Soria of Sigüenza was accused of cooking **sheep's** heads for several hours, chopping them finely, sprinkling them with **cheese and spices,** and making meat pies to fry in **olive oil** and soak in **honey.**[10]*

Hernando de Soria's Lamb Pies*

Makes 10 pies

Filling

1–2 tablespoons olive oil	½ teaspoon salt
1 onion, chopped	½ teaspoon pepper
¾ pound lamb, cut into 2-inch pieces	⅓–½ cup water
½ teaspoon ground cardamom	⅓ cup raisins (optional)
½ teaspoon crushed fenugreek	

Spice Mixture

¼ cup chopped fresh cilantro or fresh parsley	½ teaspoon salt
⅓ cup chopped onion	¼ teaspoon pepper
¼ teaspoon ground cloves	½ cup grated hard cheese, such as Manchego
½–¾ teaspoon cinnamon	

Dough

⅓ cup water	Pinch of salt
⅓ cup olive oil	1⅓ cups unsifted flour
2–4 tablespoons olive oil	Honey for garnish

Make the filling:

1. In a large frying pan, heat the olive oil over high heat. Add the onion and lamb and fry until lightly browned, about 8 minutes.

2. Stir in the cardamom, fenugreek, salt, and pepper.

3. Add just enough water to barely cover the mixture (about ⅓–½ cup). Cover the pan and simmer over low heat for 2 hours, stirring occasionally. If you are using the raisins, add them during the last 15 minutes of cooking. The meat will be very tender.

4. Drain the meat mixture. You may reserve the broth for use in a stew some other time.

5. Slice or chop the meat into small pieces. Place the meat mixture in a medium bowl.

6. Combine the spices and cheese. Mix them thoroughly into the meat. Set aside or refrigerate.

*For some Jewish groups, this recipe is not kosher.

Prepare the dough:

7. Bring the ⅓ cup water, oil, and salt to a boil in a medium pan. Remove from heat.

8. When the liquid is tepid, add the flour all at once to the water mixture. Stir until all is well mixed.

9. Place an egg-size lump of dough on a lightly floured bread board. With a rolling pin, shape it into a ⅓-inch-thick oval.

Assemble the pies:

10. Place 1 tablespoon of meat mixture onto a piece of dough. Fold and pinch the fold to seal the pie.

Fry the pies (see Notes):

11. Heat 2 tablespoons olive oil in a large frying pan over medium heat. Place the pies in the hot oil and gently fry, turning them once or twice, until golden brown on both sides, about 6 minutes. You may have to do this in batches, adding more oil as needed.

12. Remove and drain on paper towels.

Serve:

13. Serve hot or cold (see Notes). Drizzle warmed honey over the top of the pies.

NOTES

The steps in making this dish may seem cumbersome, but the actual preparation time is not long.

These meat pies are best eaten hot. If you wish to prepare them ahead of time for serving at a later date, we suggest that you halt the preparation after you have formed the meat pies, but before you actually fry them. They are also good cold.

Diego García Costello's Wife's Empanadas de Pescado

In 1488 Diego García Costello's wife was accused in Aranda by a neighbor of making "fish pies on Friday for the Sabbath." [14]

Diego was a surgeon who had previously been a tailor. The family was originally from Aranda (in Soria), but later moved to Palenzuela (in the province of Palencia). We have no knowledge of the circumstances or the reasons for their conversion, but it is clear that they were the sort of *conversos* who preserved close ties with the Jewish community in those years prior to the establishment of the Inquisition. They thought of themselves as Jews, despite the fact that they were nominal Christians and entirely subject to Christian law. When the Inquisition began to function ca. 1480, everything changed. During the next decade or so before the 1492 expulsion, although Jews were not normally subject to Christian religious law, Jews who abetted *conversos* in preserving their Jewish customs were liable to severe penalties. This, as intended, drove a wedge between the Jewish and *converso* communities. Many Jews wished the converts would get on with their assimilating and leave the remaining Jews alone.

Thus it is not surprising that the four witnesses who detailed the family's Judaizing customs to the Sorian Tribunal included three Jews. Teresa López noted how, for the fifteen years she had known them, Diego lit candles on Friday night, and on Saturday he invited Jewish neighbors to his home. She said she had seen him pray swaying back and forth while reading from a Hebrew book. Jacob Amillo confirmed this, and added that Diego and his wife set their Saturday table on Friday night, and that on both days they ate Sabbath stews. Judah Hazai, rabbi of the Segovian town of Cuéllar, said that when he lived in Aranda he frequently saw Diego in the synagogue reciting the Kaddish. He added that on Passover Diego used to go house to house through the Jewish quarter asking for matza so that he could celebrate the holiday. Jamila, the widow of Simón abén Farax, who is the woman who reported this recipe, said that the family used to buy their meat from the kosher butcher.

We give two versions of this recipe. One encases a large portion of fish in a bread-like dough; the other wraps a biscuit-like dough around minced fish. Both are delicious.

Diego García Costello's Wife's Individual Fish Pies*

Makes 4 small pies

Filling

½ pound fresh swordfish or other
  steak fish
1–2 teaspoons olive oil
3 tablespoons minced onion
½ teaspoon pepper
½ teaspoon cinnamon

¼ teaspoon mace
Pinch of cloves
3 tablespoons chopped fresh cilantro
2 tablespoons chopped almonds
2 teaspoons capers

Dough

½ package yeast (not rapid-rise)
3 tablespoons hot water
¾ cup sifted flour
¼ teaspoon salt

¼ teaspoon pepper
1½ tablespoons olive oil, plus more if
  needed

Make the filling (see Notes):

1. Dice the fish. In a small saucepan, simmer it in water to cover about 10
   minutes. Drain, reserving 2 tablespoons of the broth. Place the drained
   fish in a medium nonreactive bowl.

2. In a small skillet, heat the olive oil over medium heat. Add the onion
   and stir-fry until it is translucent, about 2 minutes.

3. Combine the pepper, cinnamon, mace, and cloves. Add them to the
   onion and stir-fry 2 minutes more.

4. Mix the onion and spice mixture with the drained fish in the bowl. Pour
   the reserved fish broth into the skillet; stir and pour it over the fish.

5. Mix the fish and spice combination with the cilantro, almonds, and
   capers.

6. Cover and refrigerate the mixture 30 minutes to overnight.

Make the dough:

7. In a medium bowl, dissolve the yeast in the hot water and let it sit
   5 minutes.

*Meat and
Fish Pies*

*This recipe contains swordfish and is not kosher.
Tuna may be substituted to make it a kosher dish.

8. Mix the dry ingredients together. Add them to the yeast mixture. Add the olive oil. If the dough is too flaky to roll, add more oil as needed.

9. Form into four balls and roll them flat.

Assemble the pies:

10. Preheat the oven to 350°.

11. For each pie, place 2 tablespoons filling in the center of the rolled-out dough and fold over the ends of the dough making a tight seal with moistened fingers.

12. Prick the tops of the pies with a fork.

13. Bake the pies on an ungreased cookie sheet 8–10 minutes, or until they just turn golden.

NOTES

It is best to allow the flavors of the various filling ingredients to meld before baking the pies. We suggest making the filling the day before.

This dough recipe is made with some yeast, but the dough is not allowed to rise. We opted for a thicker, crunchier pie that will hold its shape while baking.

These fish pies are so sturdy that they can be eaten with the fingers.

Diego García Costello's Wife's Large Fish Pie

Serves 4

Dough

½ package yeast (not rapid-rise)
½ teaspoon sugar
¼ cup warm water
1½ cups flour

¼ teaspoon pepper
½ teaspoon salt
1 egg, beaten

Filling

2 tablespoons chopped onion
3 tablespoons chopped fresh cilantro
2 tablespoons water
½ teaspoon pepper
½ teaspoon cumin
1½ teaspoons thinly sliced fresh ginger

1 tablespoon Pennyroyal Almorí
  (page 21)
1 egg, beaten
1 tablespoon olive oil
¾ c chopped mushrooms (optional)

1 (¾ pound) fish fillet, such as cod,
  sole, pollack, perch

5 teaspoons cinnamon-sugar

Make the dough:

1. Combine the yeast, sugar, and warm water in a small bowl and let the dough sit 5 minutes.

2. In a larger bowl, place the flour, pepper, and salt. Add the egg and the yeast mixture. Knead for 2 minutes on a lightly floured board.

3. Let the dough sit, covered with a damp towel, in a warm place for 30 minutes. It will double in size.

4. Knead the dough again to remove the bubbles. Then roll it out flat on a floured board. Roll it so that the dough is 4 inches longer and 8 inches wider than the fish fillet.

Prepare the filling:

5. Puree the chopped onion and cilantro with 2 tablespoons water in a food grinder.

6. In a spice grinder, combine the pepper, cumin, ginger, and *almorí* and grind until fine.

Meat and Fish Pies

235

7. In a small bowl, combine the beaten egg, olive oil, the onion–cilantro mixture, and the ground spices. Add the mushrooms if you wish. Mix until the ingredients are thoroughly combined.

Assemble the pie:

8. Preheat the oven to 350°. Lightly grease a cookie sheet.

9. Spread one third of the filling onto the center of the dough where the fish will lie. Lay the fish on top. Pour the rest of the sauce over all of the fish.

10. Fold the pastry sides and ends over the fish. Pinch them to seal.

11. Place the fish pastry on the prepared cookie sheet. Lay a piece of aluminum foil over the pastry, to keep it from browning too quickly.

12. Bake 25 minutes.

13. Remove the aluminum foil. Sprinkle the cinnamon-sugar over the pie. Return the pie to the oven and bake it, uncovered, another 15 minutes. Serve hot.

María García's Palominos en Pan

Almazán, a medium-size town on the Duero River in the province of Soria, in the later Middle Ages housed the second-largest Jewish community in the province. Documents suggest that most of the Jewish community converted during the latter years of that century, and remained intact in Almazán as new-Christians. In 1505 four local clerics presented the Inquisition with a complaint alleging that the Almazán new-Christians "have not dispersed nor drawn away from living one next to the other just as when they were Jews, nor have they paid any attention at all to what the Lord Inquisitor has ordered."[16] Their complaint lists 102 *conversos* by name and place of residence, convincingly demonstrating that 90 percent of the houses on the five major streets of the former Jewish quarter—about half of the area within the walls of the city—were occupied by *conversos*.

This document together with Inquisition trial testimony studied by Carrete Parrondo and Fraile Conde give a nice portrait of the professional activities of a representative large *converso* community. Altogether some 252 *conversos* are mentioned by name in the documents, 156 of them men, 58 of whom arc identified by professions. Of these 58:

26 (45 percent) worked in the clothing industry as tailors, furriers, weavers, carders, or shearers;

9 (15 percent) were other sorts of artisans: shoemakers, silversmiths, or makers of wineskins or ink;

7 (12 percent) were merchants;

6 (10 percent) were bureaucrats or administrators: they included a scribe, a majordomo, a household accountant for a local noble, a couple of toll takers, and a city official;

5 (9 percent) were involved in the medical professions: doctors, surgeons, or druggists;

2 (3 percent) were soldiers;

1 man ran a tavern and another an inn; and there was 1 laborer.

None seem to have entered another profession popular among *converso* intelligentsia: the clergy.

In Almazán in the early 1500s Martín García's wife María was observed on one Sabbath during Lent eating "some **doves in bread.** *"*[15]

Meat and Fish Pies

What emerges for Almazán is a portrait entirely consistent with *converso* communities in urban centers all over the Peninsula: a community composed largely of an urban lower middle class, dominated by artisans—principally in the clothing industry—and petty bureaucrats and administrators, with a sprinkling of professionals, and some minor crossover into professions for the most part dominated by old-Christians: innkeeping, soldiery, and common labor. Still, despite these primary professions, it seems likely that some *conversos* continued to serve as informal bankers for Almazán's Christian populace, for the clerics' census closes with the allegation that "it is well known to the public in Almazán that many of these new-Christians continue to lend money for interest just as they did when they were Jews."[17]

María García's Dove Pie

2 doves or Cornish hens, quartered

Spice Ingredients

1 cup chicken broth
½ teaspoon saffron threads
½ cup raisins
1 teaspoon sugar
1 teaspoon cinnamon
½ teaspoon ground cloves

½ teaspoon ground cardamom
1 tablespoon finely chopped fresh ginger
⅓ cup slivered almonds (optional)
1 egg plus 2 egg yolks, beaten
1 teaspoon rose water

Dough

3 cups sifted flour
2 teaspoons salt
¾ teaspoon pepper

1 cup olive oil
4 tablespoons water

Prepare the fowl (see Notes):

1. Quarter the fowl. Roast the pieces at 375° for 20 minutes. Place the pieces under the broiler for 5 minutes and allow them to turn crisp and golden.

2. Remove and cool.

3. Debone the meat and shred or cut it into bite-size pieces. Discard the bones and place the meat in a bowl and set it aside.

Prepare the filling:

4. In a small pan (or in a microwave-safe bowl if you're using a microwave), combine the chicken broth and the saffron threads. Over medium heat, heat the liquid to nearly boiling. Remove the pan from the heat and let it sit for 5 minutes.

5. Add the raisins to the chicken broth and let it sit for 20 minutes more.

6. Combine the sugar, cinnamon, cloves, cardamon, and ginger and mix them with the reserved meat.

7. Drain the raisins, reserving the liquid. Add the raisins and the almonds to the meat mixture.

Meat and Fish Pies

239

8. Combine 6 tablespoons of the reserved broth with the beaten eggs. Make sure the saffron threads are left in with the egg mixture. Pour it into the meat mixture, add the rose water, and stir thoroughly. The mixture should be moist but not soupy. Cover and refrigerate until you are ready to make the pie.

Make the dough (see Variation):

9. Preheat the oven to 475°. Sift the dry ingredients together into a medium bowl. Mix the wet ingredients thoroughly. Combine the wet ingredients with the dry ones all at once. Stir quickly with a fork.

10. Divide the dough into two balls, one slightly larger than the other. Take the larger dough ball and with a spoon press it into an 8-inch ovenproof casserole dish to a thickness of ¼ inch. Prick the bottoms and sides with a fork. Bake it for 15 minutes. Take it out of the oven and set it aside until it cools, about 5 minutes. Lower the oven temperature to 350°.

11. Meanwhile, roll the other dough ball flat between two pieces of waxed paper, to about ⅛-inch thickness.

Assemble the pie:

12. Fill the prebaked shell with the filling.

13. Place the remaining piece of dough on top of the pie and trim the edges to fit the casserole. Crimp the edges together. Prick the crust with a fork. Cook the pie for 20 minutes or until the crust is just turning brown.

NOTES

Serve hot or cold.

You can prepare most of this dish ahead of time: you may stop after having cooked and deboned the fowl or you can stop after having mixed all of the filling ingredients.

VARIATION

You can make this recipe as four small (or one large) *empanadas*, using these ingredients for the dough:

4 cups flour, sifted	*1 teaspoon pepper*
2 tablespoons salt	*1½ cups water less 1 tablespoon*

2 teaspoons chopped fresh parsley	*2 teaspoons chopped fresh mint*
2 teaspoons chopped fresh oregano	*Olive oil for oiling pies if needed*

Make the dough:

1. Combine the flour, salt, and pepper in a large bowl.
2. Add the water and the fresh herbs.
3. Mix to a stiff dough. Knead it on a lightly floured board until it is satiny, about 5 minutes.
4. Cover it and let sit 30 minutes.

Prepare the filling following the directions in steps 4–8 above.

Make the *empanada(s)*:

5. Preheat the oven to 475°. Grease a baking sheet.
6. Divide the dough into eight balls. On a board, between two sheets of waxed paper, roll out two of the dough balls in a round or oval shape as thin as you can get them (about ⅛ inch).
7. Place one quarter of the meat mixture in the center of one of the dough pieces. Place the other dough piece on top. Press together all around the edges. Take a fork and crimp the edges. Repeat for the remaining dough balls.
8. Place the pies on the greased baking sheet. Bake for 15–20 minutes or until the bottoms begin to brown. Oil the tops of the pies if they are not browning.

Breads

In medieval Iberia bread was a staple, accompanying every meal. Families had their own source of wheat, which they had ground into flour at a commercial mill, and from which they made their dough at home. In the crowded wooden cities the risk of fire was great, so most people had their dough baked in a commercial oven. Wealthier families, with enough space to be able to maintain a detached oven, baked at home. Since the bread that Jews and Judaizing *conversos* prepared and ate had no characteristics distinguishing it from the bread that the rest of Christian Iberia consumed, no attention is drawn to it in the literature. For example, we have found no Iberian references to the braided, egg-rich Sabbath white bread known to Ashkenazi Judaism as *challah*.

Two things are, however, specifically identified with Jews and *conversos*. One is the unleavened Passover matza.[1] The other is the custom of Jewish bakers of pinching off a small piece of the risen dough and throwing it into the fire before baking. The separation of this piece of dough, which is discussed in both the Talmud (Shab. 2:6) and the *Shulhan Arukh* (OH 457), was commonly practiced, at least among the expulsion generation and their children. A checklist of Judaizing customs, compiled for the Inquisition in the 1480s, explains the practice in some detail:

> *The rabbi says that throwing a piece of dough in the fire is in memory of the bread that the people of Israel were obliged to give to the High Priest in sacrifice. It was one piece of bread every time that they baked in memory of the priesthood that the people of Israel lost.*[2]

In 1502 in Almazán a servant of the Laínez family was observed tearing off a piece of dough and throwing it in the fire. When she was asked why, the servant replied, "Forget it, it's just a little trifle that my mistress makes me do."[3] In 1569 Beatriz Rodrigues, of the Portuguese village of Lamego, was accused of "throwing three pinches of dough into the fire as a sacrifice and Jewish ceremony."[4] The custom was reported in Mexico in 1639,[5] and in the 1670s on the island of Majorca, where the new-Christians would accompany the act with a muttered prayer: "May God cause my bread to rise."[6]

Bakers nourished a yeast culture for leavening their bread. They would pinch off a piece of today's dough and store it in a cool dark place to use as a starter for tomorrow's. Jewish home bakers, in the days before the expulsions, and Judaizing *converso* bakers of the same period, always shopped out their yeast starter at Passover. Those *conversos* who did not purge their houses of leaven at Passover sometimes helped out their more observant brethren. Pedro Abella, of Barbastro, was typical. According to testimony in 1491, "after Passover he sent the Jewish women leavened bread and bread starter in exchange for the matza that the Jews gave him."[7]

For medieval diners bread was a universal tool. In northern countries flat slices of day-old bread—called "trenchers" or "sops"—often substituted for plates; if the trencher had been cut from fresh bread, after the meat was gone the gravy-soaked plate was consumed. Since bowls were often shared, and metal utensils were scarce, slivers of bread were used to dip sauces; pieces of thick crust could serve as spoons. This was common in the rest of Europe and most likely occurred in Iberia as well. The Portuguese and *Sent soví* cookbooks occasionally cite bread as sops,[8] but we have found no Inquisition references to this practice in Iberia. The porous quality of bread was especially useful in another way. In Portugal, Cistercian monks were enjoined "not to wipe their hands or knives on the tablecloth unless they had first cleaned them with bread."[9] Slices of bread could even be used as potholders to carry iron vessels from the fire.[10]

Although the four breads that follow are associated with Judaizing *conversos* in the documents, really they are typical of the breads that Jews, Christians, and Muslims would have eaten in fifteenth-century Iberia.

Mayor González's Panezicos

Mayor González,
the wife of Pedro
Núñez Franco of
Ciudad Real, "put
on her Sabbath table
some **little, folded
white breads,**
and they were
delicious!"[11]

Nothing but the best for the Sabbath was the credo of Judaizing *conversa* housewives of the expulsion generation like Mayor González. On Fridays Mayor had her slave María, the slave's daughter Isabel, and her hired servants Juana González and her sister Elena García sweep and decorate the house from top to bottom.[12] In summer they sprinkled water to keep the dust down.[13]

It was young Isabel's duty to clean the Sabbath lamp and place a new wick in it. Friday evenings the family extravagantly lit three oil lamps: one for the kitchen, one that the servants carried through the house, and in the bedroom another one, which they insisted had to burn out of its own accord. One of their servants was scandalized at Mayor's wastefulness: "Sometimes I went and put out that lamp when my master and mistress had gone to sleep, but my mistress ordered me not to do it."[14] According to this servant, Mayor's husband Pedro also disapproved. "He scolded her for not allowing it to be put out, asking her why she insisted on having it lit all night."[15]

Several servants confirmed that on Friday evenings the normal household bustle came to a halt. What Mayor and Pedro most enjoyed then, the servants noted, was to stretch out near the fire on a bench that had been plumped with pillows, and just loaf and do nothing.[16] Then they would go to bed early and not get up until late on Saturday morning.[17]

But what the servants liked best about the Sabbath was that on Friday nights their masters' tempers sweetened. According to Juana González, "Friday nights they never scolded me or the other serving girls or slaves like they did on weekdays, when my mistress used to scold me and my sister and the slaves for not doing any work, and she used to curse at us and say that we weren't earning our keep. But Friday nights when they were loafing they never scolded us or said anything like that."[18]

The Mayor González trial mentions several sorts of Sabbath *adafinas*.[19] The accompanying white rolls could be taken fresh from the oven before sunset on Friday evening without risk of violating the Sabbath prohibitions against work. We give one recipe with suggestions for a second, sweeter version.

*A Drizzle
of Honey*

Mayor González's Bread Rolls

1 package dry yeast
2 tablespoons warm water
¾ cup milk
2 tablespoons butter or olive oil

½ teaspoon salt
1 tablespoon sugar (see Variations)
1 egg
2½ cups white flour (approximately)

1. Stir the yeast into the warm water. Set aside for 10 minutes.

2. In a medium pan, heat the milk, butter, salt, and sugar over medium-high heat until the point of boiling. Remove the pan from the heat and let the mixture cool until it feels warm, not hot, to the touch. Pour the liquid into a large bowl. Beat in the egg. Add the yeast water.

3. Sift the flour into the liquid. Stir until it forms a shaggy mass, then knead with the hands, on a lightly floured board, adding more flour when it gets sticky. Knead until it forms a satiny dough. Cover it with a towel and let it rise until it doubles in size (about 40 minutes on a warm day). Meanwhile, grease two baking sheets.

4. Knead out the bubbles. For each roll: cut off an egg-size piece. Roll it into a circle, 6 inches in diameter. Fold the circle once in half, then in quarters. Do not press the folds together. Place the rolls on the greased baking sheets. Let them rise to double their bulk in a warm place for about 30 minutes.

5. Preheat the oven to 400°. Bake for 10 minutes until light gold in color. Serve hot.

VARIATIONS

For richer, sweeter folded rolls do any, or all, of the following:

substitute 2 tablespoons honey for the sugar;

use two eggs rather than one and reduce the milk by 2 tablespoons;

sprinkle liberally with cinnamon-sugar just before baking.

María González's Torta Blanquesca

Saturday gatherings

at the home of María

González were for

talking, eating, and

sometimes bathing

together. María

"used to make a

white flat bread,

and she gave a piece

of it to the first person

who entered . . .

and the bread was

tasteless and white,

and this witness

believed that it was

unleavened, although

no one who was there

called it that." [20]

Let's listen to the words of another María González, the wife of Pedro de Villarreal, as she testifies on March 30, 1512, in Ciudad Real about her aunt, María González, widow of Diego de Teva. As was customary, the scribe recorded the testimony in the third person.

All the ladies used to gather in the house of her aunt María González, the wife of the knife-sharpener Diego de Teva, deceased, on Friday evenings. . . . Those Friday evenings [María] used to light two clean lamps with new wicks some two hours before twilight; and she cleaned and decked out her house very nicely those Friday evenings to honor the Law of Moses. . . . Sometimes the women talked about church things, and the Catholic faith, and they made fun of the mass. She knows that the women did not believe in the mass or want to listen to it, and that when they did go to church to hear mass they only went to fulfill their obligations. . . . The ladies used to keep some of the Jewish weekday fasts, which she believes were Monday and Friday, or Thursday, she doesn't remember which. . . . Each one fasted at home during the day, and then ate dinner, and after dinner they gathered at Diego de Teva's wife's house, and together there they gossiped about how they had fasted. . . . Some of them fasted more than others, and she herself, because she was always pregnant or had just given birth, rarely fasted.

And when they gathered there in Diego de Teva's house on Saturdays they used to eat little cakes, which were as white as snow, and tasteless, . . . which Diego de Teva's wife gave them. And she herself believed that Diego de Teva's wife prepared and baked them in her home, because her house had an oven. . . . Sometimes when she went into Diego de Teva's wife's house she found her eating these little cakes, and she ate some too, and she remarked that they were very tasteless, and Teva's wife would say, "Eat it, it's good."

And the reason they gathered in Diego de Teva's wife's house is that she was a widow and didn't have anyone around from whom to hide these practices. . . .

All these things happened when Teva's wife lived next door to the witness. Later, when Teva's wife moved to the Moorish neighborhood, they still gathered there, but seldom, because it was a long way away. [21]

María González's Flatbreads

Makes 4 flatbreads

1 tablespoon salt

2 tablespoons sugar or honey

2 cups warm water

½ cup whole wheat flour, sifted

5½ cups white flour (approximately),
   sifted

The day before serving:

1. Stir the salt and sugar into the warm water. Stir in the whole wheat flour. Beat for 3 minutes (or count three hundred strokes) with a wooden spoon.

2. Stir in the white flour ½ cup at a time, until the dough is too thick to stir. Then add flour by hand until the dough loses its stickiness and becomes kneadable. Knead it on a floured board by pushing the dough flat and folding it over. Do this at least two hundred times.

3. Cover the dough with a damp towel and let it sit overnight in a warm place. This allows the dough to begin to ferment, making the bread lighter by causing it to rise slightly.

The day of serving:

4. Grease two cookie sheets. Knead the dough another twenty to thirty times. Divide it into four balls. Press each into a flattened oval or rectangle about ½–¾ inch thick. Place them on the greased cookie sheets. Cover with a damp cloth and let them rest for 45 minutes. Score the top of each bread deeply with a knife in parallel lines or like the spokes of a wheel. The cooked bread can be broken apart along these lines.

5. Preheat the oven to 375°. Brush the breads with water before baking. Bake for approximately 30 minutes. The breads are done when they have a hollow sound when tapped. Remove them to a rack to cool.

NOTE

This unyeasted bread will not rise much; it will have nice crisp crusts and a softer inside.

Tortitas de Harina de Cebada

*In the Canary Islands the Sabbath meal was goat meat stewed with lots of onion and olive oil, accompanied by **unsalted barley cakes**.*[22]

Medieval Europeans—no matter where they lived or their wealth or station—tended to consume about two pounds of bread daily. By and large, the difference between rich and poor was not the amount of bread they consumed, but the type.[23]

Differences in soils and in climate meant that there was some variance in the sorts of grains that flourished in different regions of Europe. Of all the edible grains, wheat forms the best gluten, will rise into the lightest loaf, and can be made to produce bread of the whitest color. Thus generally in Europe, and certainly in Iberia, wheat was the most prestigious and costly grain. Even so, it was by far the most frequently consumed, even by the lowest classes. Records for the Barcelona poorhouse in 1284–85 show that 97 percent of the grain purchased that year was wheat.[24] Rye, according to Covarrubias's 1611 Spanish dictionary, was mainly for "rustic folk"; barley "for horses," and for people "only in times of great want." Oats were eaten by humans only in the direst circumstances, since normally they were used green as fodder for horses or dry for fowl.[25]

Wheat was the most commonly used whole grain, without separating the bran from the kernel, which was time consuming and thus an expensive process. Wheat would be stone-ground by commercial millers in mills powered by wind or water. Since the cracked bran spoils quickly in heat or moisture, the flour would be used fresh rather than stored. The flour was whitened by forcing it through a fine cloth several times to remove most of the flecks of wheat hull. The finer the cloth and the greater number of times the flour was bolted—as this process was called—the whiter and the more costly the flour.[26] Since the milling and bolting were complex processes, and since in the cities only the wealthy had home ovens, both milling and baking were generally handled commercially.

Of course wheat, rye, and oats were not the only grains consumed in Iberia. The Portuguese cookbook contains recipes using both millet and rice flour.[27] When times were really tough, chickpeas, beans, or peas could be ground to stretch the precious wheat flour. In the Canary Islands, as we can see by this recipe, and probably in the rest of Iberia as well, despite its low status bread was also made from barley.

Unsalted Barley Cakes

Makes 8–12 barley cakes

2 cups barley flour (rye flour can be
substituted)
2 teaspoons sugar

2 teaspoons baking powder
1 cup light cream or evaporated milk
2 tablespoons butter, melted

1. Combine the dry ingredients in a medium bowl.
2. Stir the cream and melted butter into the dry ingredients.
3. Preheat the oven to 450°. Grease two cookie sheets.
4. Lightly flour a board or countertop. Spoon out an egg-size lump of the dough, which will be tacky to the touch. Flour your hands, and pat the dough into a circle about ½ inch thick. Lightly score the top into eight wedges, to facilitate breaking apart the baked bread, and prick each bread several times with a fork to allow the steam to escape while baking.
5. Bake on the greased cookie sheets for 10 minutes or until the breads begin to brown. Remove them immediately and cool on a rack. Break them apart after they have cooled.

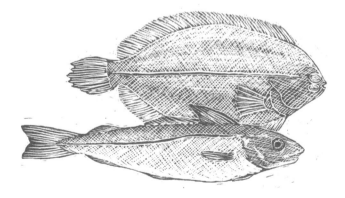

Breads

249

María Alvarez's Pan Cuez

*Master Bernal and his wife allegedly made "**cuez bread** in this fashion: they put **coriander** in a frying pan with **garlic and ground spices and water and oil** and threw in **bread crumbs and green coriander,** and stirred it up and from this they made this **cuez** bread for Saturdays and Fridays."[28]*

In 1505 in Almazán, Soria, the Inquisition tried Master Bernal, a physician married to María Alvarez[29] and the father of four children, who were themselves later tried as Judaizers. Bernal socialized with don Antonio de Mendoza, the Count of Monteagudo, one of whose servants reported having heard Bernal say that he would not recite the *"Ego pecator"* prayer because he was not a sinner. One of Bernal's neighbors said he overheard the physician assert that it was all right for every man to worship his own God, and one of Bernal's own servants said he overheard him talking in Hebrew with several other *conversos*. A barber, who was bleeding Bernal one day, said he heard him say "ouch" in Hebrew when he pricked his skin.

Bernal owned some medical books in Arabic. He also kept some Hebrew books at home. After his death his widow, fearful of the Inquisition, burned them.

A local carpenter's wife named Magdalena, who had worked for the Bernal family twelve years previously, complained about how the physician used to gouge his patients, selling them purges for two or three *reales* that she had bought at the pharmacy for a half *real*.

Magdalena provided inquisitors with this family recipe for *cuez* bread, a sausage recipe,[30] and the family Passover matza recipe.[31]

María Alvarez's Cuez Bread

1 small loaf day-old bread (see Notes)

Spice Mixture

2 teaspoons coriander seeds
1 teaspoon cumin seeds

1 teaspoon caraway seeds

3 tablespoons olive oil
3 cloves garlic, finely diced

5 tablespoons water
½ cup chopped fresh cilantro

1. Take the bread and chop it in a food processor or by hand into ¼-inch cubes. Chop enough to make 4 cups.

2. Grind the ingredients for the spice mixture together in a grinder. Mix them into the bread cubes.

3. In a large frying pan, heat the olive oil over medium heat. Add the garlic and stir-fry about 2 minutes or until it begins to brown.

4. Add and stir-fry the bread cubes until they begin to brown, about 3 minutes. Then add the water, 1 tablespoon at a time, stirring the mixture and allowing the liquid to evaporate before adding another tablespoon, at approximately 1-minute intervals.

5. After all the water has been added, add the cilantro, stir to combine, and continue to fry about 1 minute more. Remove from the heat and serve immediately.

NOTES

Use French bread or any other bread that becomes hard and crumbly when no longer fresh.

This dish is great for sopping up the juices of a Sabbath stew.

Desserts and Snacks

Today we think of desserts as those little somethings, frequently sweet, that finish off a substantial meal. The medieval French term *dessert* (literally "un-serving") reminds us that these tidbits were presented as the table was being dismantled (literally "un-tableclothed"). The Spanish term for dessert, *postre,* underscores its location at the end of the meal. In late medieval Iberia, as the seventeenth-century lexicographer Covarrubias reminds us, *postres* tended to be "the fruits or cooked sweets given at the end of dinner or supper."[1]

From the nature and slim number of the scattered references to Jewish or *converso* desserts we draw two conclusions. The first is that Iberian Jewish desserts—with the exception of Passover desserts that were made with ground-up matza— were precisely like those of their Christian neighbors. And the second is that they were so commonly appended to major meals that they did not merit anyone's special attention.

Therefore to understand how Iberian Jews and *conversos* finished their meals, we must look to the overall culinary culture of the Peninsula.

Fresh fruit was eaten for dessert so commonly that it is rarely cited in culinary treatises, though fruits do appear regularly in documents referring to markets and occasionally in household accounts, such as a sixteenth-century Madrid record that includes expenditures for fruits and salads for openers and desserts.[2] Mexican *conversos* were also fond of fruit. The Mexican *conversa* Ana de León Carvajal testified in 1600 that for the first day of Passover a friend sent her a mamey and a large melon.[3]

Even in ancient times, other desserts tended to be sweet. The ancients sweetened principally with honey. But by the thirteenth century an exotic Islamic sweetener, brought to northern Europe by returning crusaders and introduced to the south by the Muslim kingdoms of Iberia, turned all of Europa gaga. Sugar. In unrefined brown lumps. In sparkling white crystals. Ground in mortars to a powdery dust. Mixed with cinnamon and sprinkled on meats, fish, eggs, pies, and vegetables in quantities that would alarm modern nutritionists. In the 1330s a Florentine merchant grew rich importing from Damascus and Cairo loaf sugar, as well as powdered, candied, refined, rose, and violet sugars.[4]

In accord with the medieval theory of the four bodily humors, sugar was classified as warm and moist, and because these qualities were thought to aid digestion, sugar in any form was considered an ideal way to end a meal.[5] Sugar was preferred over honey for two reasons: it combined splendidly with almost anything, and because it was durable, foods preserved with it could be kept for a very long time. Most important, sugar was made into sweets. Desserts that combined sugar with fruit or baked it into pastries were known generically by the Latin verb for blending: *conficio*. For Covarrubias, *confites* were "confections of almonds, hazelnuts, pine-nuts, or any other fruit or seed incorporated with or covered with sugar."[6]

By the mid-fourteenth century these sugary confections were all the rage, and by the next century master chefs were compiling their recipes into books like the Catalán *Libre de totes maneres de confits,* which gives thirty-three recipes for candied fruits and nuts, fruits preserved in sugar syrup, nougats, and hard candies of diverse flavors.[7] These were not uniquely Iberian, for similar sweetmeats are cited all over Europe at that time. They appear similar to modern candied fruits and nuts, except that our late-medieval ancestors had palates much broader than ours. A price list of *confituras* for sale in Madrid in 1567, for example, lists candied almonds, pine nuts, hazelnuts, anise, lemon peel, quinces, coriander, roses, citrons, squash and lettuce hearts, and borage greens.[8]

Dessert pastries also tended to be sweet. Whether they were yeasted or unleavened, fried or baked or boiled, they were commonly soaked in honey, or liberally sprinkled with sugar and cinnamon or other flavorings. Deep-fried puff pastries similar to our doughnuts were popular, as were wafer-like cookies and sweet ring-shaped pastries stuffed with fruit or nuts.

Allusions to crypto-Jewish snack foods are rare, since *conversos,* like everyone else, munched on the finger foods at hand. Still, references to snacks consumed in special circumstances sometimes made their way into the documents. This chapter's garlic snacks and bread and olives are examples. Mexican *conversos* were fond of snacks, even in jail. In 1601 Ana Rodríguez, in a cell next to Jorge Rodríguez, pulled a stone from the wall through which she could pass him fruit, radishes, and cheese,[9] while Ruy Díaz Nieto kept a bowl of raisins and almonds on his table.[10]

Membrilla

Quince (Latin: *Pyrus cydonia*) was not only Ruy Díaz Nieto's favorite fruit. Ancient authorities lauded it as both healthful and pleasing. In Roman mythology it was dedicated to the goddess of love. In the mid-ninth century Charlemagne ordered that it be grown in France. Chaucer knew it.[12] There are recipes for quince in fifteenth-century English and French cookbooks. Although quinces are grown throughout Iberia, those of Toledo were particularly prized, as can be seen in this well-known proverb: "Quinces, swords, and girls, the ones from Toledo are pearls!"[13] Recipes for quinces abound in the medieval Peninsular cookbooks, from *Al-Andalus* to Nola. Many of these are for quince preserves, which even today are frequently served as a sweet dessert, but the fruit was also added to meat or fowl stews. There is some thought that quinces existed in both the Old World and the New, and that unlike its European cousin, the American variety—sweeter and larger—was edible raw.[14]

According to Genesis, man's first recorded snack was an apple, and ever since that little nibble, fruits have been a universal part of the human diet. Their variety, color, texture, juiciness, sweetness, and versatility make fruit ideal for a snack, an appetizer, a dessert, or as a component of an infinite variety of complex dishes. Fancy meals were bracketed by fruit. As Lobera de Avila's 1530 *Banquete de nobles caballeros* states on the first line in the first chapter, "In a good banquet there must be a lot of fruit as a first course. . . ."[15] In addition, the role of fruit in maintaining and restoring health was well known in the Middle Ages: if the apple a day didn't work, when the doctor did visit he was likely to prescribe fruit.[16]

Quinces were but one of some three dozen fruits that were commonly eaten in Iberia. Some thirty fruits are discussed in the sixth-century encyclopedia of St. Isidoro, much of whose information is derived from classical authorities such as Dioscorides. Villena's *Arte cisoria* mentions about a dozen fruits—the same ones found in the earlier *Tacuinum sanitatis*—including pomegranates, quinces, apples, cherries, plums, and peaches. By the later Middle Ages some of the exotic Eastern fruits like oranges, pomegranates, and lemons, which had been introduced by the Muslims, were fairly widely cultivated on the Iberian Peninsula and incorporated into recipes for sauces in Catalán, Andalusian, and Portuguese cookbooks.

How widely were they eaten? In season—June through September— they were probably consumed daily by people of all regions and stations.

*Ruy Díaz Nieto lived on **quince** and cheese for months while imprisoned by the Mexican Inquisition in 1603.[11]*

The accounts of a summer journey from Estella to Seville in 1352 show that the travelers bought two kinds of cherries, blackberries, apples, pears, and plums, as well as some generic "fruit." In sixty-eight days they bought fruit seventy-two times. Presumably they also helped themselves to what they found along the way, for as the proverb states, "Fruit by the roadside never gets ripe."[17] Iberians also ate preserved fruits. Apples, like onions and turnips, were stored in cool rooms for later consumption. Sweet fruits like pears and peaches were put into sugared syrups to conserve them. Some fruits, like berries and quinces, were sugared and boiled down into jams. Others, such as grapes, plums, and figs were dried, with the dried versions sometimes renamed, as with raisins and prunes. In Andalucía, as in the Maghreb, lemons were salted and preserved for use in stews. The Portuguese cookbook has recipes for conserves for citron, lemon, peach, pear, pumpkin, and quince. The *Manual de mugeres* suggests conserving peaches until Christmas by covering them with honey and sealing them in an airtight container.

Fruit, then, seems to have been an important, routine part of the diet of medieval Iberians. Its very universality probably explains why we find so few references to it in Inquisition documents. Since Jews and *conversos* ate fruit like everybody else and, with the exception of an occasional reference to the consumption of citrons at Sukkot, fruit seems to have had no ritual importance, what was there to notice?

The following recipe for quince paste—which because it is so cheap and easy and tasty may well have been what Ruy Díaz Nieto was given to eat in prison—is based on one found in the *Al-Andalus* cookbook and our own preference for a fruity preserve that is more on the tart side than the sweet.

10–12 quinces   *Sugar (see Variations)*

1. Wash the quinces and remove the stems and leaves. Put the fruit in a large pot and add barely enough water to cover (see Variations). Bring to a boil, then cover and simmer until the fruits have become completely mushy and are falling apart, about an hour. Turn the heat off, and set the pot aside to cool.

2. Carefully run the liquid and fruits through a fruit strainer into a large pan. Be sure to strain out the seeds and skins.

3. Measure the resulting pulp and then put it into a heavy, clean pan. Add sugar equal to one half the amount of pulp (see Variations). Stir well. Place over low heat and simmer gently, stirring often, until the pulp thickens to a consistency between apple butter and jelly, about 30 minutes.

4. Remove from the heat and pour into hot sterilized jars. Let cool. Seal tightly. Jars of quince paste may be stored in the freezer for several months.

VARIATIONS

Add ¼ cup cider vinegar to the water in step **1**.

Instead of using white sugar, use a combination of white and dark brown sugars or a combination of ¾ white sugar and ¼ honey.

Add more sugar for a sweeter paste.

Add 2 teaspoons rose water at step **3**.

Add one or both of the following spices to step **3**:

1 teaspoon cinnamon
¼ teaspoon cloves

Pedro Abella's Azuquaques

In 1491 Pedro
Abella, of Barbastro,
was accused of
having "**sugar
cakes and nougat
candy** brought from
the Jewish quarter;
he would eat them
only if Jewish
women had
prepared them."[18]

Abella was accused in Teruel of keeping the Sabbath by putting on clean clothes, lighting candles, eating *hamin*,[19] and not working. Witnesses heard him praying in the synagogue, and the indictment even accused him of praying to the Torah. They said that he observed Purim, Yom Kippur, Passover, and Sukkot. He was said to attend circumcisions and Jewish weddings, to eat only koshered meat, to contribute charity—the indictment uses the Hebrew word *cedaqua*—to poor Jews, and to sit at home for the traditional mourning period when a Jewish relative died. In addition, he was accused of ignoring Church festivals, of not going to mass, of violating the Sunday rest, and of being totally ignorant of Christian prayers like the "Our Father" and the "Hail Mary."

Despite the fact that Abella was a part of the preexpulsion Jewish community, and so overtly rejected the most visible trappings of Christianity, he, like many of his *converso* contemporaries, had already absorbed the Christian concept of the personal salvation of the soul, and he believed that the souls of Jews could be saved only in their ancient law.[20]

It is also clear that he had a sweet tooth.

Although the word *azuquaque* is not found in contemporary dictionaries or other culinary sources, it is clearly derived from the Arabic word for sugar. Every contemporary Islamo-Hispanic source leaves no doubt that sugar cakes—compressed, flavored confections of sugar and nuts—were a staple of Islamic sweet making. The following candy recipe for *azuquaques* is derived from one in the thirteenth-century *Baghdad Cookery-Book*.[21] The cookie recipe is an adaptation of one in the Portuguese cookbook.[22]

Pedro Abella's Sugar Candies

½ cup plus ⅓ cup sugar
¼ cup almonds

1 teaspoon almond extract
2 teaspoons rose water (see Variation)

1. Grind the ½ cup sugar and almonds together. Mix in the almond extract.

2. Place the ⅓ cup sugar in a medium saucepan or heatproof glass dish. Over low heat dissolve the sugar, shaking occasionally until the sugar is all melted. The mixture will turn golden brown. Remove from the heat.

3. With a fork, mix the ground sugar and almonds into the dissolved sugar. Add the rose water, and work the mixture into a dough.

4. Cut off an olive-size piece and, on a board, using the flat edge of a knife as a tool, press the piece flat (about ¼ inch high) and press the sides so as to form the desired shape. Triangles are easy to form. The candies should be of a size to pop into your mouth whole.

5. Let the candies cool on a plate. To store, place them in a covered container.

NOTES

You will need to work fairly quickly to shape the candies before they harden.

Do not double this recipe. If you want more candy pieces, make the recipe twice.

VARIATION

For the rose water, substitute 1 teaspoon water and 1 teaspoon of any other extract flavoring.

Pedro Abella's Sugar Wafer Cookies

Makes 24 cookies

½ cup sugar
⅓ cup butter
1 tablespoon white wine or sherry

1 tablespoon hot water
2 teaspoons orange extract
⅞ cup flour, sifted

1. Cream the sugar and butter until smooth.

2. Mix in, one at a time, the wine, hot water, and orange extract.

3. Add the sifted flour, ¼ cup at a time. Mix until smooth.

4. Preheat the oven to 375°. Drop the batter by teaspoonfuls onto an ungreased cookie sheet, about 2 inches apart. Six to eight will fit on a sheet.

5. Bake for about 7 minutes, or until the edges turn brown. Remove them from the oven. Allow them to cool on the cookie sheet before placing them on a plate.

6. Repeat with the remaining batter. Store the cookies tightly covered.

NOTE

The cookies spread out while cooking to make a thin wafer. Be careful not to overbake.

A Drizzle
of Honey

Sephardic Holiday Turrón

The Santángel family of Teruel was typical of the Judaizing converts of the late fifteenth century who, before the founding of the Inquisition, mingled freely with their Jewish friends and neighbors and tended to live their Jewish lives pretty much as they had before their conversion. Jaime Martínez de Santángel and his wife, Rita Besante, converted around 1413 in the wake of the preaching campaigns of the Dominican Vicente Ferrer (who was later canonized as a saint). As children their daughters Brianda and Alba were given a Jewish education, but as they reached their maturity they moved in the direction of assimilation to Christianity. The eldest, Brianda, so thoroughly rejected her childhood practices and was so forthcoming in testifying against her parents that the Inquisition absolved her of heresy and let her off with minor penances.

With simple ingredients—principally nuts, honey, and sugar—nougat candies are found in cultures all over the world. The Spanish varieties of nougat, called *turrón,* derive their name from the verb *turrar,* which means to boil in the embers of a fire.[24] *Turrón* is traditionally molded in small, rectangular wooden boxes in which the bottom and sides are covered with paper that has been dusted with flour. Sometimes the bottom and top are covered with a thin cookie wafer instead.

Although nougat is made in dozens of Spanish cities, *turrón* from the Mediterranean coastal city of Alicante is particularly famed. The original *turrón alicantino* contained only almonds and honey.[25] Modern versions feature hazelnuts, add egg whites to the liquid, and are known for their crunchiness. In one of the plays of Miguel de Cervantes, a poor man dreams of an ideal feast that ends with *turrón* from Alicante.[26]

A maid servant of the converso *Santángel family said that on Passover in the 1480s Jewish friends "used to send them matza and* **turrón.** *"*[23]

Holiday Nougat Candy

Makes 2 7 × 3-inch bricks of candy

Flour for dusting
2 egg whites
¾ cup honey
¾ cup sugar

¾ cup toasted nuts (¼ cup slivered
    almonds, ¼ cup pine nuts, ¼ cup
    walnuts or hazelnuts) (see Notes)
1 tablespoon cinnamon

Prepare the nougat boxes:

1. Choose one of the following molds for the nougat:

   • a traditional *turrón* box, 8 × 3 × 1 inches

   • some other small box: a cigar box with an added central strip of wood will do

   • a small metal loaf pan, 7 × 3 × 2 inches

2. Cover the bottom and sides of the mold with baking paper. Dust it with flour.

3. Prepare a piece of baking paper to cover the top of the mold.

Prepare the nougat:

4. Beat the egg whites stiff.

5. In a medium saucepan, combine the honey, egg whites, and sugar and bring to a boil. Once the mixture begins to boil, stir constantly for about 10 minutes. The syrup is ready when a drop of the mixture dropped into cold water forms a ball, or when a drop falling on a tilted plate forms a sticky ball rather than a runny liquid.

6. Remove the syrup from the heat. Let it cool to lukewarm.

7. Stir in the nuts and cinnamon.

8. With a spatula, spread the syrup into the nougat boxes. When the nougat has nearly hardened, dust it with flour and cover it with paper.

9. Let the nougat cool until it is hard. Remove it from the mold. Wrap it in wax paper and cover it with plastic wrap.

NOTES

To toast nuts: Place them on an ungreased cookie sheet in a 300° oven for 3–5 minutes, turning frequently to avoid scorching. Remove them as soon as they begin to color. Toast each variety separately.

Nougat may be eaten immediately or stored almost indefinitely.

To eat it, break pieces off as you would peanut brittle.

VARIATIONS

To line the molds, use a thin cookie wafer instead of baking paper.

To cut the sweetness, try adding a few drops of lemon juice.

For intensified flavor, add a few drops of almond extract or rose water to the mixture as it cools.

Halvah de Mexico

*Friday night meals in colonial Mexico frequently ended with **halvah.**[27]*

Another confection contributed to the European sweet tooth by Islamic kitchens is the combination of ground nuts—almonds, hazelnuts, and pistachios—or of nuts combined with sesame seeds. The varieties must have been nearly infinite. The thirteenth-century *Baghdad Cookery-Book*'s entire ninth chapter is devoted to these *halwa'*, with nine recipes that run from a smooth, pasty confection similar to what today's Levantine markets call halvah, to individual nut cookies called *alfajores,*[28] to the molded and decorated almond paste figures that today are called marzipan.

Liebman's generic reference to Mexican halvah is in no way a recipe. In fact it is not unlikely that these Mexican new-Christians purchased commercially-prepared halvah in the street or the local market. But most of the medieval Iberian cookbooks we have consulted contain recipes for making one or another variety of halvah at home. The *Al-Andalus* cookbook thickens its almond-sugar paste confection with starch and then flavors it with rose water, honey, or julep, or, in another case, with clove or camphor.[29] Nola's *marzapanes,* made of ground almonds and sugar syrup, are sometimes baked and sometimes just set to cool and harden.[30] The Portuguese cookbook's *maçapaaees* [sic] are bound with a little flour, cooked into a soft paste, and then molded into shapes.[31] Granado gives two recipes for a *maçapán* confected of almonds, sugar, and eggs, and then flavored with rose water or cinnamon.[32]

These desserts have not lost their popularity in the Muslim or former-Muslim territories that stretch from central Asia to the Maghreb and Iberia. Marks presents a sesame-seed based Sephardic recipe from Uzbekistan,[33] while any visitor who gapes at the bake shop windows in modern-day Toledo knows that Alfonso the Wise's capital city is still the marzipan center of Europe.

Mexican Halvah

½ cup sesame seeds, plus 2 tablespoons sesame seeds for topping
1 cup sugar
1½ cups sliced almonds

1 tablespoon sesame oil
1 teaspoon water
½ cup honey

1. Grind the ½ cup sesame seeds, sugar, and almonds as finely as possible.

2. In a medium saucepan, heat the sesame oil, water, and honey. Bring the mixture to a boil over medium heat. When it foams, turn the heat down to simmer.

3. Stir in the ground nuts, sugar, and sesame mixture. Cook over a low heat, stirring constantly, about 5 minutes, until the mixture thickens and begins to set.

4. Pour into a heatproof glass or metal pan. Smooth with a spatula. Sprinkle with the 2 tablespoons sesame seeds.

5. Let the halvah cool, and then cut into squares.

NOTE

If the halvah becomes too hard, soften it in a microwave oven about 30 seconds at medium power. If it is too soft, refrigerate it for a while.

María de Luna's Rosquillas

*A servant testified in Almazán in 1505 that María de Luna, "fifteen days after her son Luisico was born, had me cook six or seven **unleavened breads,** and then she grated these breads . . . and made **round pastries** and poured **sugar** and **honey** over them; and . . . gave them to the guests who returned from her son's baptism."[34]*

Seven generations after Luisico's baptism, in Toledo, in 1677, Isabel Rodríguez concluded the meal that broke her Yom Kippur fast with honeyed pastries.[35]

In Hispanic cooking the term *rosquillas*—which means "little coiled things"—embraces a multitude of round pastries. They can be made of diverse doughs. They can be boiled, fried, or baked. They can be of any size, soft or crunchy, sweet or bland, filled or plain. Granado's recipe for *rosquillas,* in which the dough is boiled and then baked, is indistinguishable from the modern bagel, except perhaps for the forty egg yolks Granado calls for.[36]

We present two versions of the *rosquilla*. María de Luna's recipe, using matza meal, describes a small, round, honey-soaked pastry that would be at home in any modern Sephardic household. The thirteenth-century *Al-Andalus* cookbook, from which our second recipe is derived, makes clear that to a large extent the mode of preparation of a *rosquilla* is chef's choice. His recipe is similar to many in medieval cookbooks in that it assumes that no cook needs to be instructed in how to make anything as basic as pastry dough, that indications of amounts or proportions are superfluous, and that the exact mode of preparation may well depend on what else is cooking for dinner:

> *Make a dough of whatever quantity you like of finely-milled flour and work it until it is well-kneaded, leave it until it has risen and then finely chop some almonds until they are like little bits of bran and mix them with a similar quantity of white sugar and knead into the two parts some rose water and scent them with pleasant aromas; roll out the dough long-wise and put the filling in it and cover it with dough, form it into a round and make it into* rosquillas; *send it to the oven or, if you like, fry it in a frying pot with olive oil and sprinkle it with sugar, and if you want it plainer, leave out the scents.[37]*

María de Luna's Round Pastries

Oil for frying

Dough

3 eggs
¼ teaspoon salt

1 cup + 2 tablespoons matza meal
  (approximately)

Syrup

½ cup honey
½ cup sugar

¾ cup water

Sugar for topping

Make the dough:

1. Beat the eggs with the salt in a medium bowl.

2. Mix in the matza meal, ¼ cup at a time for the first cup, then tablespoon by tablespoon, until you have a stiff dough that can be rolled in the hands.

3. Take a 1-inch diameter piece. Roll it into a snake 5 inches long and ½ inch thick. Form it into a circle. Repeat until all the dough has been used.

Fry the *rosquillas:*

4. Pour oil to about a ½-inch depth into a large skillet. Heat the oil to frying temperature (a tiny piece of dough will sizzle when it is hot enough).

5. Fry the *rosquillas* for about 5 minutes per side, until golden brown.

6. Remove them and drain them on paper towels.

Make the syrup:

7. Mix the three syrup ingredients in a small saucepan.

8. Heat the liquid to a boil, then reduce the heat to its lowest setting and simmer the syrup for 3 minutes.

9. Remove from the heat.

Serve the *rosquillas:*

10. Put the *rosquillas* into the saucepan. Soak them in the hot syrup for about 10 minutes, about 5 minutes per side.

11. Remove them to a plate, and dust them with sugar.

Andalusian Rosquillas

Makes 2 (10-inch) <u>rosquillas</u>

Dough

½ teaspoon saffron threads
½ cup hot water
⅓ cup shortening or butter
½ cup sugar

1 teaspoon salt
5½–6 cups flour
1 package dry yeast

Filling

½ cup chopped almonds
½ cup sugar

1 teaspoon rose water

1 egg, plus 1 egg white

Make the dough:

1. Soak the saffron threads in the hot water for 5 minutes in a large bowl.

2. Stir in the shortening. It need not thoroughly dissolve.

3. Sift in the sugar, salt, and 2 cups of flour. Add the yeast and beat for 2 minutes.

4. Gradually add enough flour to make a soft dough: 3½–4 cups more. Knead on a lightly floured board for 6 minutes. Cover and let rise in a warm place for 30 minutes, or until it has doubled in bulk.

Make the filling:

5. In a separate bowl, mix the filling ingredients. Set aside.

Form the pastries:

6. Divide the dough in half. With the hands, roll each into a long, thin roll, and then with a rolling pin flatten each into a long rectangle.

7. Reserve ⅕ of the filling mixture. Spoon the rest into the center of the two rectangles. Roll them up lengthwise and pinch the seams to seal. Curve them into a circle, and pinch the ends together. Place them on a greased cookie sheet.

8. Let them rise in a warm place for 15 minutes, while you preheat the oven to 350°.

Bake:

9. Beat the egg and egg white together. Score the tops of the *rosquillas* with a knife; brush the tops with the egg mixture, and sprinkle on the reserved filling mixture.

10. Bake for 30 minutes or until they are golden brown.

11. Remove the *rosquillas* to a rack to cool.

Buñuelos

Nowadays these honeyed puff fritters, because they are fried in olive oil, are a Hanukah tradition among Sephardic communities all around the Mediterranean, where they are generally called *bimuelos*. However, Hanukah, judging from Inquisition testimonies and from other documents relating to the Jews, seems to have been an extremely minor holiday in late medieval Iberia, for references to its celebration are exceedingly rare. Instead the puff fritters seem to have been associated with a number of other holidays, including Passover and Yom Kippur, as well as festive family celebrations. Margarita de Rivera's family in Mexico in 1643 considered the consumption of "fritters and honey" an essential part of the wedding ceremony. [39]

Of course these pastries are not unique to Sephardic cooking. They are common to nearly all European cultures: in the Tunisian Maghreb the fried puffs are known as *yoyo*, [40] while in the eastern Mediterranean they are known as *tiganites* (in Ioannina, Greece), *zvingous* (among the Greek Romaniote communities), or *loukoumades* (among Greeks in general). [41] Northern and central Europeans make a variety of doughnuts, crullers, and funnel cakes as well. Modern Spaniards devour two versions: the round puffs resembling an American doughnut hole are called *buñuelos,* while the ring pastries still go by María de Luna's term, *rosquillas.* [42]

The term *buñuelo* seems to have been linked fairly early to fried dishes meant as a dessert. They are further evidence of the pervasive popularity of fried, sweet things in Islamic cooking. One can consider the popular *buñuelos* of Mexican restaurants as the modern vestige of this Hispano-Arabic world of sweets.

We offer two versions of these *buñuelos:* a puff-pastry made with flour and, for Passover, a round matza-meal fritter which, because of its shape, could also be called a *rosquilla.*

Honeyed Fritters

Dough

1 package dry yeast	2 eggs, well beaten
1⅓ cups warm water	½ teaspoon salt
3 cups unsifted white flour	1 tablespoon olive oil

Syrup

3 cups honey	¼ cup water

Olive oil (enough to cover a deep pan
to a depth of 1 inch) (see Variation)

Topping

Cinnamon	Powdered sugar

Mix the dough:

1. Dissolve the yeast in ⅓ cup warm water. Let sit for 10 minutes.

2. Place the flour into a medium bowl. Stir the yeasted water, the beaten eggs, salt, and olive oil into the flour all at once. Gradually add the remaining 1 cup water to make a slightly tacky dough.

3. Cover and let rise in a warm place for 1 hour until doubled in bulk.

Make the syrup:

4. Mix the honey and water in a medium saucepan and bring to a hard boil. Reduce the heat to low. Simmer for 5 minutes and then turn down the heat to its minimum setting so that the syrup remains hot but does not boil again.

Fry the fritters:

5. In a large deep skillet or saucepan, heat the olive oil to approximately 375° or hot enough for a drop of water to sputter.

6. Dip a tablespoon into the oil to coat it. Dip out a scant teaspoon of the dough and drop it into the boiling oil. You can fry several *buñuelos* at one time as long as you do not crowd them in the pan. As they fry, turn them

*Desserts
and Snacks*

several times until they puff up and become golden in color, about 8 minutes.

7. Remove them with a slotted spoon and drain them on paper towels.

Serve the fritters:

8. Place the fritters on a plate. Drizzle the hot honey syrup over them, and sprinkle them with cinnamon and powdered sugar.

NOTE

These are best when eaten fresh. In a pinch, or for a crowd, the fritters can be made ahead, and then dipped into the honey syrup just before serving.

VARIATION

Sephardic cooks would have used olive oil to fry the fritters. We suggest a mixture of 1¾ cups vegetable oil and ¼ cup olive oil.

Passover Fritters

Dough

1 cup milk	3 eggs, well beaten
1 tablespoon butter	½ teaspoon salt
1 tablespoon grated lemon rind	2 cups matza meal (approximately)

Syrup (see Variations)

1½ cups honey	2 tablespoons water

Olive oil (enough to cover a deep pan to a depth of 1 inch) (see Variations)

Topping

½ cup almonds or walnuts, finely chopped	½ cup cinnamon-sugar mixture

Mix the dough:

1. In a large saucepan, bring the milk, butter, and lemon rind just to a boil.

2. Remove the liquid from the heat and cool for about 10 minutes.

3. Stir in the beaten eggs. Stir in the salt. Stir in enough matza meal to make a thick dough that can be worked with the hand.

Form the fritters:

4. Break off a piece of the dough the size of a walnut. Roll it into a cylinder about ½ inch thick. Curl it into a circle and press the ends together.

5. Place each fritter on waxed paper while you form enough to use all of the dough.

Make the syrup:

6. Mix the honey and water in a small saucepan and bring them to a hard boil. Reduce the heat to low. Simmer the liquid for 5 minutes and then

Desserts and Snacks

turn the heat down to its minimum setting so that the syrup remains hot but does not boil again.

Fry the fritters:

7. In a large deep frying pan or saucepan, add enough oil to cover the pan 1 inch deep. Heat the oil to approximately 375° or hot enough for a drop of water to sputter.

8. Drop the fritters one by one into the boiling oil. You can fry several at one time as long as you do not crowd them in the pan. Fry them about 3–4 minutes per side, until they become gold in color.

9. Remove them with a slotted spoon and drain them on paper towels.

Serve the fritters:

10. With kitchen tongs, dip each fritter into the hot honey syrup. Place the fritters on a plate and sprinkle with the chopped nuts and cinnamon-sugar.

VARIATIONS

Boil a ½-inch length of cinnamon stick with the honey.

Add 1 teaspoon rose water to the syrup.

Sephardic cooks would have used olive oil to fry the fritters. We suggest a mixture of 1¾ cups vegetable oil and ¼ cup olive oil.

These fritters are also good in a cold syrup which may be made ahead, as follows:

1 cup water	*½ cup sugar*
¼ cup honey	*Juice of 1 lemon*

Boil the water, honey, and sugar together for 5–10 minutes, just long enough so that the mixture pills when dropped onto a plate, or will coat the back of a wooden spoon dipped into the mixture. Remove the mixture from the heat and add the lemon juice. Cool and then chill it for at least 2 hours in the refrigerator.

Alfajores de Mexico

By their name, and by their combination of finely milled nuts and honey, *alfajores* are inescapably one of the Andalusian Islamic contributions to Iberian cuisine. These cookies, common throughout Spain, were defined by Covarrubias in 1611 as "a certain paste made by the Moors of bread crumbs, honey, and spices,"[44] and a century later by the *Diccionario de autoridades* as "a dough made of almonds, walnuts (and sometimes pine nuts), grated toast, and fine spices, held together with boiled honey." This recipe is almost exactly the same as one for cookies called *alhagues,* which is found in the *Manual de mugeres,* written shortly after the Jewish expulsion from Spain. It produces a chewy almond cookie very close to a modern macaroon.[45]

The *alfajor* offers an object lesson in how names can change their meaning over time. The *alfajor* common today in Latin America is a thin, powdery sugar cookie, about the size of an Oreo Creme, generally filled with *manjar blanco*. This sweetened condensed milk filling, in turn, is similar only in color to the medieval chicken and almond-based *blancmange* from which its name obviously derives.

Alfajores *were a popular treat among new-Christians in Mexico in the early seventeenth century.*[43]

Mexican Almond Cookies

Makes 36 cookies

¾ cup almonds
¾ cup chopped walnuts
½ cup sesame seeds
¾ cup honey
2 eggs, well beaten

½ teaspoon almond extract
1 teaspoon cinnamon
¼ teaspoon cloves
½ cup finely ground bread crumbs

1. Finely grind the nuts and sesame seeds together in a food processor.
2. Heat the honey in a medium saucepan over medium heat until it foams. Turn off the heat. When the foam has subsided, fold in the nut mixture.
3. When it has cooled so that it is warm to the touch, stir in the beaten eggs, almond extract, spices, and bread crumbs.
4. Preheat the oven to 325°. Grease and flour two cookie sheets. Using a teaspoon, drop the batter onto the prepared cookie sheet, at least 1½ inches apart.
5. Bake until lightly browned, 20–25 minutes. Let the cookies cool on the cookie sheet until firm and then remove them to a plate.
6. Repeat with the remaining batter. Store the cookies tightly covered.

VARIATIONS

Dust with cinnamon before baking.

Place a sliver of almond in the center of each cookie before baking.

The Spanish *frutas del sartén* literally means at one in the same time "fruits of the skillet," and "skillet-fried dish." Some *frutas del sartén* are main courses: a chicken liver "fruta" is found in Nola's cookbook, and the Catalán *Sent soví* gives a recipe for an herbal concoction called "ffrexols."[47] But most of the recipes we have found for *frutas del sartén* describe light fried dishes.

By far the majority of the recipes include a main ingredient of cheese, mixed with or dipped in eggs or egg yolks. The mixture is then either coated with a spiced flour mixture or it is wrapped in a thin piece of bread dough. The *fruta* is then fried in oil, butter, or lard; when it is done, it is coated with honey, rose water, and cinnamon and sugar before serving. Spanish proverbs corroborate the importance of the honey coating and speak to the *frutas'* importance among Christians as a common treat of the Christmas season.[48] Nola's recipe for cheese, sliced about a finger's width, then coated with flour before frying, has resonances in a mid-fifteenth century Austrian cookbook's cheese sticks[49] and in any modern restaurant's appetizer of fried mozzarella.

In Ciudad Real in the 1480s the converso families used to gather on Friday evenings to talk and snack on **"fried desserts,** *and other things, according to the season and what there was. Other times they ate fruits and other things."*[46]

Skillet-Fried Sweets

Makes 10–12 pieces

6 ounces cheese, such as Swiss, goat
    cheese, cream cheese
2 tablespoons bread crumbs
1 tablespoon dried mint
1 egg yolk

3 tablespoons butter (approximately)
Honey
Cinnamon-sugar
Rose water (optional)

1. Cut the cheese into finger pieces, approximately 2½ inches long and ¾ inch thick.
2. In a grinder, pulverize the bread crumbs and the mint together. Place the mixture in a 5- or 6-inch wide flat bowl.
3. Beat the egg yolk and place it in a small bowl.
4. Roll the cheese pieces in the egg yolk; then coat them with the bread crumb mixture.
5. Heat the butter in a medium skillet over medium-high heat. Place the coated cheese pieces in the butter and fry quickly, turning once or twice until they are golden brown.
6. Remove the cheese and place on paper towels to remove the excess butter.
7. Place the cooked cheese on a second plate and drizzle with honey and sprinkle with cinnamon-sugar and rose water, if you are using it.

NOTES

Any cheese is good prepared this way. Try a combination of flavors.

Goat cheese and cream cheese become very soft in the frying process. Be careful when moving them so they don't fall apart.

Let the cheeses cool somewhat before serving so that they will retain their shape. These sweets should be eaten with a fork.

Manjarejos de Ajos

One of the most detailed contemporary portraits of Jews and *conversos* was penned by Andrés Bernáldez, a cleric who chronicled year by year the major events in the reign of Ferdinand and Isabel, the Catholic Monarchs. In addition to his writing career, Bernáldez served as a cathedral chaplain to the archbishop of Seville, Diego de Deza, who followed Torquemada to become the second Grand Inquisitor. He was also a parish priest of the Andalusian village of Palacios for a quarter of a century. Even today Bernáldez's chronicle makes fascinating reading, particularly his first-hand accounts of interactions he had personally witnessed. As he prepared the chronicle, among his many confidants was Christopher Columbus, who lent him important documents relevant to the discovery of the Indies.

Bernáldez was no friend of the Jews or *conversos*. He enthusiastically supported the racial policies of his monarchs and looked forward to the day when the Inquisition fires had burned so fiercely "that all the Judaizers are consumed and dead, and none of them remains."[51] Nonetheless, his powers of observation and analysis are often startlingly fresh, and his narration of events—if not always their causes or effects, which he overlays with a rhetoric of anti-Semitism—has in its main points been confirmed by modern historians.

His poignant description of the expulsion of 1492 highlights the economic chaos that ensued from the suddenness of the order. "There were Christians who acquired their property and fine houses and lands for very little money, and they even had to go begging to find buyers, for there was no one who would buy them. And they sold a house for a donkey, and a vineyard for a little cloth."[52] He lauded the sense of community responsibility by which "the rich Jews paid for the journey of the poor Jews, and in that departure they all treated one another with much charity."[53] "And they joined in marriage all the boys and girls age twelve and older, the ones to the others, so that all the females of that age and older would go in the company and shelter of a husband."[54] Bernáldez criticized what he saw as the unreasoned stubbornness that kept most Jews from converting, but he was clearly moved by the sad pageant of the expulsion itself:

> *Confiding in the vain hopes of their blindness, they set forth to the difficulties of the road, leaving the lands of their birth: the great and the small, old men and children, on foot and mounted on asses and other beasts and in wagons, each*

Andrés Bernáldez says that the conversos "ate and drank a great deal, and never lost the Jewish custom of snacks and pots of adafina, *snacks of* **onion and garlic, refried with olive oil.** . . ."[50]

proceeding in their journey to the ports where they were to embark. With great trials and difficulties they went on roads and across fields, some falling down, others helping them up, some dying, others being born, others falling sick, such that there was no Christian who did not feel grief on their account. Wherever they went they invited them to be baptized, and some under the stress converted and stayed behind, but very few. The rabbis went along encouraging them, making the children and young people sing and play tambourines and timbrels to cheer the people up.[55]

In another place he describes how the conditions for the refugees in North Africa were so terrible that many returned to Iberia seeking baptism, a hundred of them to his own village of Palacios, where he personally baptized ten or twelve rabbis.[56]

Bernáldez seems to have taken a special interest in cooking, judging from his comments about *adafina* and garlic, cited above, and his disgust for the Jewish predilection for cooking meat in olive oil.

6 large whole heads garlic
Kosher salt
½ cup finely diced onion, such as red
    or Vidalia

1–2 tablespoons olive oil for frying

1. Preheat the oven to 350°. Place the whole garlics closely together in a Pyrex pan and pour the salt over them until only the tip of the garlic shows. Roast them about 35 minutes, or until you see garlic bubbling on top of the salt. Remove from the oven and cool.

2. Peel the cooled garlics.

3. Over medium heat, heat the olive oil in a medium skillet and add the diced onion. Stir-fry just until it begins to brown, about 6 minutes. Turn down the heat to medium-low. Add the peeled garlic cloves and gently stir-fry 1–2 minutes more.

4. Serve warm with crackers or bread.

NOTES

For color, add a little diced parsley or cilantro.

These are good as appetizers when served warm.

They are good when complemented by a bland cheese.

The roast garlic cloves are good when eaten alone, hot out of the oven.

Pan y Aceitunas / Bread and Olives

*Judaizers in Majorca in the 1670s who were unable to make a Sabbath stew ate only **bread and olives**.*[57]

Olives were and are still today extremely popular in the Iberian Peninsula, where they are called both by their Roman (*olivos*) and Arabic (*aceitunas*) names. The fruits gathered green, before they have fully ripened, or become black, are cured in a variety of pickling sauces which impart a nearly infinite variety of flavors to the olives. Surprisingly, olives do not seem to have been much used in the fifteenth or sixteenth centuries in cooked foods, for they are rarely mentioned in any of the contemporary cookbooks.

Olive oil, however, pressed and filtered and bottled, was widely used both for cooking and for flavoring. Since for frying Christian cooking tended to prefer rendered fat, particularly lard, and since lard was forbidden to Jews,[58] frying meat in olive oil became an important indicator of crypto-Jewish cuisine. Andrés Bernáldez, the chronicler of Ferdinand and Isabel, found this a particularly nauseating custom:

> They cooked their meat in olive oil, which they used instead of salt-pork or other fat, so as to avoid pork. Olive oil with meat and other fried things leaves a very unpleasant odor, and so their houses and doorways stunk with the odor of that food. The Jews too gave off the same odor, on account of those foods, and because they were not baptized. . . .[59]

Converso preference for olive oil over lard was used as a diagnostic both by inquisitors and by crypto-Jews hoping to discover if a colleague Judaized or not. Francisco Delicado incorporated this strategy into his 1528 novel-in-dialogue *Retrato de la Lozana andaluza*. The *conversa* Lozana has just come from Spain to Rome and enters the house of some old women:

LOZANA: *What are you talking about?*

TERESA: *About how we want to make some braided fritters for tomorrow.*

LOZANA: *Do you have some fresh coriander? Let me. With a handful of flour and some olive oil, if you have some of good quality, I'll make you a tray full.*

BEATRIZ: *(By God, she's one of us!)*[60]

Olive oil was also burned in lamps, and dozens of Inquisition cases from the years just prior to the expulsions testify to the crypto-Jewish custom of donating oil for synagogue lamps. Some rich *conversos,* such as Diego Arias

Dávila in the 1450s, were widely known to contribute "as much olive oil as the synagogues of Avila and Segovia might happen to need."[61]

We give no recipe here, for these days there is little call for the home-curing of olives. Many local supermarkets or ethnic groceries stock a good array of flavored olives for putting out as snacks.

Holiday Foods

Inquisitors were particularly attuned to Jewish holiday observances, and they tended to notice both special foods consumed during the holidays (e.g., matza) or ordinary foods consumed in relation to some ritual observance (e.g., visiting a booth at Sukkot). Passover, whose central act is a ritual family meal and whose observance requires special foods like matza, drew the most attention. Occasionally we find a description of an entire seder plate, such as this one, reported by the Mexican *converso* Diego Díaz Nieto in 1601, remembering his years of residence among the Jews in Italy: "They set out a basket in which there are lettuce, celery, and others of the most bitter greens, and a piece of roast meat in memory of the [Passover] lamb, and a little dish with balls of [*haroset*]. . . . And they dampen the lettuce and celery in vinegar and eat it, but they do not eat the meat, which is only in remembrance. And the wine they drink that night has to be kosher, which means clean wine."[1] All of the recipes in this section are for special Passover foods.

Still, the trials contain sporadic information about other holiday foods as well. The most common references are to the meals preceding or following the twenty-four-hour fasts of Yom Kippur and Esther (Purim). In these cases what was at issue was not the content of the meal but the timing, and the fact that it was of special character. A maidservant in Majorca, for example, noted in 1678 how the crypto-Jewish *chueta* family of Margarita Martí before Yom Kippur "cooked all night many different dishes . . . and they ate in their main room, where they did not eat on other days, at a large table more splendidly set than on other days."[2] At most of these occasions the foods consumed were quite ordinary (and therefore are found in other sections of this book). Before fasting, crypto-Jews in Teruel in the 1480s fortified themselves with chicken.[3] In Mexico, the Gabriel Granada family in the 1640s ate fish, eggs, and vegetables,[4] while the Machorro family bulked up on eggs and meat pies.[5]

Although in Castile Judaizers might "break their fast with fowl and other meat,"[6] in Aragon, Portugal, and the colonies, fowl and fish seem to have been the preferred foods. In the late fifteenth century Rabbi Simuel of Teruel testified that "after the fast, in the evening, [his family] ate chicken."[7] The family of Aldonza Deli of Teruel broke their fast with doves.[8] Gabriel Gomes Navarro in Lisbon in 1673 reported that his family would break the Yom Kippur fast with anything except meat: grapes, fruit, fish, bread, or wine.[9] In Mexico, Tomás Treviño de Sobremonte declared to the Inquisition in 1624 that on Yom Kippur eve he and his mother and her friends ate "some fish dish, which was required because it was a ceremony of said Law."[10]

At the harvest holiday of Sukkot, which is usually celebrated in September or October, traditionally four varieties of fruits are displayed in a small, open air booth that each observant family builds near its house. These four fruits (palm, myrtle, willow, and citron) appear in descriptions of some crypto-Jewish observances from the late fifteenth century, but rarely thereafter. When *converso* children visited booths in the Jewish quarters in Iberian cities prior to the expulsions of the 1490s, they were often given fruit or candy.[11]

Pan Cenceño

For crypto-Jews, matza essentially defined the Passover, a fact reflected in many of the names commonly given to the holiday. Among Spanish speakers it was *Pascua del pan cenceño*;[12] among the Portuguese, *Pascua do pão asmo* and *Jejum das filhós*;[13] and in Cataluña, *Pasqua del pa alís*.[14] Eating the flat, unleavened matza fulfills the commandment given in Exodus 12:17–20 to commemorate annually the hurried departure from Egypt. References to matza appear in nearly every description of crypto-Jewish Passover observances.

Since in the wooden tenements of Iberian cities most people could not have ovens in their homes because of the danger of fire, matza was usually prepared in a communal oven. Prior to the expulsion, Judaizing *conversos* could buy their matza from Jewish bakers; afterward they had to be baked and distributed clandestinely, often at great risk.

Most matza, such as the *pan de la aflicción* (bread of affliction) prepared by Antonio Cardoso, of Barajas (Madrid) in the 1650s, was simply a **plain dough of flour and water, mixed without salt or yeast**.[15] Beatriz Enríquez described to Mexican inquisitors in 1642 the care with which her mother prepared matza using the same simple ingredients:

> *Three days before Easter . . . having sent the house slaves to see the processions, her mother laid on the table new tablecloths or towels, and then the new knife, and in the new bowl put the [white] flour, and from the new pitcher poured some cold water, and mixed and kneaded the flour with both hands, with a fire already kindled in the new brazier; and after having blessed each separate thing, and having kneaded the flour, she broke three small pieces off of the dough, reciting certain prayers over each one . . . of which she only remembers the following: "Blessed art Thou, Adonai, who gave us your laws, holy and blessed, blessed and holy." Then she kneaded the three pieces together and threw them into the fire, reciting the same prayers, and if the dough popped when she threw it in, her mother said that that was a sign that the God of Israel had approved the festival, and had accepted the hala . . . And she made three flat cakes, or she could make five or six or as many as she wanted. . . .*[16]

Matza came to be such an important ritual food that its consumption was not limited to the Passover season, as can be seen in the case of Francisco Suárez, a toll taker in Almazán (Soria) in the early 1500s. According to an old-Christian neighbor, Francisco's wife used to make matza with this recipe every year not at Passover but around St. Michael's day (September 19), which suggests that it may have been eaten in connection with Rosh Hashanah, or with breaking the Yom Kippur fast. They made some of the dough into flat cakes, and from the rest made little meat pies.[17] Suárez's wife's friends used to enrich their matza with eggs: "[they] prepared flat bread, i.e., **unleavened bread,** and they kneaded it with an **egg,** and put **olive oil** in the dough."[18]

Antonio Cardoso's Matza
Makes about 12 matza

2 cups flour, sifted
12 tablespoons water

2 teaspoons olive oil

1. Preheat the oven to 400°.

2. Place the flour in a small bowl.

3. Add the wet ingredients gradually and mix to form a very dry dough. You may not need all the water or you may need a bit more. Don't overmix.

4. Form the dough into walnut-size balls. Roll them flat and thin on a floured surface. Prick them several times with a fork.

5. Bake them on a nonstick cookie sheet for 10 minutes. You may have to use two cookie sheets.

6. Remove them immediately from the cookie sheet and cool on a rack.

Francisco Suárez's Matza
Makes about 12 matza

2 cups flour, sifted
8 tablespoons water

2 teaspoons olive oil
4 egg yolks, beaten

1. Preheat the oven to 400°.

2. Place the flour in a small bowl.

3. Add the wet ingredients gradually and mix to form a very dry dough. You may not need all the water or you may need a bit more. Don't overmix.

4. Form the dough into walnut-size balls. Roll them flat and thin on a floured surface. Prick them several times with a fork.

5. Bake them on a nonstick cookie sheet for 10 minutes. You may have to use two cookie sheets.

6. Remove them immediately from the cookie sheet and cool on a rack.

All of the matza recipes that appear in the trials use flour and water as their base, but they could be enriched in a number of ways. Some Iberian crypto-Jews used spices to introduce flavors into their matza. Angelina, the wife of Christóual de León of Almazán (Soria), "made the dough of **flour and eggs, and formed some round, flat cakes with pepper and honey and oil.** She cooked them in an oven and she did this around Holy Week."[19]

Juana de Fuente, also of Almazán, said in 1505 that she and Beatriz, the wife of Ruy Díaz Laínez, "made some cakes separately of another dough that had no leavening and they kneaded it with **white wine and honey and clove and pepper,** and they made about twenty of those and they kept them . . . in a storage chest."[20] Beatriz and Ruy Díaz Laínez's fondness for matza seems to have been matched by their strong aversion for the consecrated host. A neighbor named Olalla, who used to sit behind Beatriz at mass, said that she saw her take the communion wafer in her mouth and then turn her head and spit it out instead of swallowing it.

One of the most curious additions to matza was finely ground dirt, perhaps to signal that the flat cakes were truly a "bread of affliction," or perhaps to suggest that the Hebrews fled Egypt in such haste and with so little flour in their baggage, that they had to stretch what they had with what they found on the road. Two trials from the 1620s from Ciudad Rodrigo, in Salamanca near the Portuguese border, refer to this custom. Isabel Núñez was accused of "making a **Passover bread** which they used to mix without leavening or salt, saying certain prayers over it, and they baked it in an oven that was in the house of another prisoner and that they had set the table for the Big Day and they mixed it with **finely sifted dirt** and after the [day-long] fast they ate that bread the next night with salad with oil and vinegar."[21] Although the reference is clearly to Passover bread, the "Big Day" was probably Yom Kippur. The closest practice we have been able to find in Jewish tradition is eating bread dipped in ashes the day before the fast of Tisha B'Av: "At the approach of evening one should sit on the ground . . . only bread and a cold hard-boiled egg should be partaken of, and a portion of the bread should be **dipped in ashes** and eaten. Care should be taken to finish this meal while it is yet day."[22] The substitution of dirt for ashes may result from a confusion of the Hebrew *epher* (ahes—with an 'ayin) with *aphar* (dirt—with an 'alif).[23] The conflation of holidays—

Passover matza, a reference to the Big Day of Yom Kippur, and a culinary custom from Tisha B'Av—may well be another sign that by the early seventeenth century, Iberian crypto-Jews were losing touch with the specifics of normative Judaism.

Isabel's friend Ana López was similarly accused of eating "**Passover bread** which they mix with **finely sifted dirt** without adding salt or leavening."[24] Ana was denounced in Ciudad Rodrigo in 1622 when she was twenty-three years old. An eighteen-year-old neighbor told how Ana used to wear around her neck a little gold and silver sheep, on which a golden knight with his sword and lance was mounted, and that she used to worship it as if it were a crucifix. After her arrest on July 1, she repeatedly told her inquisitors that she knew nothing about crypto-Judaism, and she gave convincing details of several incidents which might have caused her neighbors to falsely denounce her. Unfortunately, one of her friends had confessed to being a Judaizer, so that the inquisitors did not believe her protestations of innocence. When they threatened her with torture she panicked, asking a cellmate "if the pain of torture was worse than giving birth." Nonetheless, the record does not indicate that torture was applied, and on April 5, nine months after her arrest, the Inquisition concluded that it could not make a case against her and set her free.

Angelina de León's Matza

Makes about 12 matza

*2 cups flour, sifted, or 2 cups matza
    cake flour*
½ teaspoon pepper
4 eggs, beaten

6 tablespoons honey
1½ teaspoons olive oil
8–12 tablespoons water

1. Preheat oven to 400°.

2. Mix the flour and pepper together in a small bowl.

3. Add the wet ingredients gradually and mix to form a very dry dough. You may not need all the water or you may need a bit more. Don't overmix.

4. Form the dough into walnut-size balls. Roll them flat and thin on a floured surface. Prick them several times with a fork.

5. Bake them on a nonstick cookie sheet for 10 minutes. You may have to use two cookie sheets.

6. Remove them immediately from the cookie sheet and cool on a rack.

Beatriz de Díaz Laínez's Matza

Makes about 12 matza

2 cups flour, sifted
½ teaspoon black pepper
Pinch of cloves
4 tablespoons honey

8 tablespoons white wine
4 egg yolks, beaten
4 tablespoons water

1. Preheat the oven to 400°.

2. Mix the flour, pepper, and cloves together in a small bowl.

3. Combine the honey, white wine, and egg yolks. Add the mixture gradually to the flour and mix to form a very dry dough. Add the water slowly. You may not need all the water or you may need a bit more. Don't overmix.

4. Form the dough into walnut-size balls. Roll them flat and thin on a floured surface. Prick them several times with a fork.

5. Bake them on a nonstick cookie sheet for 10 minutes. You may have to use two cookie sheets.

6. Remove them immediately from the cookie sheet and cool on a rack.

Matza de Castanbas

One of these Judaizing women was Graça Lopes, age seventy, tried in Coimbra in 1567. According to inquisitors, among her other Jewish practices was keeping the Sabbath and the principal fasts. Twice daily she recited twelve Psalms (leaving off the Catholic "Gloria Patri") to commemorate—she said—the twelve paths through the Red Sea that God opened for the Jews at Moses' behest. Graça seems to have been steadfastly unrepentant of her Judaizing. Even while in prison she fasted on Mondays and Thursdays so that God would free her, and she prayed while standing, swaying back and forth, her eyes raised to heaven, and her hands open and extended upward. She was sentenced to be burned.[26]

Almost identical charges were brought three years later in Lamego against twenty-four-year-old Felipa Cardosa, who was said to believe that her soul could be saved only in the Law of Moses. The inquisitorial scribe, most likely confusing the Jewish holidays, recorded that it was on Sukkot, the "Feast of Branches," when she substituted for the matza some chestnuts that had been cooked in a new pot. When confronted, she confessed her sins and asked for forgiveness. Consequently she was sentenced to be jailed and instructed in the ways of Catholicism.[27]

Cecília Cardosa, age sixty, was accused in 1569 in Porto of having celebrated Passover by eating matza, grains, and chestnuts cooked in a new pot. She was sentenced to publicly abjure her heresy, and then to house arrest, and to never appear in public without wearing her penitential robe, or *sambenito*.[28]

Other Portuguese new-Christian women accused in Lamego in 1569 of eating chestnuts on Passover were Beatriz de Costa (age thirty; abjuration, house arrest, *sambenito*); Catarina Cardosa (age fifteen; march with a candle to the local church and publicly abjure); and Violante Gomes (age thirty; abjuration, house arrest, *sambenito*, instruction in Catholicism).[29]

In Mexico a different solution was found for the problem of the lack of matza. Luis de Carvajal told the Inquisition there in 1589 that on Passover "because he did not have unleavened bread he ate **corn *tortillas,*** since they had no yeast."[30] Two generations later, in 1642, Catalina de Rivera similarly reported that one Passover Juan de León ate "**corn *tortillas,*** fish, and vegetables" with his crypto-Jewish friends. Juan was not so scrupulous, however, for when the *tortillas* dried out he ate ordinary bread.[31]

*When materials for traditional matza could not be obtained, crypto-Jews substituted local foods that did not contain leaven. For example, Judaizers in Portugal in the late sixteenth century sometimes "substituted **cooked chestnuts** for matza."[25]*

Chestnut Matza

Coimbra Chestnut Matza
Makes 12–14 matza

1 jar cooked chestnuts (about 14.8 ounces) (see Notes)

3 eggs, beaten

3 tablespoons olive oil

3 tablespoons honey or sugar

1 teaspoon cinnamon

½ teaspoon pepper

1. Preheat oven to 450°.
2. With a large spoon or fork, mash the chestnuts until they are in small pieces.
3. In a food processor, place one third of the chestnuts, one egg, and 1 tablespoon oil. Process until they become a thick paste. Add one third more of the chestnuts, another egg, and 1 tablespoon oil. Continue to process. Repeat until the remaining chestnuts, egg, and oil are used up and the mixture is a well-combined paste.
4. Add the honey, the cinnamon, and pepper. Process until they are mixed in.
5. Generously grease a cookie sheet or aluminum foil covering a cookie sheet.
6. Place 2 tablespoons of the mixture onto the sheet and press with a spatula or other flat utensil until the mass is about ¼–½ inch thick. Repeat for each matza. Leave about 1 inch around each matza.
7. Bake for 12–15 minutes. The matza should brown. You may have to use two cookie sheets.
8. Remove immediately from the cookie sheet and cool on a rack.

NOTES

If you are using fresh chestnuts, use about twenty-five. Boil them, covered, in water to cover for 20–25 minutes. Cool. Remove the shells and skin.

For crisper matza, bake for 6 minutes and then turn each matza over and bake another 6 minutes.

María Alvarez's Rollillos

Several documents from around the year 1500 that allude to crypto-Jewish Passover customs in the Aragonese province of Soria hint at a second common Passover bread in addition to matza. The most common name given to this bread—*rollillos*—suggests that the unleavened dough was rolled or pressed into cakes, which in Aragon were generally called *tortas*. In addition to María Alvarez, Angelina de León was said to make some *rollicos* with the same ingredients—olive oil, pepper, and honey—that she used to make her matza.[33] When Beatriz de Díaz Laínez made her *rollillos,* she used to hide them in a chest.[34]

*When María Alvarez "made **rolled biscuits,** she made some matza from the same dough."*[32]

María Alvarez's Passover Biscuits

Makes 4 large rolls

8 tablespoons water, plus more if needed

2 teaspoons olive oil

½ teaspoon pepper

6 tablespoons honey, warmed

4 eggs, beaten

3½ cups flour, sifted

1. Preheat the oven to 375°. Cover a cookie sheet with aluminum foil.

2. Beat the first five ingredients together in a small bowl.

3. Place the flour in a large bowl. Add the liquid mixture to the flour all at once using a fork, beating as little as possible. If necessary to get the dough to form a mass, add more water, a tablespoon at a time.

4. Divide the dough into four equal pieces. On a floured board, press each piece into a ¾-inch thick cake.

5. Bake them on the prepared cookie sheet for 15–20 minutes or until they are a light brown color.

6. Remove them to a rack.

Dalmau de Tolosa's Pa Alis Picat

Dalmau de Tolosa was a cleric from Tarragona who served as a canon in the cathedral of Lleida (Lérida). Both his father, Gabriel Tolosa, and his mother, Isabel, were Judaizing *conversos*. And, in fact, at the time of Dalmau's trial his mother was classified as a fugitive heretic. The bill of indictment against the Tolosa family lists the practices common among *conversos* of the late fifteenth century: observance of the Sabbath and the major Jewish festivals, keeping a kosher kitchen, and the like. Like many trials, Dalmau's adds an occasional picturesque detail that helps us to visualize his family and circle of friends. For example, at the end of Yom Kippur, after fasting barefoot all day, the Tolosas "would go outside to a place where they could see the sky and they would fall on their knees on the ground and say their prayers while kneeling and do their other Jewish ceremonies. Afterward, when the stars had come out, they would all run inside to eat, and Dalmau would ask pardon of each person in the company." The bill of indictment also alleges that Dalmau used to carry on his person a circular amulet that enclosed some parchment written in Hebrew to protect him against harm. On Passover, when he used to eat the matza fritters described in this recipe, he kept leavened bread on the table in order to show his servants that he was a good Christian. The trial also notes that Dalmau had been circumcised.[36]

Evidence of such activities in a priest was fatal. In 1505 Dalmau was stripped of his titles, benefices, and estate, and "relaxed to the secular arm of justice" to be burned at the stake.

*"They made matza cakes and gave them to Tolosa's ancient mother who broke up the **unleavened cakes** in a mortar and then mixed them with **spices** and **eggs** in a new bowl."*[35]

Dalmau de Tolosa's Matza Fritters

Serves 4

6 matza	1 teaspoon sugar
2 eggs, beaten	½ teaspoon grated nutmeg
1 teaspoon cinnamon	3 tablespoons oil or butter for frying

Topping

Cinnamon-sugar	Honey

1. Soak the matza in water to cover for 5 minutes, or until soft. Remove them from the water and with your hands squeeze out as much liquid as possible. Put them in a large bowl.

2. Mix in the eggs and spices.

3. Heat the oil or butter in a large skillet.

4. With a tablespoon, drop spoonfuls of the mixture into the hot oil. Pat each flat into a cake ½ inch thick. Fry on both sides until done, about 6 minutes total. Drain on paper towels.

5. Serve hot topped with cinnamon-sugar or a drizzle of honey.

Diego Díaz Nieto's Albóndigas de Pesach

In many ways Diego Díaz Nieto typifies late sixteenth-century international *conversos*. Many were merchants who tended to live double lives: as Jews with the Jews and as Christians with the Christians. They often had family members living in a half-dozen countries. The wealthy among them frequently engaged in large-scale importing and exporting and the sorts of lending and money transferring activities that today we call banking. The poor peddled what they could on street corners. Most of the émigrés deliberately made it difficult for the Iberian authorities to track them by adopting numerous aliases.

The tangled networks and conflicting allegiances can be clearly seen in the far-flung Díaz Nieto clan. Diego's grandparents fled Portugal in 1535, going first to Flanders and then to Ferrara, Italy, which the Dukes of Este had permitted to become a refuge for Iberian *conversos,* even allowing them to revert openly to Judaism. Thus, in Ferrara, Manuel Díaz (aka Ruy Gómez Nieto) and Francisca Rodríguez (aka Cecilia Rodríguez Cardoso) became Itzhak and Rivkah Nieto.[38] They had eight children, several of whom remained in Portugal as Christians. The most prominent, Antonio Gómez, imported spices from India. A Jewish son, Ferrara-born Yosef Gómez, sailed to India as Antonio's agent. Another Christian son, Domingo Hernández, lost his life fighting alongside the Portuguese King Sebastian in the Moroccan battle of Alcázarquivir. Yet another son, Yaakov (aka Ruy Díaz or Ruy Gómez), was Diego Díaz Nieto's father. Yaakov/Ruy had other sons as well. Two, bastards from before his marriage to Diego's mother, were taken prisoner at Alcázarquivir and sold as slaves in Constantinople.

As was common in those times, marriages were used to advance family business interests and to protect the family's crypto-Jewish network. Thus when he reached puberty, Yaakov/Ruy's son, Diego, was married to Rivkah Gómez, his own cousin, who had been brought to Ferrara from Portugal for that purpose. Her family was big in the Portuguese pepper and sugar trade with India and Brazil.

Around 1589 the family's business ventures went sour. Suddenly impoverished, father and son devised a novel scheme: they would live by begging ransom money for family members—and other Portuguese Christians—who were being held as slaves in Muslim lands. To this end Ruy (age sixty) and Diego (age sixteen) went first to Venice, where they approached the

In 1601 the Mexican converso Diego Díaz Nieto reported to inquisitors that during the time he lived in Ferrara, Italy, at Passover the Portuguese Jews who lived there made "balls of **sweets, apples, ground chestnuts, and other ingredients,** *which they ate dissolved in vinegar."*[37]

Jewish community for money. From there they went to Rome, where, in 1592, using their Christian identities, they secured a bull from Pope Clement VIII licensing their fund-raising activities. From Rome they journeyed to Genoa, Barcelona, and Madrid, where they met—using one or another of their identities—with both Christian and crypto-Jewish contacts. From there they journeyed to Portugal, where they arranged for forged documentation proving that the Díaz Nietos were of ancient Christian lineage. With these papers in hand, they returned to Madrid, where Diego seems to have lived in vacillation between crypto-Judaism and more or less sincere Christianity. But since in Spain they had little success in raising money, and they became convinced that the fabled wealth of Mexico offered greener pastures, with King Philip II's permission, in 1594 they embarked for the New World.[39]

Haroset is the mixture of fruit, nuts, and wine that traditionally symbolizes the mortar prepared by Jewish slaves for the builders of the pyramids in Egypt. Although the illuminations of several pre-expulsion Iberian *Haggadot* depict Passover scenes that include haroset, Diego Díaz Nieto's testimony is the only Inquisition document we know of that refers to the actual preparation or consumption of haroset during Inquisition times.

Diego Díaz Nieto's Haroset Balls

2 apples, cored and finely diced

6 tablespoons chopped almonds

6 tablespoons chopped dates

6 tablespoons raisins

12 chestnuts, cooked and peeled

¾ teaspoon cinnamon

3 tablespoons sugar

5 tablespoons white vinegar

1. Place the diced apples, almonds, dates, raisins, and chestnuts into an unbreakable bowl. With a potato masher or similar utensil, mash the ingredients together.

2. Add the cinnamon and 1 tablespoon sugar and mix well.

3. Place the remaining sugar in a small bowl.

4. With your fingers, form the haroset mixture into 1-inch balls. Roll them in the sugar and place them on a plate.

5. Serve immediately or refrigerate until serving.

6. To serve, arrange the haroset balls on a platter or on individual plates. Spoon the vinegar over them, allotting approximately 1 tablespoon to three haroset balls. Let them stand until most of the vinegar is absorbed. Like all haroset, eat with a fork or serve on matza.

NOTES

Any kind of apple works well. We prefer red-skinned ones for the visual impression.

Do not use an electric grinder or processor for these balls. They won't hold together if they are ground to a pulpy paste.

VARIATIONS

Use brown sugar or a combination of brown and white sugars in the preparation of the haroset.

Substitute 5 pitted prunes or figs for either the dates or the raisins.

ENDNOTES

Preface

1. AGN vol. 1531, fol. 222r.

2. See the Introduction for more information on the sources.

3. All the trial testimony translations from Spanish, Portuguese, and Catalán are Gitlitz's and all the medieval cookbook translations are Davidson's, unless otherwise indicated.

Introduction

1. Culinary practices also identified crypto-Muslims to the Inquisition. For example, in 1538 Juan de Burgos and a group of his *morisco* friends were denounced "for gathering in the evening to play and dance and eat couscous" (Espadas Burgos 547).

2. Edict of Faith, Las Palmas, Canary Islands, 1524 (Wolf 26–8).

3. Edict of Faith, Cuenca, 1624. Translated by Gitlitz, *Secrecy and Deceit* 626.

4. See page 159, María Alvarez's Olla de Carne.

5. See page 91, Isabel Núñez's Caldo de Garbanzos y Pescado.

6. We think our conclusion more likely than Newman's, who posits that the lack of garlic and onion in the Portuguese cookbook was due to their identification as "Jewish" foods (xv).

7. Sass's edition contains fewer than two hundred recipes; Hieatt/Butler/Hosington's new edition of *Pleyn Delit* has two hundred five.

8. Marks's *Sephardic Cooking,* for example, includes chapters on the "Sephardic" cuisines of Kurdistan, Iraq, Iran, Georgia, Uzbekistan, Calcutta, Cochin, Yemen, and Ethiopia.

Cooking Medieval in a Modern Kitchen

1. Directions from a medieval English cookbook indicate that the mixture should steep ten days (Scully, *Art of Cookery* 68 citing *Noble Boke of Cookry for a Prynce Houssolde or eny other Estately Houssolde*). Cosman quotes another recipe, but gives no source (52). Nola mentions this starch twice for making pottages. We have not attempted to replicate this starch thickener.

2. Nola doesn't use rice flour often.

3. On occasion Nola insists that the bread be well toasted, leading us to intuit that it was nearly burned and thus very dark, nearly black, before it was soaked in vinegar.

4. This easy, modern thickener seems to have been used less commonly by medieval cooks. We include it here based on the several references to flour in the *Al-Andalus* cookbook.

5. See Roden 428–30. Hieatt notes that she made use of this method in Britain some years ago when electricity was limited to only a few hours a day (Personal letter, November 28, 1997).

6. For more about almond milk and other, similar, recipes, see Hieatt/Butler, *Pleyn Delit,* recipe 6; Renfrow 1:223; Sass, *To the King's Taste* 116–17, and "Preference for Sweets"; Scully, "Tempering" 11–14.

7. See especially Alonso 1:275. Alonso cites its use in the thirteenth-century *Libro de montería* [3: part 2, c. 10 (Ed. Bibl. venat, 2: 175)]. See also the *Enciclopedia universal ilustrada* (4:865).

8. Although the seventeenth-century lexicographer Covarrubias does not list the word *almorí,* he defines *salmuera,* the modern word for brine, as a combination of the two words *sal* (salt) and *muria* (923). He also states that it is a coating for preparing meat or fish. See also the *Enciclopedia universal ilustrada* 53:289.

9. Perry estimates that 30 percent of the *Al-Andalus* manuscript's recipes require *almorí* ("Medieval" 171). The late medieval Arabic treatise about food, *Al-Kalam 'alà l-Agdiya,* written in Almería (Spain), speaks of two kinds of *almorí,* one of which is made of fish. According to the treatise, both kinds warm and clean the stomach and aid in digestion (Díaz García, 10–11:22). The resemblance of this liquid to the Roman *garum,* the rotten sauce incorporating fish, has been noted by scholars.

10. 1:235. This is the only reference we have found to "palm hearts" as an *almorí* ingredient.

11. Perry, "Medieval" 169. Here is Arberry's translation without Perry's correction:

"Take 5 *ratls* each of penny-royal and flour. Make the flour into a good dough without leaven or salt, bake, and leave until dry. Then grind up fine with the penny-royal, knead into a green trough with a third the quantity of salt, and put out into the sun for 40 days in the heat of the summer, kneading every day at dawn and evening, and sprinkling with water. When black, put into conserving-jars, cover with an equal quantity of water, and leave for two weeks, stirring morning and evening. When it begins to bubble, leave it to settle, then strain, and put the lees back into the trough. Leave in the sun another two weeks, covered with an equal quantity of water, stirring morning and evening: then strain it into the first murri. Add cinnamon, saffron and some aromatic herbs. [Another recipe] Take salt, and bake into a loaf with a hole in the middle. Wrap in fig leaves, stuff into a preserving-jar, and leave in the shade until fetid. Then remove, and dry" (Arberry 36, n.1). Perry translates twenty-one recipes for the three major kinds of Arabic rotted condiments we mention here. One recipe, declared "undesirable" in the *Al-Andalus* cookbook (88), starts with boiled honey and contains quinces, walnuts, and carob, in addition to the half dozen spices used in the other recipes.

12. Perry, "Medieval" 170. He conducted the experiment in 1987. In a phone conversation, Perry compared the heavy salty flavor to the mold on salami. He continues to experiment with the recipes, this time to test for toxicity (Phone conversation, December 17, 1997). Friedman/Cook have derived from Perry's translation of a Byzantine *murri* a recipe for "a fake *murri*" developed in medieval times as a substitute for the real thing (3–4).

13. Although several of the recipes mention saffron, we feel its taste would be lost with the other stronger flavors. We substitute safflower to retain coloring ability.

14. We thank Michelle LaRoche for her help in clarifying the toxicity of pennyroyal oil.

Salads and Vegetables

1. The Portuguese cookbook gives instructions to boil the lettuce stalks in sugar for fifteen days (fol. 32v, Newman xxxiii and 26–7).

2. Villena 55. Since Villena is concerned with carving, diminutive foods such as peas and chickpeas are omitted.

3. These are Covarrubias's definitions: *Hortaliza:* "Whatever fruit ones takes in the garden . . . like radish, lettuce, cabbage, etc." (701). *Ierva [hierba]:* "Everything that grows in the earth but has nothing but leaves without stalks." The term also "is used to refer to vegetables that grow in gardens that are thrown into a pot and also are used to make salad" (728). Covarrubias also relates a broader meaning of *ierva,* which encompasses anything green that animals graze. *Legumbre:* "Everything whose fruit or seed is in a pod, like chickpeas, lentils, beans, *frisoles,* and other things" (758). *Verdura:* "Whatever is green, but commonly . . . those which are grown in gardens, such as lettuce, radishes, etc." (1001). Scully's *Art of Cookery* wrestles with the same problem (69–70). See the discussion about herbs and spices on page 341.

4. *". . . yervas diferentes, carnes, saladas, pescados, azeytunas, conservas, confituras [,] yemas de huevos, flor de borraja, grageas y de mucha diversidad de cosas . . ."* (Covarrubias 522).

5. Covarrubias 522.

6. Sass, *To the King's Taste* 80–81. One manuscript, cited in Hieatt/Butler/Hosington's *Pleyn Delit* (1996), includes lettuce in this list.

7. Mateo Alemán in *Guzmán de Alfarache,* cited in "La Cocina del Teatro en el Siglo de Oro," a Parador menu complementing Almagro's Theater conference, July 1996.

8. Francisco de Quevedo in "Boda y acompañamiento en el campo," cited in "La Cocina del Teatro en el Siglo de Oro," a Parador menu complementing Almagro's Theater conference, July 1996. We are grateful to Elma Dassbach for this and the previous reference.

9. Covarrubias 756.

10. *"Para hacer una buena ensalada, cuatro hombres hacen falta: para la sal, un sabio; para el aceite, un pródigo; para el vinagre, un avariento, y para revolverla, un loco . . ."* (Martínez Kleiser 235).

11. Granado 93.

12. *"Nabos con col, nada hay mejor."* Another proverb indicates that a good year is a year with turnips (*"Año bueno, año de nabos"* Martínez Kleiser 511).

13. *"El rábano tierno, de cualquier tamaño es bueno"; "No hay vida buena sin rábanos y candela"* (Martínez Kleiser 615).

14. Covarrubias 893.

15. Other vegetables common on the modern table came from the Americas and were successfully introduced to European cuisine after the time of this cookbook's recipes.

16. *Al-Andalus* 193–94.

17. "Most medieval English cookery manuals have few vegetable dishes; but almost all have some" (Cosman 47). See also Scully, *Art of Cookery* 71. Neither the fifteenth-century *Manual de mugeres* nor the Portuguese cookbook includes any vegetable recipes. One must bear in mind that there are manuscript pages missing from the Portuguese work and we cannot be sure that there were no vegetable recipes in the complete text. Banquet menus from late fifteenth-century Valladolid occasionally mention onions, asparagus, and eggplant, but generally as condiments or seasoning for meat dishes (Rucquoi 302).

18. Granado, 376–82. See our recipe page 19 for Almond Milk.

19. See the discussion about food restrictions in Catholicism on page 99.

20. *"Que les daua la dicha su ama a merendar lechugas e ravanos e queso e mastuerço e otras cosas que este testigo no se acuerda"* (Beinart 3:324). For the entire trial testimony, see Beinart 2:466–538.

21. See page 189 for more information on Juan de Teva.

22. *"Estavan muchas conversas comiendo verdura con vinagre a las puertas"* (Baer 2:417).

23. Baer 2:448.

24. Baer 2:447–48.

25. *"Los viernes fasía . . . su ama açelgas sancochadas en agua e después ahogadas en aseyte e con çebollas, e allí, en el azeyte, reheruir; e después echaua allí su agua e pan rallado e espeçias y yemas de hueuos; e cozía fasta que se para muy espeso"* (Carrete Parrondo/Fraile Conde 27). See also Arbós Ayuso 78. See biographical information on María Alvarez on page 159.

26. Covarrubias 728. See page 27 for a discussion of greens in medieval cuisine.

27. Peterson cites a medieval Italian recipe for twelve portions that uses half a pound of various spices (328–29).

28. *Al-Andalus* 53.

29. Nola 141.

30. *Sent soví* 215 and Nola 44.

31. Nola 45. See page 159 for the medieval recipe and our adaptation of it.

32. *Sent soví* 216.

33. García i Fortuny 67–68.

34. Covarrubias 552–53.

35. See Scully's translation of the 1268 Parisian trade guild statutes about selling fresh meat (*Art of Cookery* 236–7). The *Al-Andalus* cookbook's comments about proper utensils include a caution about keeping meat untainted (90).

36. *Encyclopaedia Judaica* 15:268–69.

37. *Encyclopaedia Judaica* 15:269–70.

38. *Al-Andalus* 85.

39. Peterson 324, 330–31. Peterson's tabular data suggest that compared to the rest of Europe Ibero-Arabic cuisine made less frequent use of honey, grains of paradise, nutmeg, mace, cubebs, sumac, anise, asafoetida, and celery seeds (334–35). Grewe's study of the *Al-Andalus* cookbook indicates that the prevalent spices were pepper, cinnamon, and spikenard, with ginger, clove, nutmeg, and galingale also common (144).

40. *Desde Estella a Sevilla.*

41. Listed in decreasing order of frequency (Allard 158).

42. *"Una caçuela con huevos e açanorias e espeçias e otras cosas"* (Beinart 2:390). Pages 378–533 contain the complete trial.

43. See pages 18 and 146 for a discussion of Sabbath stews.

44. *"Come por cerimonia judayca del sábado vn comer vulgarmente llamado Hamyn . . . garuanços e espinazas o uerças"* (Llorca 130–31). Later in the document the dish is called *hamía* (135). See pages 18 and 146 about Sabbath stews.

45. In context this can be identified as Shavuot.

46. Llorca 129–34.

47. *". . . vna olla guisada de açelgas con queso e pan rallado"* (Carrete Parrondo/Fraile Conde 63; also 116). Trial data relating to Almazán's extended Vélez family is found in Carrete Parrondo/Fraile Conde 115–22.

48. Carrete Parrondo/Fraile Conde 116.

49. Carrete Parrondo/Fraile Conde 117.

50. Carrete Parrondo/Fraile Conde 122.

51. Liebman 97.

52. Carrete Parrondo/Fraile Conde 116–17. For further information about *converso* funeral customs, see Gitlitz, *Secrecy and Deceit* 277–315.

53. Sperling 294. In 1642 in Mexico Margarita de Ribera explained that "close relatives eat hard-boiled eggs as a sign of mortification of the flesh [in honor of] the death of the deceased" (AGN vol. 408, fol. 79v).

54. Beinart 2:309; Moreno Koch 353. See Gitlitz, *Secrecy and Deceit* 294.

55. Cortes i Cortes 290; Selke de Sánchez 100.

56. Beinart 2:176.

57. *"Pasas, almendras, ensalada, pan cassero . . . y chocolate y otras cosas, y ninguna de carne . . ."* (AGN vol. 411, fol. 207v).

58. *"Cuando se ayunaba por algún difunto observante de la Ley de Moisés, se come lo primero, cuando se cena a la noche, una sopa de*

pan mojado en agua con sal" (Lewin, *Singular proceso* 223).

59. *"Mucha verengena y açafrán con açelguilla"* (Cota 105).

60. For a history of this family, see Gitlitz, *Los Arias Dávila de Segovia.*

61. *"Cazuelas de verenjenas con huevos"* (Moreno Koch 355). This reference is from a document dated 1489.

62. Sturtevant 541.

63. Herrera, *Obra de agricultura* (3:155–56). Dubler states that there are two types of eggplant, the edible *Solanum melongena L* and the *Solanum ovigerum Dun* (371). The *Enciclopedia universal ilustrada* describes the latter as an annual with red, yellow, or white ovoid berries, originally from India and having poisonous fruits (8:220–21).

64. The *Baghdad Cookery-Book,* written about the year 1226, has several recipes as well.

65. Recipes 149, 151, 152, 153.

66. Tannahill 279.

67. Covarrubias 206–07.

68. "Garlic, from Quero, and eggplant, from Toledo" (*"Ajos, de Quero, y berenjenas, de Toledo,"* Martínez Kleiser 23).

69. 2:2.

70. *". . . merendando de vna caçuela de verenjenas rellenas, las quales estaban frias, e vbas e fruta . . . fecha de vn dia ante fianbre"* (Beinart 2:259). See pages 18 and 146 for information on Sabbath stews.

71. Beinart 2:251, 256. Graçia de Teva was burned as a Judaizer on September 7, 1513.

72. Beinart 2:257, 259–60. Leonor Alvarez was tried separately in 1513. Though there was no doubt about her Judaizing, since some of the testimony against her was found to have been perjured she was not executed but rather sentenced to life imprisonment, a sentence later reduced to house arrest, and the observance of certain fasts and penances (Beinart 2:320).

73. *"E las vezes con verengenas e con çebollas y culantron y espeçias"* (Beinart 2:163; the complete trial is on 155–88). See pages 18 and 146 for information on Sabbath stews.

74. Beinart 2:169.

75. Beinart 2:163.

76. Beinart 2:164.

77. *"Que nos diese de la olla vnos nabos y que los echase vna ralladura de queso"* (Carrete Parrondo/Fraile Conde 19).

78. *"Asentada a la entrada de la . . . cocina, y tenía ençima de las rodillas, sobre las faldas, vn paño blanco, de lienço, ençima dél vna pierna de carnero o macho, redonda, y la tenía hendida por*

medio y vn cuchillo junto con ella; y con las vñas o dedos de la vna mano estaua quitando toda la gordura e vna vena larga, y con la otra mano la tenía" (Carrete Parrondo/Fraile Conde 20).

79. Carrete Parrondo/Fraile Conde 23.

80. Carrete Parrondo/Fraile Conde 19–21.

81. Carrete Parrondo/Fraile Conde 24.

82. *"Cenaron çebollas con almodrote"* (Moreno Koch 353). See also Beinart 2:163.

83. Apicius 58, 59. Rue is now considered unsafe. The term *moretum* persists: Smith's *Smaller Latin-English Dictionary* defines it as "a country dish made with garlic, vinegar, oil, etc.; a salad. . . ." (445).

84. Corominas, *Diccionario crítico etimológico* 1:155.

85. Nola 62.

86. *Sent soví,* chapters 141 and 142.

87. *"Cierta salsa que se haze de azeyte, ajos, queso y otras cosas"* (100).

88. AHN Clero, leg. 1423 (no pagination). We thank Julie A. Evans for transcribing this reference.

89. Stavroulakis's Greek recipe uses zucchini (216); Marks's recipe from Turkey contains eggplant (18). Roden gives a recipe for Turkish *Almodrote de Berengem* ("Eggplant Flan") which also consists of eggs and cheese (521–22), later adapted by O'Neill (54).

90. See, for example, the recipe in the Sephardic Sisterhood, Temple Tifereth Israel's cookbook (67) and Marks 50.

91. *". . . echar garvanços y cebollas, espeçias y miel a la olla"* (Cantera Burgos/Carrete Parrondo 262). See pages 18 and 146 for information on Sabbath stews.

92. Sturtevant 165–66.

93. *Historiae naturalis* (cited in Scully, *Art of Cookery* 191).

94. Recipe 76 (cited in Scully, *Art of Cookery* 193).

95. Fol. 27v in the Liège manuscript, black-and-white illustration 25 in the Arano edition.

96. Because there are gaps in the manuscript, we cannot be sure that some vegetable recipes have not been lost.

97. In an imprecise poll, we found only two uses of the chickpea, one for the red variety.

98. 87.

99. *". . . holgaron e comieron habas"* (Beinart 2:302). See page 77 for more about María González.

100. Beinart 2:301.

101. Beinart 2:302.

102. *"Faen la Pascha dels juheus del pa alis la qual durava vuyt dies e la dita sa mare los dits vuyt*

dies sempre manjava pa alis e arros e peix e faves tenres o galines degolades empero no manjava carn de la carneceria" (Bofarull y Sans 2:99–100).

103. Bofarull y Sans 2:101.
104. Bofarull y Sans 2:101
105. *Sent soví* 141.

Eggs

1. Carrete Parrondo/Fraile Conde 22. For a 1602 Mexican example, see Uchmany 331a.

2. Renfrow adapted one hundred of the recipes into modern English. Even in a cursory reading it becomes obvious that eggs, bread, and saffron are the three ingredients cited most frequently.

3. See illustration 208 in Arano. In 1387, King Richard II's list of provisions included eleven thousand dozen eggs (Cosman 42). A thirteenth-century English baronial manor purchased three thousand seven hundred eggs around Easter time and they lasted only part of the week (Labarge 82). In feudal times, serfs were often required to give certain numbers of eggs as part payment of taxes.

4. *"Por San Antón, huevos a montón." "Por la Candelaria, ponen la gallina buena y la mala"* (Martínez Kleiser 358–59). St. Anthony's feast day is January 17. *Candelaria* is a feast day on February 2.

5. Book VII, "The Gourmet."

6. See the examples given by Scully, *Art of Cookery* 211–12.

7. The Portuguese cookbook contains three egg recipes in a special section entitled "Folder of Egg Dishes," (*Cadernno dos mamgares de ovoos* [sic]). While the fourteenth-century *Libre de sent soví* is not divided into chapters, several egg recipes are grouped together. Recipe 173 lists nine possibilities for preparing eggs. The six recipes that follow (recipes 174–79) cover most of the standard preparations. Six additional recipes are scattered elsewhere in the text. Granado's large cookbook is divided into sections, but there is no specific egg section, even though some recipes feature eggs (366–70).

8. Nola 79.

9. The cooked eggs are stuffed with yolks, cilantro, onion, and cinnamon. The egg halves are then put back together, secured with sticks, covered with saffron, dusted with flour, and fried (152).

10. Paris (fol. 61) and Casanatense (fol. 125) manuscripts. See Arano, illustrations 206 and 207. In the five *Tacuinum sanitatis* manuscripts studied by Arano, the Rouen manuscript mentions no eggs, but of the other four manuscripts, the chicken egg is mentioned in all four, the partridge and goose eggs in three, and the ostrich egg only in the Liège manuscript. Given the limitations of modern markets and our need to calculate exact amounts—a pressure not felt by medieval cookbook writers—we have used exclusively large chicken eggs in this cookbook.

11. See Scully, *Art of Cookery* 62 for information on the evolution of the brightly colored Easter egg.

12. *"Después de haberse bañado merendaron huevos asados, pan, queso y vino . . . estando a la lumbre asando los huevos. . . ."* (Lewin, *Singular proceso* 236–37). For Juan de León, see also page 96. A good brief biography of the Treviño family, in English, can be found in Liebman 238–51.

13. Lewin, *Mártires* 126.

14. *"Hamin y huebos hammados"* (Baer 2:463).

15. Baer 2:463.

16. I.e., Jesus.

17. I.e., beyond the prescribed limits of a Sabbath day's walk.

18. Baer 2:463–4.

19. Blázquez Miguel, *Inquisición en Castilla* 57. Zubaida interprets the term *haminado* to mean oven cooked (45).

20. Blázquez Miguel, *Inquisición y cripto Judaísmo* 59.

21. Sephardic Sisterhood, Temple Tifereth Israel 31; Stavroulakis 23; Marks 37–38.

22. *"Caçuelas . . . hechas de huevos e queso e perexil e calantares e espeçias, e que algunas vezes las hazian de verenjenas e otras vezes de çanahorias, como hera el tienpo, y que comian frias las dichas caçuelas"* (Beinart 2:251; see also 479). For other examples see Beinart 3:390, 482. We have not been able to discover the meaning of *calantares*. For the entire trial, see Beinart 2:240–319.

23. The disposition of María González's case is discussed on page 64.

24. See page 39, Mayor González's recipe for eggs and carrots, as another example.

25. Both Marks, about Turkey (15), and Stavroulakis, about Greece (213), note this change. The French term might be *soufflé* or perhaps *quiche*.

26. Or VeShalom Sisterhood. See pages 58 and 123, 70–72.

27. The recipe is for "*Tyropatinam*," 170–73.

28. This is a special cheese from Auvergne, France. See Benbassa 62 and David 38.

29. Nola 104.

30. Nola 104, 108, 109. See the information about *fruta del sartén* on page 277.

31. Nola 97.

32. *Al-Andalus* 101–2.

33. *Al-Andalus* 130.

Fish

1. A document dated 1490 lists fish received by Queen Isabel's cook, including *"peçes byuos que se echaron en el alberca"* (Domingo 13).

2. AHN Clero, leg. 1423 (no pagination). Our thanks to Julie A. Evans, who transcribed the pertinent information from this document for us.

3. Rucquoi 301. See page 99 for more on Christian proscriptions.

4. See page 43 about funerals.

5. *"Sienpre acostunbrava . . . la dicha Ysabel Gonsales guisar los dichos viernes para los sabados caçuelas de pescado y sardinas"* (Beinart 2:163). See page 52 for Isabel's biography. For information on Sabbath meals, see pages 18 and 146.

6. *"Vna caçuela de verenjenas e pescado e huevos"* (Beinart 2:295). See pages 18 and 146 about Sabbath stews.

7. Beinart 2:274–75, 293–97.

8. Beinart 2:294.

9. Beinart 3:377.

10. *". . . guisaba los biernes caçuelas de pescado e açanorias e espeçias e huevos, e lo guisaban por mandado de la dicha su ama e comian dello los biernes e guardavan dello para el sabado e lo comian frio el sabado los dichos sus amos"* (Beinart 3:418). The family of Alfonso Alvarez, of Ciudad Real, also used to eat a cold Sabbath stew of fish and carrots and eggs and ground spices [*"Vna caçuela fecha de pescado e çanorias e huevos e espeçias fianbre . . . fria e seca"* (Beinart 2:256)]. For more information about Mayor González, see pages 38 and 199 For more on Sabath meals, see pages 18 and 146.

11. Beinart 3:417.

12. *"Cenaban caldo de garbanços y pescado"* (Sierro Malmierca 178). See pages 18 and 146 for information on Sabbath stews.

13. *"Adreçar despues de medio dia mucha comida de garbanços, hueuos, pescado salado y pescado fresco, y atún"* (AGN, vol. 276, exp. 14, 422v). See pages 18 and 146 about Sabbath stews. For further biographical information, see Uchmany. Preparation of this recipe was filmed for the forthcoming documentary *Los ocultos* (Dir. Daniel Goldberg [1999]).

14. AGN vol. 271, exp. 14, 437v.

15. AGN vol. 271, exp. 1, 10r–12r.

16. Liebman 191–97.

17. *"Les dio a cenar a todos un poco de escabeche que tenía guardado, aceitunas, queso, pan, frutas y vino . . ."* (Lewin, *Singular proceso* 81). See also page 72 for more on León/Machorro.

18. Recipes for preserving cooked and raw fish call for vinegar (50, 51); for meat pieces, several spices are mixed with *liquamen,* a briny sauce (158, 159); for venison, a combination of vinegar, *liquamen,* spices, herbs, and raisins (184, 185).

19. *Baghdad Cookery-Book* 34, 200; *Al-Andalus* 36–37.

20. One recipe to conserve rabbits for "many days" adds ginger, cloves, and saffron (112). Another recipe for fish *escabeche* contains several more spices and combines them with honey (143–44).

21. 27–28; other recipes on pages 205 and 218. Many times Granado simply says that a specific fish is good in *escabeche* without giving a detailed recipe for it. The Mexican Ruy Díaz Nieto was also fond of eggs, and fish cooked in oil and vinegar (*"huevos y pescado cozido con azeyte y vinagre"*) (AGN vol. 276, exp. 15, fol. 425v–426r).

22. 532.

23. *"Fritio vnas sardinas rellenas con huevos"* (Beinart 2:244). For the biography of María González, see page 64.

24. Scully, *Art of Cookery* 59.

25. García Marsilla 75; Henisch 30.

26. Scully, *Art of Cookery* 62–64. The best Spanish example is found in the *Libro de buen amor,* a work of the fourteenth-century Castilian cleric poet Juan Ruiz. See the introduction to this chapter.

27. García Marsilla 74.

28. Carrete Parrondo/Fraile Conde 19. In the 1480s in Guadalupe, Fray Juan de Andujar was surprised when Fray Juan Platero had some roasted eggs (*huevos estafados*) served for dinner on a Friday evening. Andújar claimed that from then on he didn't have a good opinion of Platero (AHN Clero, leg. 1423 [no pagination]). Our thanks to Julie A. Evans, who transcribed this document's pertinent contents for us.

29. See those associated with recipes on pages 41, 110, 134, and 185, for example.

30. Espadas Burgos 560. *Morcilla* is a kind of blood sausage often made with pork.

31. Carrete Parrondo/Fraile Conde 39, 41, 50, 73, 81, 100.

32. *". . . truchuela, fruta, potaje de garbanzos, aceitunas, hojuelas de masa con miel y chocolate con bizcochos"* (Blázquez Miguel, *Toledot* 215).

Blázquez Miguel does not cite the document, but summarizes the information.

33. *"Guebos, ensalada, aceitunas, y chocolate, y no carne"; "ensalada, guebos, pescado, y chocolate, y empanadas"* (AGN vol. 411, fol. 201r, 210v); *"pescado guisado, ensalada y unas empanadas de pescado y guebos cocidos y no cossas de carne"* (AGN vol. 414, exp. 13, fol. 561r).

34. *"Merendando . . . la víspera antes dulce, frutas y chocolate . . . [y a] la noche de ellos . . . cenó ensalada, huevos, dulce y chocolate"* (67). The night before Yom Kippur and in the bathhouse they ate *"huevos asados, vino y marquesotes"* (69). In another description of the same meal, *"merendaron huevos asados, pan y queso y vino; . . . y antes bebieron chocolate que hizo el mismo Juan de León"* (80–81) (Lewin, *Singular proceso*).

35. *Desde Estella a Sevilla.*

36. Martínez García 354.

37. See Rucquoi 298, 301–4, and Molénat 316–17.

38. Díaz 110–11.

39. *Goodman of Paris* 226–36; Brereton/Ferrier 174–90. See also Cosman 20–25.

40. See the introduction to sausages, page 210, for information about this Arabic preparation.

41. See page 19 for *almorí*.

42. *Don Quijote* 2:20.

43. Book I, chapter 15 (no pagination).

44. Fray Bernardino de Sahagún, *Historia general de las cosas de la Nueva España,* cited by González de la Vara 293–94.

45. González de la Vara 302–3.

46. Giovanni Francesco Gemelli Careri in his *Viaje a la Nueva España,* cited by González de la Vara 297.

Fowl

1. Castro Martínez 267.

2. Granado's cookbook (1599) also offers several recipes for *gallo de las Indias* (guinea birds), suggesting that these New World birds need two to four days of hanging before they can be cooked.

3. According to extant account books in fifteenth-century Toledo, chicken was the preferred dish of high officials (Molénat 317). In the 1438–69 accounts of a Valladolid confraternity, chicken was served at 70 percent of official banquets (Rucquoi 300–1).

4. See Scully, *Art of Cookery* 106.

5. See page 140.

6. Carrete Parrondo/Fraile Conde 75. For more on the extended Laínez family see pages 54 and 178.

7. *"Señor, ya venimos de las vyñas y no podemos hazer nada, que está elado y ymonos agora acostar para yrnos a la mañana a ver sy podriemos hazer algo y no bolueremos a vuestra merçed hasta la noche, y yo lleuo pescado y sardinas y todo recabdo para los peones, y para vuestra merçed dexo su gallina cozida con su caldillo . . . e dexo su vyno de la odrinita en su jarrico, bien atapado"* (Carrete Parrondo/ Fraile Conde 75).

8. Carrete Parrondo/Fraile Conde 72.

9. *"Un santbenetillo asul de estameña, como los judíos honrados lo solían traer a manera de çeçí; . . . vio vnas cuerdas blancas que colgauan de los cabos del sanbenito"* (Carrete Parrondo/ Fraile Conde 74).

10. Carrete Parrondo/Fraile Conde 71–77.

11. *"Para enfermos caldo destilado, y para debilitados, muy singular"* (82–83).

12. *"ansarones como otras aves"* (Beinart 3:433).

13. *"La dicha Mayor Gonçales e otra çierta persona mandavan degollar las aves que se matavan en su casa, asy gallinas como pollos e palominos"* (Beinart 3:446).

14. *"Facía los tres ayunos de la Reina Ester y enllas comía buenas gallinas o huevos duros con perexil"* (Sánchez Moya, "Inquisición" 173). For the biography of Mayor González, see page 38.

15. Beinart 3:461–65.

16. See the discussion of *almorí* on page 19.

17. *"Ráuanos buenos . . . papillos rellenos"* (Castillo, poem 994).

18. *Cancionero de obras de burlas* 78.

19. *Cancionero de obras de burlas* 100–1.

20. Márquez Villanueva 397.

21. In Perry's translation the chicken is roasted, not fried (*Anonymous Andalusian Cookbook* A-15).

22. *Al-Andalus* 71–72.

23. *Al-Andalus* 75–76. Perry translates "a quarter of a pound of water" where Huici Miranda's Spanish says "four pounds." When we made this recipe we found that the coating works better without any water at all.

24. See Balducci Pegolotti (415–16).

25. Since nowadays cassia is much less available for purchase, cinnamon may be substituted for cassia without substantially affecting the recipe. See Norman 30. See page 203 for the Jewish eggplant recipe.

26. *Al-Andalus* 70, with the bracketed addition from Perry (*Anonymous Andalusian Cookbook* A-15).

27. Platina, Book 3, chapter 6 (no pagination).

28. *Al-Andalus* 73–74.

29. *". . . que avía comido en quaresma vna pierna de perdís . . ."; "comer huevos en las vegilias de ayunar . . . e que vn sábado le vido comer de vnos palominos puestos en pan"* (Carrete Parrondo/Fraile Conde 49).

30. See page 99 for more about Christian food prohibitions.

31. *". . . en entrando, olido carne asada, y que se asomó en la cozina e que vio asar vn ansarón . . .* (Carrete Parrondo/Fraile Conde 74).

32. *Cancionero de obras de burlas* 99. See also page 119.

33. Castro Martínez 269.

34. Prices recorded in 1472 in Zaragoza show that a chicken cost 2 *sueldos* 9 *dineros*, a hen 2 *sueldos* 6 *dineros*, and a goose 3 *sueldos*, 6 *dineros* (Castro Martínez 267–70).

35. One of the recipes is for an Ashkenazi Sabbath stew, called cholent. Her acute observations about the value of goose fat are interesting and worth keeping in mind while preparing Sabbath goose stew.

36. Arbós Ayuso, 79.

37. *Cancionero de obras de burlas* 77.

38. *"merecia accusada e quimada por que era huma má judia que comia a carne fria com azeite . . . comia a carne e a gallinha fria molhada no azeite"* (Furtado de Mendoça, *Primera visitação* 1925, 260–61).

39. *"millor li sabia la vianda freda que calda"* (Fort i Cogul 178). This testimony is from 1496.

Beef

1. O'Callaghan 618.

2. Rucquoi 298.

3. Molénat 317.

4. See page 4. One can salt and soak the beef for any of the recipes in this chapter. We suggest some directions for the process on page 161.

5. Lera García 93. For additional information about crypto-Jewish koshering practices, see Gitlitz, *Secrecy and Deceit* 542–48.

6. Leviticus 3:17, 7:23–25.

7. Santa María 184.

8. AGN vol. 271, exp. 1, fol. 9v.

9. Santa María 184.

10. Furtado de Mendoça, *Primera visitação* 31.

11. *"Se acostumbraba a hacer con carne gorda, garbanços, fabas, judías, huebos duros, y de otro cualquier legumbre"* (Santa María 187).

12. Roden (430) points out the universality of hard-boiled eggs in Sabbath stew in modern North African and Levantine traditions, but our sources do not substantiate this practice quite so globally for medieval Iberia: in the nearly thirty stews clearly identified as "Sabbath stews," fewer than one quarter of the references mention eggs specifically.

13. Llorca 130–31.

14. Carrete Parrondo, *Proceso* 98.

15. Castillo, poem 994.

16. García Fuentes 275. Espadas Burgos defines *boronia* as a stew of eggplant, tomato, squash, and pepper all chopped up and mixed together (542). His definition is anachronistic, given that the tomato is a New World product.

17. 184. The *Baghdad Cookery-Book* also refers to this dish in a poem, calling it *buran* (23). Espadas Burgos affirms that the dish is cited in the *Thousand and One Nights* as *alboraniya*. Both he and Grewe repeat the datum with which the *Al-Andalus* cookbook begins the recipe: that the name derives from Buran, the wife of the khalif Mamoun, who had a great fondness for the dish (Espadas Burgos 542; Grewe, "Hispano-Arabic Cuisine" 146).

18. Jiménez Lozano calls this a "culteme," which he defines as a remnant usage that indicates a broad assimilation, popularization, and ultimately trivialization of a custom which—in this case—had once been an explicit indicator of Judaizing (362). Angel gives one recipe for a Sabbath stew, calling it *adafina*. The ingredients for the Moroccan stew include both Old World and New World ingredients, but notably eggs, which are put in the stew pot uncooked still in their shells (177). Perry ascribes *adafina* to the Arabic *madfun*, meaning "buried" or "buried treasure" (*Anonymous Andalusian Cookbook* A17, note 42). See also Roden for other terms for Sabbath stews current in modern Sephardic communities (428–30).

19. *". . . carne con perejil, cebollas, berzas y yerbabuena"* (Blázquez Miguel, *Toledot* 195).

20. Although presentation may have been an important part of the Roman banquets, color is seldom highlighted. Apicius gives several recipes for "white sauce" (*jus album*) (Book V, iii, and Book VII, vi).

21. A few lines later the poet describes a dish having "Meat . . . in slices white and scarlet laid" (Arberry 22). From the same dinner, given before the year 950 in the court of Mustakfi, Caliph of Baghdad, comes this example about rice: "Purer than snow . . . / . . . / White as the whitest milk that heart could

wish, / Its brilliance dazzles the beholding eye . . ." (Arberry 27). See also Wilson 16–18.

22. Marín 206.

23. An early fourteenth-century cookbook written on the Iberian Peninsula by Ibn Razin seems less concerned with the "aesthetic aspects of a meal" (Marín 210).

24. See the discussion of "white" dishes on page 197.

25. "Blue Jelly" in *Goodman of Paris* (280; Brereton/Ferrier 251–2); "Golden soup" in Granado 51. Scully mentions a recipe for a food of "cheery green" color ("gawdy grene" in the English source). He also describes a recipe for a blue mush found in a German cookbook (*Art of Cookery* 114–15).

26. *"Manjar real"* (47).

27. For example, *"Potaje llamado jota"* (125).

28. Nola 121; "Green sauce" in *Forme of Cury* 68; *"Jurvert"* in *Sent soví* 179–80.

29. Nola 47, 54, and 115, for example.

30. See page 70 for more about eggs in medieval cooking.

31. Norman 33.

32. Covarrubias 640. See, for example, Nola 60 and *Sent soví* recipe 56 (100). The latter recipe uses a combination of rice and saffron. See also *Goodman of Paris* (265; Brereton/Ferrier 219) and Scully, *Art of Cookery* 199.

33. One must remember that tomatoes and chile peppers were not yet part of European cooking, so the feat of turning a food red was not easily accomplished.

34. See the recipe Vermilioned Eggs (page 76).

35. 289. The recipe, for *yuwaris,* is in a section of drinks and syrups located at the end of the collection. Wilson also notes that all of these ingredients for red coloring were from the Arab culture (18).

36. See, for example, the recipe Goose Stew (page 142).

37. *"Facía guisar a sus mozas carne con garbanzos e berzas para el sábado"* (Sánchez Moya, "Inquisición" 173). The complete trial can be found on 146–99. For similar examples see Carrete Parrondo *Tribunal* 155. María and Martín García, of Almazán, made their Sabbath stew of "ox hooves with chickpeas" (*"pesuñas de buey con garvanços"*) (Carrete Parrondo/Fraile Conde 49, 87, 132).

38. *"La amostraron a guisar vna olla . . . en la qual echauan garvanços e avas; y carne de lo más gordo que se podía aver o ubre, echávase en la dicha*

olla, e si era tiempo de berengenas echáuanlas, y echauan más culantrillo seco e alcaravea e cominos e pimienta e çebolla; e aquestas espeçias e çebolla, llamávanlo guesmo, e la dicha olla se començava a guisar desde ora de bísperas fasta otro día a la ora de comer; quando la querían cubijar antenoche, echauan azelgas cochas e picadas e machacadas, y si no avía acelgas, echauan hojas de rávanos. . . ." (León Tello 2:70–71). Pages 69–80 contain the trial information that we summarize here.

39. This custom is discussed on page 242.

40. Blázquez Miguel, *Inquisición y criptojudaismo* 60.

41. Blázquez Miguel, *Inquisición en Castilla* 58.

42. *". . . echaua garuanços e çebollas y espeçias, e cozía fasta que todo estaua desfecho, como formigos"* (Carrete Parrondo/Fraile Conde 27). See page 250 for more information about this family.

43. *"Mandó . . . quitar el sebo de la carne con las vñas e toda la flor, que non le dexaua ninguna gordora, e fasta que lo quitaua este testigo non se quitaua de allí . . . su ama. Y algunas veses, porque no lo quitaua del todo, . . . le daua de bofetadas; y después . . . se lo fasía lauar con çinco o seys aguas fasta que todo quedaua magro, como carne blancusca, mortezina"* (Carrete Parrondo/Fraile Conde 27).

44. *"¿Qué diablo ha andado con esta carne? Dívosla sana e florida y traésmela piscada, que paresçe que pollos o ratones lo han comido e picado"* (Carrete Parrondo/Fraile Conde 35).

45. *"¿Por qué avía fecho aquéllo?, que avía echado la carne a perder y no podía faser la çena por lo gordo que le avía quitado . . ."* (Carrete Parrondo/Fraile Conde 57).

46. *"Muchas vezes trayan carne en verano de la masiada [casa de campo], y porque no se perdiese la lauaua y la echaua sal algunas vezes en el ayre e otras vezes en vna çesta; y que no fazía por çeremonia"* (Carrete Parrondo/Fraile Conde 26).

47. *"Leonor tenía vna pierna de carne en las rodillas sobre sus faldas, fendida por medio, y con vn cuchillo la estaua sacando de dentro de la . . . pierna el sebo e lo echaua fuera . . . y le dixo este testigo: 'Esto fasiedes quando judíos, que quedaua para quando hérades judíos', y la susodicha respondió: '¿Cómo? ¿esto no podemos faser?'"* (Carrete Parrondo/Fraile Conde 80).

48. *"Gingibre blanco dos onzas; galangal medio quarto de onza; canela vna onza; pimienta luenga vna onza; nuezes de xarque vna onza; nuezes moscadas vna onza; azucar fino vna libra; todo esto sea bien molido y passado por vn sedazo delgado"* (45).

49. *"Al tienpo que avia verengenas la dicha su ama le hazia coser a este testigo las verenjenas e freyrlas en azeyte y las hechaua en la olla con la carne, syn toçino"* (Beinart 2:491). For information on Juana Núñez, see page 30.

50. Coelho 207.

51. Roth 19.

52. García, *Autos de fe* 59.

53. *"Que su limpieza exagere, / porque anda el mundo al revés, / quien de puro limpio que es / comer el puerco no quiere"* ("Letrilla 651," *Obras completas 702).*

54. *"Yo te untaré mis obras con tocino, / porque no me las muerdas, Gongorilla"* ("Soneto 841," *Obras completas* 1195).

55. *"Puerco en casa judía, hipocresía"; "Con misa ni tocino no convides al judío"; "No temblés tocino, decía el judío; que no hay en casa quien mal os haga"* (Martínez Kleiser 394–95).

56. *"Mari Gómez, ¿tocino comes? ¡Guay de mi casa: no te me ahogues!"* (Martínez Kleiser 149).

57. *Cancionero de obras de burlas* 106–7.

58. Montoro, *Poesía* 202. Note how his bitterness intensifies in the sixth line with his shift to a first-person verb.

59. *"Que tomase las tripas de carnero o vaca e manos e pies de carnero e vñas de baca, que avían tomado el jueves antes, las cozinase en vna olla para otro día sábado, . . . y que echaua nabos al tienpo que los avía, y que asy se estaua la olla al fuego coziendo fasta otro día, sábado"* (Carrete Parrondo/Fraile Conde 78).

60. Carrete Parrondo/Fraile Conde 26. For more about María Alvarez see the recipe on page 159.

61. Carrete Parrondo/Fraile Conde 78, 92, 98.

62. *"Era amarella . . . que se fazia com grãos pisados, e a carne picada e adubos"* (Furtado de Mendoça, *Denunciaçoẽs* 31). See also Wiznitzer 25. The Fernandes family is also discussed in Lipiner 165–78.

63. Furtado de Mendoça, *Denunciaçoẽs* 282; Lipiner 166–67.

64. Furtado de Mendoça, *Denunciaçoẽs* 282; Lipiner 168.

65. *"Não cozinhava a carne em panella senão em tijella, dizendo que era assi mais gostosa e com a carne mesturava grãos e os pisava y lhes lançava adubos sem lhe botar couve e . . . diziam que aquillo era cousa de judia"* (Furtado de Mendoça, *Denunciaçoẽs* 25, 261).

66. *"Tomava a carne de vaqua e ella a fregia no azeita com cebola e lhe lançava dentro grãos"* (Furtado de Mendoça, *Denunciaçoẽs* 25, 494).

67. *"Fregir cebola com aceite e botaia na panella da carne pere comerem todas"* (Furtado de Mendoça, *Denunciaçoẽs* 25, 361).

68. *"Le guisava las dichas ollas, echando en ellas vaca y carnero y espinazo de puerco e çebolla e garvanços y espeçias, y otras vezes echava con la baca y el carnero repollo cortado muy menudo e su çebolla . . . , azafran y pimienta e su sal, e algunas vezes echava toçino y otras no"* (Cantera Burgos/Carrete Parrondo156).

69. Cantera Burgos/Carrete Parrondo147, 156–57.

70. *"Una aue de tierra rellena con hueuos y toçino"* (AGN vol. 271, exp. 1, fol. 10r). For Leonor de Cáceres see Uchmany 240a.

71. *"El viernes en la noche, echava vnas pelotas cozidas e sancochadas e otra olla de açelgas con sus espeçias e garvanços, e quando se yvan acostar dexavan vna caldera sobre la dicha olla con lunbre, e otro día, sábado, hallavan descocha la dicha olla e comían della"* (León Tello 70–1). See page 155.

72. Meatballs were evidently fairly popular in medieval Europe. In the British Isles recipes for *pommes* (the French for "apples"), generally meant to be cooked in broth, are scattered throughout the cookbooks.

73. Joaquín de Val in Granado (xl). Covarrubias states the same and adds other possible etymological origins: *bunduqun* for *avellana* (hazelnut); and, citing a Padre Guadix, *albóndiga* as a corruption of the Arabic *albidaca,* "chopped meat" (67–68).

74. Cantera Burgos/Carrete Parrondo156.

75. Espadas Burgos (552) citing Fray Diego de Mérida, *Viaje de Oriente.*

76. See Roden 407; Benbassa for French recipes; Stavroulakis for Greek recipes. Marks offers recipes from Turkey, Tangiers, and Uzbekistan.

77. *"Picauan vna poca de carne cruda e la echauan en vn mortero, e allí echauan espeçias e algunos hueuos, e majauan aquello e, después de majado fasían vnos como bodoques redondos, e los freyan en vna sartén con azeyte o en vna olla, e los llamauan albondequexos"* (Carrete Parrondo/Fraile Conde 43). No last name is given for Beatriz, who in the documents is merely called wife of Ruy Díaz Laínez.

78. Carrete Parrondo/Fraile Conde 42–43.

79. Carrete Parrondo/Fraile Conde 91.

80. Beinart 3:556.

81. Beinart 2:163.

82. See page 229.

83. See pages 34–36 for more about spices.

84. *"Estrellaban los huevos en una sarten de ambre [sic] y apres que eran fechos echaban encima carne picada sofreida con cebolla, y apres batian otros huevos y los echaban encima, y tomaban otra*

sartén con rescaldo y ponianla encima, y asi se oleaba todo" (Sánchez Moya/Monasterio Aspiri 131).

85. "Plato judío relleno oculto" (79). We keep the punctuation of the Spanish version.

86. ". . . carne e figado de vaca . . . sabados estando de saude" (Azevedo Mea 241).

87. The recipe is called "Vinagrea que es higado adobado" (59).

Lamb and Goat

1. The 1438–69 accounts of a Valladolid confraternity indicate that mutton was reserved for the poor, while the confraternity officials preferred goat (Rucquoi 301). Lamb, in small quantities, was also prescribed for the sick (Molénat 315).

2. O'Callaghan 304.

3. Coelho 208.

4. Blázquez Miguel, Inquisición en Castilla 67.

5. Lewin, Singular proceso 32. See page 96 for more about Juan de León. The Mexican conversa Ana de León Carvajal testified in 1600 that when they couldn't secure lamb for Passover they ate kid (Uchmany 230b).

6. "Quando trayan pierna de carnero de la carniçeria, veya este testigo como al dicho Juan de Teva, e otras vezes Alonso de Teva, su hermano, endian la dicha pierna a lo largo, y no sabe sy sacauan la landrezilla o lo que se hazian" (Beinart 2:490; 3:324–25).

7. For information about Juana Nuñez, see page 30.

8. Beinart 3:328.

9. Beinart 3:322.

10. Beinart 3:325.

11. Beinart 3:326.

12. Beinart 3:331.

13. ". . . una certa vianda en què mettia spinachs, ciurons, moltó, carn salada e ous" (Fort i Cogul 182).

14. For a brief review of the preexpulsion Jewish demographic controversy, see Gitlitz, Secrecy and Deceit 74.

15. ". . . spinachs com ciurons, e ous, e altres coses" (Fort i Cogul 183).

16. ". . . huevos e espeçias e carnero" (Beinart 3:403).

17. "Pies de carnero . . . el biernes en la noche lo hazía poner a su olla con garvanços e huebos en el forno . . . como lo hazían los judíos; e se cozía allí toda la noche" (Carrete Parrondo, Tribunal 155).

18. "Algunos sábados comían vientres e pies de carnero . . . e que lo cozían con garvanços" (Fita y Colomé 299). For more on Beatriz Núñez, see page 219.

19. Carrete Parrondo, Tribunal 70.

20. Carrete Parrondo, Tribunal 155–56.

21. Carrete Parrondo, Tribunal 155.

22. ". . . caçuela de carnero. E que no sabe de que hera la dicha caçuela mas de quanto le pareçio que estaba blanca . . . y que [Pedro Nuñez] repartio arrevanadas de la dicha caçuela por todos los susodichos, e que estaba fria quando comieron la dicha caçuela" (Beinart 3:386–87). This information was given by Miguel Rodrigues, testifying in the Mayor González trial in 1511. See page 39 for more on Mayor González and page 199 for more on Pedro Núñez.

23. See page 149 for more about color and food.

24. See the recipes for white rolls (page 245) and white bread (page 247), both from kitchens in Ciudad Real. The person who had tasted the white rolls remembered them to be "delicious," but the person who mentioned the white bread found it "tasteless."

25. Al-Andalus 92. Tafaya is a meat stew. Díaz García explains that in Arabic cooking there are two kinds of tafaya: "green," made with fresh cilantro, and "white," made with dried coriander (13).

26. Goodman of Paris 253; Brereton/ Ferrier 200–1. The writer carefully explains that this dish is made with the white of leeks. Porray is a kind of greens. Among his other porray recipes are one for green and another for black.

27. Granado 24. The sauce is made primarily of peeled ginger, so that, as the recipe states, it remains white. The Roman Apicius also lauded the attractiveness of a white dish: one recipe calls for "chalk used for cleaning silver" so that the ingredients become "equally white" (recipe II, ii, 10; Flower/ Rosenbaum 66, 67).

28. Al-Andalus 255.

29. Al-Andalus 245.

30. Scully describes the evolution of blanc-mange dishes, noting that many were created with spices that would have made the dish not white. He posits that the original form of the words was blant mange, or gentle, bland eating (Art of Cookery 207–11).

31. "Mato vn ansaron, e otro dia sabado comieron el menudo con vn pedaço de carnero" (Beinart 3:386).

32. Beinart 3:396. Information from the trials is found in Beinart 3:378–535.

33. See pages 38, 89, and 199.

34. Beinart 3:387.

35. Beinart 3:437.

36. Beinart 3:399.

37. Beinart 3:464–65.

38. 32.

39. For information about the two different types of cinnamon, see page 127.

40. An Arabic measure of weight equivalent to 3 grams. See Lane-Poole xii.

41. *Al-Andalus* 248. Our translation replicates the punctuation found in the Spanish edition. Perry's translation uses spikenard instead of lavender, and rue for heather (A46).

42. Blázquez Miguel, *Inquisición y criptojudaismo* 60. For the barley cakes, see page 248.

43. Blázquez Miguel, *Inquisición y criptojudaismo* 286.

44. Kamen 212.

Sausages

1. *"Cada puerco tiene su San Martín."*

2. Arberry 199. The translator notes that both names for this dish, *Sukhtur* and *Kiba,* are of Persian origin and refer to stuffing sheep's or goat's intestines.

3. See page 19 for more about *almorí.*

4. *Al-Andalus* 15. Another recipe for *mirkas* adds not-very-fresh cheese to the meat mixture (19). Two other recipes, one for *mirkas,* another for *morcillón* (the Spanish term) are meat free, having eggplant, and onions and eggs, respectively (189, 32).

5. *Al-Andalus* 92–94.

6. 71.

7. Scully notes that there is a recipe for green sausages in the *Mittelniederdeutsches Kochbuch,* a fifteenth-century collection (*Art of Cookery* 114).

8. *Goodman of Paris* 226, 227; Brereton/Ferrier 175.

9. Granado 33.

10. *Manual de mugeres* 53, 77.

11. *"Rreceita das murcellas"* (fol. 6v, Newman xxv, 4).

12. Espadas Burgos 560.

13. Cited in Scully, *Art of Cookery* 237.

14. Marks 211; Stavroulakis 179.

15. *Goodman of Paris* 308; Brereton/Ferrier 279.

16. *". . . tomaron la cabeça del buey . . . la cozió vna noche, e a la mañana . . . su ama la picó bien y echó en ella ajos picados y culantro seco y tomó de las tripas del buey y rellenólas de aquello, como longanisas"* (Carrete Parrondo/Fraile Conde 121).

17. *"Las cabeças del buey e cabrones las echase a cozer el domingo en la noche, e después de cozidas las picaua . . . su ama y las echaua en los aluillos de los cabrones e las ponía a sahumar, e después comía dellas"* (Carrete Parrondo/Fraile Conde 32).

18. The other culinary customs she reported included removing the vein from legs of meat and soaking and salting the meat to remove all traces of blood. She also reported how the León family prepared their own matza during the Christian Holy Week. See Holiday Foods, page 289.

19. *". . . vnos aluillos de la carneçería e liuianos e carne, e dáuanlos a . . . Leonor, su fija, la qual los fasía como torteruelos, todos atados en vna cuerda, de manera que los judíos lo solían faser . . . y los comían en los días de carne"* (Carrete Parrondo/Fraile Conde 117). For more about Pedro Vélez, see page 43.

20. *"Cabaheas de lyvyanos de vaca e de cabeça de vaca y de las entrañas, y con sus ajos y espeçias, y las hazían y las comían los sábados"* (Carrete Parrondo/Fraile Conde 37–38).

21. *"Mataron dos vacas e de los baços e de las cabeças de las . . . vacas lo cozieron, e después de cozido lo picaron con ajos y lo echaron en las tripas de las vacas e las colgaron al humo"* (Carrete Parrondo/Fraile Conde 42).

22. *"Mataron tres vacas y que fisieron dellas cabaheas cosidas, . . . que cosieron en tres ollas . . . que este testigo las vio colgadas"* (Carrete Parrondo/Fraile Conde 43).

23. *". . . cabaheas de cabeça e coraçón de baca y baço de vaca, e lo cozía e picaba con culantro"* (Carrete Parrondo/Fraile Conde 67, 91).

24. *". . . de cabeças de buey, cochas e picadas con espeçias"* (Carrete Parrondo/Fraile Conde 96).

25. *". . . mandó traer . . . vn baço de cabrito e lo cozió e vn poco de cabrito con él; e después de cozido lo picó e echó culantro seco e sal e ajo e lo echó en vn aluillo de carnero que avía traydo. . . . Esto fixieron vn domingo por la mañana e lo cozieron, e a la tarde lo comieron"* (Carrete Parrondo/Fraile Conde 47).

26. Carrete Parrondo/Fraile Conde 24. Carrete Parrondo believes *cabaheas* to be similar to the modern *skamba* of various eastern Sephardic communities, and to the *bojillo* common on the flatlands of the Spanish provinces of Zamora and León.

27. *"Su ama picaua la . . . carne con espeçias e tomaua de las tripas del carnero que trayan en los . . . jueues, e rellenáualas con aquella carne e atáualas con hilos e quedauan como redondas, e las freya con manteca de vacas"* (Carrete Parrondo, *Tribunal* 115–16).

28. A convert who was working for the Inquisition at that time.

29. Carrete Parrondo, *Tribunal* 67.

30. Carrete Parrondo, *Tribunal* 66–67.

31. Carrete Parrondo, *Tribunal* 67.

32. *"Trayan algunos alvillos de carnero y del*

baço picado e huevos cozidos e las alburas picadas, e las yemas enteras echauan en los aluillos e fasían vnos torterillos, y echáuanlos a cozer, e después comían de aquéllos los sábados e otros días de carne" (Carrete Parrondo/Fraile Conde 43–44).

33. ". . . en una tripa de carnero o macho echar hígado machado e yemas de huevos e espeçias" (Fita y Colomé 301).

Meat and Fish Pies

1. Díaz García 165. This datum is undocumented. He calls them *panes de boca*.

2. Henisch 78, citing H. T. Riley, *Memorials of London and London Life* 438.

3. Quevedo, *"Poema 644," Obras completas* 665.

4. Sephardic Sisterhood, Temple Tifereth Israel 2–3; Stavroulakis 103.

5. Sephardic Sisterhood, Temple Tifereth Israel H10.

6. Stavroulakis 69–70.

7. *"Lançavão a carne picada na panella com azeite e cebolla e grãos e adubos e outras cousas, e barravão lhe o testo com massa ao redor e metiamla dentro em hum forno onde estava até se cozer"* (Furtado de Mendoça, *Denunciaçoẽs* 57). The Fernandes family is profiled on page 169.

8. Novinsky 144–45.

9. Judaizers represent only 21 percent of the total Brazilian Inquisition indictments (Siqueira 227–28).

10. Blázquez Miguel reports this from trial documents he cites as ADC, leg. 146/1782 (*Inquisición en Castilla* 71–72).

11. Blázquez Miguel refers to ADC leg. 119/1621 (*Inquisición y criptojudaismo* 59).

12. ". . . *carne picada frita en aseyte e cabeças de carnero descosidas fazían vnas enpanadas"* (Carrete Parrondo/Fraile Conde 122).

13. We have found one Catalán reference from just prior to the expulsion which seems to refer to this custom (Fort i Cogul 182). In addition, the Mexican crypto-Jew Diego Díaz Nieto, reporting in 1601 on customs he had observed in Italy, spoke with precision about the separation of milk and meat. "After eating meat it is forbidden to eat cheese, butter, or milk until six hours have passed. But one can eat those things before eating meat . . . provided one dries the mouth and washes the hands. And the pots in which meat is cooked and the plates on which it is served must not cook or touch any of those three things; rather the dishes and pots have to be kept separate" (Uchmany 368a). Similarly, Diego Pérez de Albuquerque, who had come to Mexico from France, reported in 1624 that

"one did not eat meat with cheese or milk until two hours had passed" (AGN vol. 348, exp. 5, fol. 435v). Since Cataluña was affiliated culturally with French Provence and the Mexican informats were talking about Judaism in France and Italy, the references leave in doubt whether this general European practice was commonly followed in Iberia as well.

14. *"Hasía empanadas de pescado el vyernes para el sábado"* (Carrete Parrondo, *Tribunal* 173).

15. *"vnos palominos puestos en pan"* (Carrete Parrondo/Fraile Conde 49). A second reference repeats the allegation: *"enpañó dos pares de palominos en vn día sábado"* (Carrete Parrondo/Fraile Conde 50). See page 134 for more about this family.

16. Carrete Parrondo/Fraile Conde 132.

17. Carrete Parrondo/Fraile Conde 133.

Breads

1. See Holiday Foods about matza.

2. Santa María 182, 184. Shatzmiller documents this custom in France in 1313.

3. Carrete Parrondo/Fraile Conde 35.

4. *"Lançava tres pelourinhos de masa no fogo por sacreficyo e ceremonya judaica"* (Azevedo Mea 113).

5. Liebman 97.

6. Braunstein 98.

7. *"En compensación del pan cotaço que le daban los judíos enviaba a las judías pan lieudo y les daba lebadura"* (Cabezudo Astraín 283).

8. See the recipes for *"Galynha mourisqua"* (Moorish chicken; fol. 4v, Newman 3), *"Dos laparos"* (rabbits; fol. 13v, Newman 12), and *"Tigelada de perdiz"* (partridge casserole; fol. 15r, Newman 13).

9. Oliveira Marques, cited by Henisch 153, note 23.

10. Henisch 160.

11. *"Y ponía en la dicha mesa vnos panezicos pequeñiitos, repregados, blancos, y tenia de plaser"* (Beinart 3:386). See page 199 for more about this family.

12. Mayor's husband dealt in cloth, and the family was fairly wealthy. In addition to these four servants, Catalina de la Villa, a sixteen-year-old girl named Francisca, and a *conversa* named Pasculina Sánchez worked in the house. They also employed several serving boys and stable hands (Beinart 3:399).

13. Beinart 3:395.

14. Beinart 3:397.

15. Beinart 3:397.

16. Beinart 3:417.

17. Beinart 3:394.

18. Beinart 3:396.

19. See page 148 for a discusion of Sabbath stews.

20. ". . . *hazia vna torta blanquesca, e que de aquella torta dava a la que primero entraba . . . e que el dicho pan de la torta era desabrido e blanco, e que este testigo creya que hera pan çençeño, avnque non gelo dixo ninguno de las que alli estavan*" (Beinart 2:294).

21. Beinart 2:484–86.

22. Blázquez Miguel summarizes information and does not quote any specific source (*Inquisición y criptojudaismo* 60).

23. Scully, *Art of Cookery* 36.

24. Echániz Sans 178.

25. Covarrubias 405, 413, 167. Some confusion results from the fact that in medieval times the Spanish term "*trigo*," like the English "corn," was used generically for all grains (Covarrubias 978). Barley is mentioned once in the Portuguese cookbook, as food for chickens (Newman x).

26. Christians used the whitest possible flour for their communion wafers and in the French territories white bread was known as "*paindemaine*," or Lord's bread. In Britain wheat flour was graded by texture and color: the master and mistress ate *pandemaine*; lesser mortals were given "monks' bread," "servants' bread," or "alms bread." High-prestige bread also had to be served fresh, while servants might get day-old loaves (Henisch 157–58).

27. Newman ix. In northern Europe sorghum, buckwheat, and spelt were also consumed (Scully, *Art of Cookery* 68).

28. "*Hasya pan cuez en esta manera: que tomavan culantro en vna sartén y ajos e espeçias molidas y agua y azeyte y echavan pan desmenuzado y el culantro verde, y lo boluían todo, y hazían aquel pan cuez para los sábados y los viernes*" (Carrete Parrondo/Fraile Conde 38). This seems similar to a modern Spanish dish usually called *migas*.

29. See page 159 for more on María Alvarez.

30. See page 213.

31. Carrete Parrondo/Fraile Conde 28, 36–38.

Desserts and Snacks

1. "*Se llaman postres las frutas y confituras que se dan al fin de la comida o cena*" (879).

2. Díaz 82.

3. Uchmany 230b. Mamey is an avocado-size, orange-flesh tropical fruit.

4. Balducci Pegolotti, cited by Scully, *Art of Cookery* 21.

5. Scully, *Art of Cookery* 131. For similar reasons, candies made of seeds considered to be warm and moist—anise, caraway, fennel, cumin—were used to open the stomach as an *apertif* (Scully, *Art of Cookery* 129–30).

6. "*La confección de la almendra, avellana, piñón o otra qualquier fruta o semilla incorporada o cubierta con el açucar*" (349).

7. See Faraudo de Saint-Germain. Recipe collections such as the *Libre* proliferated during the next two centuries.

8. Díaz 81–82.

9. AGN vol. 1529, fol. 135.

10. AGN vol. 271, exp. 1, fol. 6.

11. Liebman 78–79.

12. Sturtevant 475.

13. "*Membrillo, espada y mujer, de Toledo deben ser*" (Martínez Kleiser 464).

14. Sturtevant 475.

15. 13.

16. See, for example, the detailed treatment ordered by Amato Lusitano for his patient Azzarias, who was suffering from stomach problems, among other things (*Centuria* 4, Cure XLI).

17. "*Fruta junto al camino, nunca llegó a madurar*" (Martínez Kleiser 280).

18. "*Se fazía traher azuquaques e turrado de la Juderia e lo fazía aparellar de judias*" (Cabezudo Astraín 283).

19. See the discussion of *hamín* on pages 18 and 148.

20. The entire history is summarized in Cabezudo Astraín 282–84.

21. The recipe is called "*Faludhaj*" (211).

22. Fol. 39r, Newman 34–35.

23. "*En las pascuas del pan cenceño los judíos y las judías enviaban a . . . sus amos pan cenceño y turrado*" (Sánchez Moya, "*Inquisición*" 172). Their neighbor, Juan Sánchez Exarch, used to eat *turrón* on Sukkot (Llorca 132). According to information in his 1491 trial, Pedro Abella of Barbastro (see page 258) also ate nougat candy that the Jewish women had made in the Jewish quarter of that town (Cabezudo Astraín 283). See pages 153 and 261 for more about the Santángel family.

24. Covarrubias 984.

25. Figueras Pacheco 35.

26. *El rufián dichoso*, Act 1, v. 110.

27. Liebman 79. Liebman provides no supporting examples.

28. See the recipe on page 276.

29. *Al-Andalus* 240–41.

30. Nola 106–7.

31. Fol. 39v, Newman 35.

32. Granado 408–9.

33. Marks 297.

34. *"Al tienpo que parió a Luysico, su fijo, dende a vn mes o quinse días que parió, mandó a este testigo que coziese seys o siete tortas syn leuadura, e que después estas tortas ralló por su mano e de aquel pan rallado fisieron rosquillas e echaron en ellas açucar e miel; e después vido como . . . sus amos las comían e dieron dellas a los que venían de bautizar"* (Carrete Parrondo/ Fraile Conde 92). See page 166 for biographical information about María de Luna.

35. *". . . fruta . . . hojuelas de masa con miel y chocolate con bizcochos"* (Blázquez Miguel, *Toledot* 215).

36. 405.

37. *"Rosquilla rellena con azúcar"* (*Al-Andalus* 263).

38. *"Ai, maestro! Gran festa! Que menjam gallines e bunyols, e arròs amb oli i mel!"* (Riera y Sans 296).

39. *"Comieron al principio por ceremonia de la ley unos buñuelos con miel de aueja"* (AGN vol. 405, exp. 1, fol. 78r).

40. Marks 502–3.

41. Stavroulakis 123–27.

42. See page 266.

43. Liebman 81.

44. *"Cierta pasta que hacen los moros, hecha de pan rallado, miel, alegría y especias"* (83).

45. *Manual de mugeres* 81.

46. *". . . frutas de sartén y otras cosas, segund hera el tienpo e de lo que avia. Otras vezes merendavan frutas e otras cosas"* (Beinart 2:485, 2:493). The Mexican *converso* Diego Díaz Nieto testified in 1601 that on Purim Jews sent one another presents of *fruita de sartén* (Uchmany 264b). For more about the Díaz Nieto family, see page 93 and 299.

47. Nola 100; *Sent soví* recipe 169 (181). A similar recipe is found in the *Forme of Cury*, "Frytours of erbes."

48. *"Que mal que bien, por Navidad la fruta de sartén, rebozadita con miel"; "Fruta de sartén, enmeladilla sabe bien"* (Martínez Kleiser 280).

49. The recipe is for a "Mockery in May" (Birkhan 87).

50. *"Ansí eran tragones y comilones, que nunca perdieron el comer a costumbre judaica de manjarejos, e olletas de adefina, manjarejos de cebollas e ajos, refritos con aceite . . ."* (Historia de los Reyes Católicos ch. 43, 599).

51. Ch. 44, 601–2. Netanyahu accurately hyperbolizes Bernáldez as an "arch-enemy of the Marranos" (216).

52. Ch. 110, 652.

53. Ch. 110, 652.

54. Ch. 111, 652.

55. Ch. 112, 653.

56. Ch. 110, 652.

57. Cortes i Cortes 286.

58. Abstention from pork was also diagnostic for crypto-Muslims.

59. *"E la carne guisaban con aceite, e lo echaban en lugar de tocino o de grosura, por escusar el tocino; e el aceite con la carne e cosas que guisan hacen muy mal oler al resuello, e así sus casas e puertas hedían muy mal a aquellos manjarejos; e ellos eso mismo tenían el olor de los judíos, por causa de los manjares, e de no ser baptizados . . ."* (Historia de los Reyes Católicos ch. 43, 599).

60. 200. Espadas Burgos has argued that Lozana is more likely crypto-Muslim than crypto-Jewish (542–45).

57 Carrete Parrondo, *Proceso* 10.

Holiday Foods

1. Uchmany 365b. For haroset, see page 284.

2. *"Guisavan de noche differentes guissados buenos . . . y çenavan en la sala prinçipal, donde otras vezes no çenan, en mesa grande más bien adereçada que otros días"* (Selke de Sánchez 98). *Chueta* is a Majorcan-Catalán term meaning *converso*.

3. Sánchez Moya, "Ayuno" 283.

4. Adler 13, 81.

5. Lewin, *Singular proceso* 25.

6. *"A la noche desayunandose con aves e otras carnes"* (Beinart 1:58).

7. *"El día de dayuno a la noche, comen gallinas"* (Sánchez Moya, "Ayuno" 283).

8. *"No comieron fasta a la noche, que comieron palomas"* (Sánchez Moya, "Ayuno" 285).

9. Da Cunha e Freitas 19.

10. *"Algunas cosas de pescado que así habían de hacer por ser también ceremonia de la dicha Ley"* (Lewin, *Mártires* 126). This rule, applied to the meals both preceding and following the fast, is frequently cited by Mexican judaizers (AGN vol. 411, fol. 203r; AGN vol. 411, fol. 210v; AGN vol. 411:2, exp. 4, fol. 554v; AGN vol. 414, exp. 13, fol. 561v). For other examples, see Willemse 29 and Adler 13.

11. Sánchez Moya, "Inquisición" 77, 180; Carrete Parrondo, *Tribunal* 66.

12. Beinart 1:58; Lewin, *Singular proceso* 294.

13. Azevedo Mea 7, 298.

14. García, *Els Vives* 61.

15. Caro Baroja 1:469.

16. AGN vol. 410, exp. 1, fol. 102v–103r. Preparation of this recipe was filmed for the forthcoming documentary *Los ocultos* (Dir. Daniel Goldberg, [1999]).

17. Carrete Parrondo/Fraile Conde 109–10.

18. *"Masar pan çençeño, conviene a saber syn leuadura; y que la masó con vn huevo e le echó aseyte a la . . . masa . . ."* (Carrete Parrondo/Fraile Conde 109–10).

19. *"Su ama fasía con masa [y] huevos vnas tortillas redondas, con pimienta e miel e aseyte, e las cozía en el forno; e quésto fasía la Semana santa"* (Carrete Parrondo/Fraile Conde 32).

20. *"Masaron otras tortas aparte, de otra masa syn leuadura e amasada con vino blanco e miel e clauos e pimienta, e que fasían e masauan dellas fasta veynte . . . y que las guardauan . . . en su arca"* (Carrete Parrondo/Fraile Conde 35).

21. *". . . pan de pascua que masaban sin levadura ni sal, diçiéndole ciertas oraçiones, y lo coçían en un horno questaba en casa de otro preso en lo alto de su casa y questa mesa la tenían puesta por la pasqua del día grande y le echaban tierra muy cernida y comían de aquel pan la noche siguiente del ayuno con ensalada con açeite y vinagre"* (Sierro Malmierca 178).

22. *Code of Jewish Law: Kitzur Shulchan Arukh* 3: ch. 123: Laws concerning the day preceding the Ninth of Ab (60).

23. We thank David Riceman for this observation.

24. *". . . pan de pasqua, el qual masan con tierra muy cernida sin echarle levadura ni sal . . ."* (Sierro Malmierca 181).

25. *"Comendo nelle castanhas cozidas em luguar do pão asmo"* (Azevedo Mea 26).

26. Azevedo Mea 26–27.

27. Azevedo Mea 186.

28. *". . . pão asmo, grãos e castanhas cozidas em louça nova"* (Azevedo Mea 112).

29. Azevedo Mea 102, 106, 162.

30. *"Por no haber pan cenceño comía tortillas de maíz, por no tener levadura"* (Toro 243). See also Liebman 73. The Mexican Ruy Díaz Nieto (1601) cooked "his unleavened tortillas in his room on a clay skillet" (*"tortillas de masa sin leva dura y aquella tarde se les ayudó a cocer en el dicho aposento en un comal"*) (Uchmany 381a).

31. *"Cenaron unas tortillas de maíz, pescado y legumbres; . . . comieron a mediodía pescado y* legumbres, y por haberse secado las tortillas de maíz comieron todas del pan ordinario . . ." (Lewin, Singular proceso 46).

32. *"Quando fasía rollillos de la misma masa fasía vnas tortas tendidas"* (Carrete Parrondo/Fraile Conde 26). Another testimony mentions that she mixed the dough with eggs (38). For information on María Alvarez of Almazán, see page 159. *Rollillos* is spelled in a variety of ways in the documents quoted here.

33. *"Fasía . . . con masa y huevos vnas tortillas redondas . . . con pimienta e miel e aseyte; . . . asymismo le vido faser . . . en la Semana Santa . . . vnos rollicos e los fasía como fasía las tortillas, e les echaua de aquellas cosas susodichas"* (Carrete Parrondo/Fraile Conde 32).

34. *"Vio masar rollillos en casa de . . . Ruy Díaz . . . las guardauan con los rollillos en su arca"* (Carrete Parrondo/Fraile Conde 35). Although Carrete Parrondo and Fraile Conde (26–27) believe that these *rollillos* were the same as a dish called *hormigos,* of which the principal ingredient was bread crumbs, and whose texture was similar to the Moroccan couscous, it seems to us that the evidence points to an unleavened rolled cake, made of the same ingredients used to prepare matza, and generally eaten during the Passover season.

35. *"Faent coques alises e les donava a la vella mare dels sobredits Tholoses lo qual pa alis los fael piquar ab un morter e lo faen coure ab species de salses e ous en una caçola nova . . ."* (Carbonell 2:191).

36. Carbonell 2:189–94.

37. *"Albóndigas que son hechas de dulce, manzanas y castañas molidas y otras cosas que en particular no se acuerda. Y estas albóndigas se deshacen en vinagre y también las lechugas y el apio mojan en el dicho vinagre y lo van comiendo"* (Uchmany 265b).

38. Uchmany 41a–56a.

39. For further information about the family's activities in Mexico, see page 93.

Bibliography

Culinary Sources

Al-Andalus. See Huici Miranda.

Allard, Jeanne. "Nola, rupture ou continuité?" *Du manuscrit à la table. Essais sur la cuisine au Moyen Âge.* Ed. Carole Lambert. Montréal: Les Presses de l'Université de Montréal, and Paris: Champion-Slatkine, 1992. 149–62.

Alonso, Martín. *Enciclopedia del idioma.* 3 vols. Madrid: Aguilar, 1958.

Amato Lusitano (João Rodrigues de Castelo Branco). *Centúrias de Curas Medicinais.* Trans. Firmino Crespo. Vol. 3. Lisbon: Universidade Nova de Lisboa. Faculdade de Ciências médicas, [1946–56; 1983].

Angel, Gilda. *Sephardic Holiday Cooking.* Mount Vernon, N.Y.: Decalogue Books, 1986.

Apicius. See Flower and Rosenbaum.

Arano, Luisa Cogliati, ed. *The Medieval Health Handbook Tacuinum sanitatis.* Trans. Oscar Ratti and Adele Westbrook. New York: George Braziller, 1976.

Arberry, A. J. "A Baghdad Cookery-Book." *Islamic Culture* 13 (1939): 21–47, 189–214.

Baghdad Cookery-Book. See Arberry.

Balducci Pegolotti, Francesco. *La pratica della mercatura.* Ed. Allan Evans. Cambridge, Mass.: Mediaeval Academy of America, 1936.

Benbassa, Esther. *Cuisine judéo-espagnole. Recettes et traditions.* Paris: Éditions du Scribe, 1984.

Birkhan, Helmut. "Some Remarks on Medieval Cooking: The Ambras Recipe-Collection of Cod. Vind. 5486." *Food in the Middle Ages: A Book of Essays.* Ed. Melitta Weiss Adamson. Garland Medieval Casebooks 12. New York: Garland, 1995. 83–97.

Brereton and Ferrier. See *Menagier.*

Castro Martínez, Teresa de. *La alimentación en las crónicas castellanas bajomedievales.* Granada: Universidad de Granada, 1996.

Centúrias. See Amato.

La Cocina del Teatro en el Siglo de Oro. Almagro: Parador, July 1996.

Cocina hispano-magribi. See Huici Miranda.

Corominas, Joan. *Diccionari etimologic i complementari de la llengua catalana.* 7 vols. Barcelona: Curial Edicions Catalanes, 1980–91.

———. *Diccionario crítico etimológico de la lengua castellana.* 4 vols. Madrid: Gredos, 1954.

Cosman, Medeleine Pelner. *Fabulous Feasts. Medieval Cookery and Ceremony.* New York: George Braziller, 1976.

Covarrubias [Cobarruvias], Sebastián de. *Tesoro de la lengua castellana o española.* 1611. Madrid: Turner, 1977.

David, Suzy. *The Sephardic Kosher Kitchen.* Middle Village, N.Y.: Jonathan David, 1984.

Desde Estella a Sevilla. Cuentas de un viaje (1352). Ed. María Desamparados Sánchez Villar. Valencia: Anubar, 1974.

Díaz, Lorenzo. *Madrid: bodegones, mesones, fondas y restaurantes. Cocina y sociedad, 1412–1990.* Madrid: Espasa-Calpe, 1990.

Díaz García, Amador "Un tratado nazarí sobre alimentos: "Al-Kalam 'alà l-agdiya" de al-Arbuli. Edición, traducción y estudios, con glosario." *Cuadernos de estudios medievales* 6–7 (1978–79): 5–37; 10–11 (1982–83): 5–91.

Diccionario de autoridades. 1726. Madrid: Gredos, 1963.

Dioscorides. *Materia medica. The Greek Herbal of Dioscorides Englished by John Goodyear.* 1655. Ed. Robert T. Gunther. 1933. New York: Hafner, 1959.

Domingo, Xavier. *De la olla al mole.* Madrid: Ediciones Cultura Hispánica, 1984.

Dubler, César E. "Sobre la berenjena." *Al-Andalus* 7 (1942): 371–89.

Echániz Sans, María. "La alimentación de los pobres, la Pia Almoina." *Alimentació i societat a la Catalunya medieval. Anuario de estudios medievales.* Anex 20. Barcelona: Consell superior d'investigacions cientifiques, 1988. 173–262.

Enciclopedia universal ilustrada europeo-americana. 70 vols. in 72. Barcelona: Espasa Calpe, 1907.

Encyclopaedia Judaica. 16 vols. New York: Macmillan, 1972.

Espadas Burgos, Manuel. "Aspectos sociorreligiosos de la alimentación española." *Hispania* 131 (1975): 537–65.

Faraudo de Saint-Germain, Lluis. "*Libre de totes maneres de confits.* Un tratado manual cuatrocentista de arte de dulcería." *Boletín de la Real Academia de Buenas Letras de Barcelona* (1946): 97–134.

Figueras Pacheco, Francisco. *Historia del turrón y prioridad de los de Jijona y Alicante.* Alicante: Turrones La Fama—Jijona, 1970.

Flower, Barbara, and Elisabeth Rosenbaum, trans. *The Roman Cookery Book. A Critical Translation of* The Art of Cooking *by Apicius for Use in the Study and the Kitchen.* London: George G. Harrap, 1958.

Forme of Cury. See Hieatt, Butler, and Hosington; Sass, *To the King's Taste.*

Friedman, David, and Elizabeth Cook. *A Miscellany.* 8th. ed. N.p.: [Authors], 1998.

García i Fortuny, Josep. "La condimentació a la Catalunya medieval. Aportacions per al seu estudi." *Alimentació i societat a la Catalunya medieval. Anuario de estudios medievales.* Anex 20. Barcelona: Consell superior d'investigacions cientifiques, 1988. 51–70.

García Marsilla, Juan Vicente. *La jerarquía de la mesa: Los sistemas alimentarios en la Valencia bajomedieval.* Valencia: Diputación de Valencia, 1993.

González de la Vara, Martín. "Origen y virtudes del chocolate." *Conquista y comida.* Coord. Janet Long. Mexico City: UNAM, 1996. 291–308.

Goodman of Paris (Le Ménagier de Paris). A Treatise on Moral and Domestic Economy by a Citizen of Paris. 1393. Trans. Eileen Power. London: George Routledge, 1928.

———. See also *Menagier.*

Granado, Diego. *Libro del arte de cocina.* 1599. Ed. Joaquín del Val. Sociedad de Bibliófilos Españoles. Valencia: Artes Gráficas Soler, 1971.

Grewe, Rudolf. "Hispano-Arabic Cuisine in the Twelfth Century." *Du manuscrit à la table. Essais sur la cuisine au Moyen Âge.* Montréal: Les Presses de l'Université de Montréal; and Paris: Champion-Slatkine, 1992.

———. See also *Libre de sent soví.*

Henisch, Bridget Ann. *Fast and Feast. Food in Medieval Society.* University Park, Pa.: Pennsylvania State University Press, 1976.

Herrera, Fray Gabriel Alonso de. *Obra de agricultura compilada de diversos autores.* 1513. *Agricultura general de Gabriel Alonso de Herrera. Corregida según el texto* [sic] *original de la primera edición publicada en 1513 por el mismo autor.* . . . 4 vols. Madrid: Imprenta Real, 1818.

Hieatt, Constance. Personal Letter. November 28, 1997.

Hieatt, Constance, and Sharon Butler, eds. *Curye on Inglysch. English Culinary Manuscripts of the Fourteenth Century (Including the Forme of Cury).* Early English Text Society SS8. London: Oxford University Press, 1985.

Hieatt, Constance, Sharon Butler, and Brenda Hosington. *Pleyn Delit. Medieval Cookery for Modern Cooks.* 1976. 2nd ed. Toronto: University of Toronto Press, 1996.

Huici Miranda, Ambrosio, trans. *Traducción española de un manuscrito anónimo del siglo XIII sobre la cocina hispano-magribi.* Madrid: Maestre, 1966.

Ibn al Awam. *Livre de l'agriculture.* Trans. J.-J. Clement-Mullet. 3 vols. in 2. Paris: A. Franck, 1864.

Ibn Bassal. *Libro de agricultura.* Trans., eds. José María Millás Vallicrosa and Mohamed Aziman. Tetuán: Instituto Muley el-Hasan, 1955.

Isidoro de Sevilla. *Etimologías.* Vol. 2. Trans., eds. José Oroz Reta and Manuel A. Marcos Casquero. Madrid: Biblioteca de Autores Cristianos, 1982.

Labarge, Margaret Wade. *A Baronial Household of the Thirteenth Century.* London: Eyre & Spottiswoode, 1965.

Lane-Poole, Stanley. *Catalogue of Arabic Glass Weights in the British Museum.* London: Longmans, 1891.

Libre de sent soví (Receptari de cuina). Ed. Rudolph Grewe. Els nostres clàssics. Collecció A. Vol. 115. Barcelona: Barcino, 1979.

Libre de totes maneres de confits. See Faraudo de Saint-Germain.

Lobera de Avila, Luis. *Banquete de nobles caballeros.* 1530. Madrid: Facsímil de Reimpresiones Bibliográficas, 1952.

Lope Toledo, José María. "Logroño en el siglo XVI. Los alimentos." *Berceo: Boletín del Instituto de Estudios Riojanos* 20 (1965): 251–68.

Malpica Cuello, A. "El pescado en el reino de Granada a fines de la edad media: especies y nivel de consumo." *Manger et boire au moyen âge.* Nice: Centre d'études medievales de Nice, 1984. 103–17.

Manual de mugeres en el qual se contienen muchas y diversas reçeutas muy buenas. Ed. Alicia Martínez Crespo. Salamanca: Universidad, 1995.

Marín, Manuela. "Beyond Taste: the complements of colour and smell in the medieval Arab culinary tradition." *Culinary Cultures of the Middle East.* Eds. Sami Zubaida and Richard Tapper. London, New York: I. B. Tauris, 1994. 205–14.

Marks, Copeland. *Sephardic Cooking: 600 Recipes Created in Exotic Sephardic Kitchens from Morocco to India.* New York: Donald I. Fine, 1992.

Martínez García, L. "La asistencia material en los hospitales de Burgos a fines de la edad media." *Manger et boire au moyen âge.* Nice: Centre d'études medievales de Nice, 1984. 349–60.

Martínez Kleiser, Luis. *Refranero general ideológico español.* 1953. Madrid: Hernando, 1978.

Le menagier de Paris. Eds. Georgine E. Brereton and Janet M. Ferrier. Oxford: Oxford University Press, 1981.

Molénat, J. P. "Menus des pauvres, menus des confrères a Tolède dans la deuxième moitié du XVe siècle." *Manger et boire au moyen âge.* Nice: Centre d'études medievales de Nice, 1984. 313–18.

Newman, Elizabeth Thompson. "A Critical Edition of an Early Portuguese Cookbook." Ph.D. thesis. University of North Carolina, 1964.

Nola, Roberto de. *Libro de cozina.* Ed. Carmen Iranzo. Madrid: Taurus, 1969.

Norman, Jill. *The Complete Book of Spices.* London: Dorling Kindersley, 1990.

O'Neill, Molly. "Out of Egypt." *New York Times Magazine* (March 30, 1997): 53–54.

Or VeShalom Sisterhood. *The Sephardic Cooks. 'Come' con gana.* 1971. Atlanta: Or Ve-Shalom Sisterhood, 1981.

Perry, Charles. *An Anonymous Andalusian Cookbook of the 13th Century.* In *A Collection of Medieval and Renaissance Cookbooks.* Vol. 2. 6th ed. N.p.: [David Friedman] 1993.

———. "Medieval Near Eastern Rotten Condiment." *Oxford Symposium on Food and Cookery, 1987. Taste. Proceedings* London: Prospect Books, 1988. 169–77.

———. Phone Conversation. December 17, 1997.

Peterson, Toby. "The Arab Influence on Western European Cooking." *Journal of Medieval History* 6 (1980): 317–41.

Platina [Bartolomeo de Sacchi di Piadena]. *De honesta voluptate.* Trans. Ann Rice. N.p.: Mallinckrodt Chemical Works, 1967.

Portuguese cookbook. See Newman.

Renfrow, Cindy. *Take a Thousand Eggs or More. A Collection of 15th Century Recipes.* 2 vols. N.p.: [author], 1991.

Riera i Sans, Jaume. "La conflictivitat de l'alimentació dels jueus medievals (segles xii–xv)." *Alimentació i societat a la Catalunya medieval. Anuario de estudios medievales.* Anex 20. Barcelona: Consell superior d'investigacions científiques, 1988. 295–312.

Roden, Claudia. *The Book of Jewish Food. An Odyssey from Samarkand to New York.* New York: Alfred A. Knopf, 1997.

Rucquoi, A. "Alimentation des riches, alimentation des pauvres dans une ville castillane au XVe siècle." *Manger et boire au moyen âge.* Nice: Centre d'études medievales de Nice, 1984. 297–312.

Ruiz, Juan. *Libro de buen amor.* Trans. Raymond S. Willis. Princeton, N.J.: Princeton University Press, 1972.

Santich, Barbara. *Original Mediterranean Cuisine: Medieval Recipes for Today.* Chicago: Chicago Review Press, 1995.

Sass, Lorna J. "The Preference for Sweets, Spices, and Almond Milk in Late Medieval English Cuisine." *Food in Perspective. Proceedings of the Third International Conference on Ethnological Food Research.* Edinburgh: John Donald Publishers, 1981. 253–60.

———. *To the King's Taste. Richard II's book of feasts and recipes.* New York: Metropolitan Museum of Art, 1975.

Scully, Terence. *The Art of Cookery in the Middle Ages.* Woodbridge; Rochester, N.Y.: Boydell, 1995.

———. "Tempering Medieval Food." *Food in the Middle Ages. A Book of Essays.* Ed. Melitta Weiss Adamson. Garland Medieval Casebooks 12. New York: Garland, 1995. 3–23.

Sent soví. See *Libre de sent soví.*

Sephardic Sisterhood, Temple Tifereth Israel. *Cooking the Sephardic Way.* Los Angeles: Sephardic Sisterhood, n.d.

Shatzmiller, J. "Droit féodal et législation rabbinique: La cuisson du pain chez les juifs du moyen âge." *Manger et boire au moyen âge.* Nice. Centre d'études medievales de Nice, 1984. 67–74.

Smith, William. *A Smaller Latin-English Dictionary.* 1855. Rev. ed. J. F. Lockwood. London: John Murray, 1968.

Stavroulakis, Nicholas. *Cookbook of the Jews of Greece.* Port Jefferson, N.Y.: Cadmus Press, 1986.

Sturtevant, E. Lewis. *Sturtevant's Notes on Edible Plants.* Ed. U. P. Hedrick. Albany: J. B. Lyon, 1919.

Tacuinum sanitatis. See Arano.

Tannahill, Reay. *Food in History.* New York: Stein and Day, 1978.

Villena, Enrique de. *Arte cisoria.* 1423. Madrid: Espasa-Calpe, 1967.

Wilson, C. Anne. "The Saracen Connection: Arab Cuisine and the Mediaeval West." *Petits Propos Culinaires* 7 (1981): 13–22; 8 (1981): 19–27.

Zubaida, Sami. "Saturday Jewish Meals." *Culinary Cultures of the Middle East*. Eds. Sami Zubaida and Richard Tapper. London, New York: I. B. Tauris, 1994. 45.

Historical Sources

Adler, Cyrus. *Trial of Gabriel de Granada by the Inquisition in Mexico 1642–1645*. Publications of the American Jewish Historical Society 7. Baltimore: Friendenwald, 1899.

AGN. Archivo General de la Nación. Sección Inquisición. Mexico City.

AHN. Archivo Histórico Nacional. Clero. Spain.

Arbós Ayuso, Cristina. "Los cancioneros castellanos del siglo XV como fuente para la historia de los judíos españoles." *Jews and Conversos: Studies in Society and the Inquisition*. Proceedings of the Eighth World Congress of Jewish Studies held at the Hebrew University of Jerusalem. Ed. Yosef Kaplan. Jerusalem: Magnes, 1981. 74–82.

Azevedo Mea, Elvira Cunha de. *Sentenças da Inquisição de Coimbra em metropolitanos de D. Frei Bartolomeu dos Mártires (1567–1582)*. Cartôrio Dominicano Português Século XVI. Fasc. 17. Oporto: Arquivo Histórico Dominicano Português, 1982.

Baer, Yitzhak. *Die Jüden im christlichen Spanien*. Berlin: Schocken, 1936.

———. *Records of the Trials of the Spanish Inquisition in Ciudad Real. 1:1483–1485*. Jerusalem: Israel National Academy of Sciences and Humanities, 1974.

———. *Records of the Trials of the Spanish Inquisition in Ciudad Real. 2:1494–1512*. Jerusalem: Israel National Academy of Sciences and Humanities, 1977.

———. *Records of the Trials of the Spanish Inquisition in Ciudad Real. 3:1512–1527*. Jerusalem: Israel National Academy of Sciences and Humanities, 1981.

Bernáldez, Andrés. *Historia de los Reyes Católicos Don Fernando y Doña Isabel*. Biblioteca de Autores Españoles 70. Madrid: Atlas, 1953.

Blázquez Miguel, Juan. *La Inquisición en Castilla-La Mancha*. Universidad de Córdoba Monografías 86. Madrid: Librería Anticuaria Jerez, 1986.

———. *Inquisición y criptojudaísmo*. Madrid: Kaydeda, 1988.

———. *Toledot: Historia del Toledo judío*. Toledo: Arcano, 1989.

Bofarull y Sans, Francisco de Asis de. *Los judíos en el territorio de Barcelona (siglos x–xiii)*. Barcelona: J. Altés, 1910.

Braunstein, Baruch. *The Chuetas of Majorca. Conversos and the Inquisition of Majorca*. Oriental Series 28. New York: Columbia University Press, 1936.

Cabezudo Astraín, José. "Los conversos de Barbastro y el apellido 'Santángel'." *Sefarad* 23 (1963): 265–84.

Cancionero de obras de burlas provocantes a risa. Ed. Frank Domínguez. Valencia: Albatros, 1978.

Cantera Burgos, Francisco, and Carlos Carrete Parrondo. "La Judería de Hita." *Sefarad* 32 (1971): 249–305.

———. *Las juderías medievales en la provincia de Guadalajara*. Madrid: Viuda de C. Bermejo, 1975.

Carbonell, Pedro Miguel. *Opúsculos inéditos del cronista catalán Pedro Miguel Carbonell*. Ed. Manuel de Bofarull y de Sartorio. 2 vols. Barcelona: Archivo del General de la Corona de Aragón, 1965.

Caro Baroja, Julio. *Los judíos en la España moderna y contemporánea*. Madrid: Ariel, 1961.

Carrete Parrondo, Carlos. *Proceso inquisitorial contra los Arias Dávila segovianos: un enfrentamiento social entre judíos y conversos*. Fontes iudaeorum regni castellae 3. Salamanca: Universidad Pontificia de Salamanca, Universidad de Granada, 1986.

———. *El Tribunal de la Inquisición en el Obispado de Soria (1486–1502)*. Fontes iudaeorum regni castellae 2. Salamanca: Universidad Pontificia de Salamanca, Universidad de Granada, 1985.

Carrete Parrondo, Carlos, and Carolina Fraile Conde. *Los judeoconversos de Almazán 1501–5: Origen familiar de los Laínez*. Fontes iudaeorum regni castellae 4. Salamanca: Universidad Pontificia de Salamanca , Universidad de Granada, 1987.

Castillo, Hernando del. *Cancionero general de Hernando de Castillo*. Madrid: Sociedad de Bibliófilos Españoles, 1882.

Cervantes Saavedra, Miguel de. *El ingenioso hidalgo Don Quijote de la Mancha*. In *Obras completas*. Ed. Angel Valbuena Prat. Madrid: Aguilar, 1962.

———. *El rufián dichoso*. In *Obras completas*. Ed. Angel Valbuena Prat. Madrid: Aguilar, 1962.

Code of Jewish Law: Kitzur Shulhan Arukh. Trans. Chaim N. Denberg. Montreal: Jurisprudence Press, 1954.

Coelho, António Borges. *Inquisição de Évora (Dos primórdios a 1668)*. Lisboa: Caminho, 1987.

Cortes i Cortes, Gabriel. *Historia de los judíos mallorquines y de sus descendientes cristianos*. 2 vols. Palma de Mallorca: La Rodella, 1985.

Cota, Rodrigo. "Epitalamio burlesco." In *Cristianos nuevos y mercaderes de Toledo*. Ed. José Carlos Gómez-Menor Fuentes. Toledo: Librería Gómez Menor, 1970.

da Cunha e Freitas, Eugénio de Andrea. "Tradições judio-portuguesas." *Douro-Litoral: Boletim da Comissão Provincial de Etnografia e História* 4th ser., 5–6 (1952): 17–22.

Delicado, Francisco. *Retrato de la Lozana andaluza*. 1528. Ed. Claude Allaigre. Madrid: Cátedra, 1985.

Fita y Colomé, Fidel. "La Inquisición en Guadalupe." *Boletín de la Real Academia de la Historia* 23 (1893): 283–343.

Fort i Cogul, E. *Catalunya i la Inquisició*. Barcelona: Aedos, 1973.

Furtado de Mendoça, Heitor. *Denunciações de Pernambuco. Primeira visitação do Santo Officio as Partes do Brasil. Pel liçenciado Heitor Furtado de Mendoça. Capellão fidalgo del rey nossa Senhor e do seu desembargo, deputado do Santo Officio. Denunciações de Pernambuco 1593–5*. São Paulo: Paulo Prado, 1929.

———. *Primeira visitação do Santo Officio ás partes do Brasil: Denunciações da Bahia 1591–3*. São Paulo: Paulo Prado, 1925.

García, Angelina. *Els Vives: una família de jueus valencians*. Valencia: Eliseu Climent, 1987.

García, Genaro. *Autos de fe de la Inquisición de México con extractos de sus causas. 1646–48*. Documentos inéditos o muy raros para la historia de México 28. Mexico City: Viuda de Charles Bouret, 1910.

García Fuentes, José María. *La Inquisición en Granada en el siglo XVI: Fuentes para su estudio*. Granada: Departamento de Historia de la Universidad de Granada—Diputación Provincial, 1981.

Gitlitz, David M. *Los Arias Dávila de Segovia: entre la iglesia y la sinagoga*. Bethesda, Md.: International Scholars Press, 1996.

———. *Secrecy and Deceit: The Religion of the Crypto-Jews*. Philadelphia: Jewish Publication Society, 1996.

Goldberg. See *Ocultos*.

Jiménez Lozano, José. "Supervivencia de cultemas islamo-hebraicos en la sociedad española o el fracaso histórico de la Inquisición." *Inquisición española y mentalidad inquisitorial: Ponencias del simposio internacional sobre Inquisición*. Barcelona: Ariel, 1984. 353–72.

Kamen, Henry. *The Spanish Inquisition*. New York: Mentor, 1965.

León Tello, Pilar. "Costumbres, fiestas y ritos de los judíos toledanos a fines del siglo XV." *Simposio "Toledo judaico."* Toledo: Centro Universitario de Toledo de la Universidad Complutense, 1972. 2: 67–90.

Lera García, Rafael de. "La última gran persecución inquisitorial contra el criptojudaísmo: el Tribunal de Cuenca 1718–1725." *Sefarad* 47 (1987): 87–137.

Lewin, Boleslao. *Mártires y conquistadores judíos en la América Hispana*. Buenos Aires: Candelabro, 1954.

———. *Singular proceso de Salaomón Machorro (Juan de León), Israelita liornés condenado por la Inquisición (México, 1650)*. Buenos Aires: Julio Kaufman, 1977.

Liebman, Seymour B. *The Jews in New Spain*. Coral Gables: University of Miami Press, 1970.

Lipiner, Elias. *Os judaizantes nas capitanias de cima. Estudos sôbre os cristãos-novos do Brasil nos séculos XVI e XVII*. São Paulo: Brasiliense, 1969.

Llorca, Bernardino. "La Inquisición española incipiente." *Gregorianum* 20 (1939): 101–42; 507–34.

Márquez Villanueva, Francisco. "'Jewish Fools' of the Spanish Fifteenth Century." *Hispanic Review* 50 (1982): 385–409.

Montoro, Antón de. *Poesía completa*. Ed. Marithelma Costa. Cleveland: Cleveland State University Press, 1990.

———. See also *Cancionero*.

Moreno Koch, Yolanda. "La comunidad judaizante de Castillo de Garcimuñoz: 1489–1492." *Sefarad* 37 (1977): 351–71.

Netanyahu, Benzion. *The Marranos of Spain, From the Late XIVth Century, According to Contemporary Hebrew Sources*. New York: American Academy for Jewish Research, 1966.

Novinsky, Anita. "A Historical Bias: The New Christian Collaboration with the Dutch Invaders of Brazil (17th Century)." *Proceedings of the Fifth World Congress of Jewish Studies*. Jerusalem: World Union of Jewish Studies, 1972. 2: 141–54.

O'Callaghan, Joseph F. *A History of Medieval Spain*. Ithaca: Cornell University Press, 1975.

Los ocultos. Dir. Daniel Goldberg. Documentary film. Mexico: *IMCINE y Producciones Goldberg Lerner,* [1999].

Quevedo, Francisco de. "Letrilla 651." "Poema 644." "Soneto 841." *Obras completas. I: Poesía original.* Ed. José Manuel Blecua. Barcelona: Planeta, 1963.

Roth, Cecil. "The Religion of the Marranos." *Jewish Quarterly Review* 22 (1931–32): 1–33.

Sánchez Moya, Manuel. "El ayuno del Yom Kippur entre los judaizantes turolenses del siglo XV." *Sefarad* 26 (1966): 273–304.

———. "La Inquisición de Teruel y sus judaizantes en el siglo XV." *Teruel* 20 (1958): 145–200.

Sánchez Moya, Manuel, and Jasone Monasterio Aspiri. "Los judaizantes turolenses en el siglo XV." *Sefarad* 32 (1972): 105–40; 33 (1973): 111–43; 325–56.

Santa María, Ramón. "Ritos y costumbres de los hebreos españoles." *Boletín de la Real Academia de la Historia* 22 (1893): 181–88.

Selke de Sánchez, Angela. *Los Chuetas y la Inquisición: Vida y muerte en el ghetto de Mallorca.* Madrid: Taurus, 1972.

Shulhan Arukh. See *Code.*

Sierro Malmierca, Feliciano. *Judíos, moriscos e Inquisición en Ciudad Rodrigo.* Salamanca: Diputación de Salamanca, 1990.

Siqueira, Sonia. *A Inquisição portuguesa e a sociedade colonial: a ação do Santo Ofício na Bahia e em Pernambuco na epoca das visitações.* Col. Ensaios 56. São Paulo: Atica, 1978.

Sperling, Abraham Isaac. *Reasons for Jewish Customs and Traditions.* New York: Block, 1968.

Toro, Alfonso. *Los judíos en la Nueva España.* 1932. Mexico City: Archivo General de la Nación, 1982.

Uchmany, Eva Alexandra. *La vida entre el judaísmo y el cristianismo en la Nueva España 1580–1606.* Mexico City: Archivo General de la Nación/Fondo de Cultura Económica, 1992.

Willemse, David. *Un "Portugués" entre los castellanos: el primero proceso inquisitorial contra Gonzalo Báez de Paiba 1645–1657.* Paris: Funcação Calouste Gulbenkian, 1974.

Wiznitzer, Arnold. *Jews in Colonial Brazil.* New York: Columbia University Press, 1960.

Wolf, Lucien. *Jews in the Canary Islands.* London: The Jewish Historical Society of England, 1926.

INDEX

Festival of Taamuz, 40–41
Festival of the Horn, 40
festivals. *See* holiday foods
feta cheese, 77
fish, 82–107
    and carrot casserole, 90
    casseroles, 149
    and chickpea stew, 92
    and eggplant casserole, 88
    in marinade, 98
    Mexican stew of, 95
    and sardine casserole, 86
fish pies, 222–41
flatbreads, 247
flour, 14, 17
Fonesca, Pedro and Leonor de, 159–60
Forme of Cury, 8, 150
four humors, 35, 99, 105–6, 253
fowl, 108–45
Francisca (servant girl), 4
freedom of worship, 225–26
friars, Christian, and the Inquisition, 2
fritada, 77, 78
fritters, 270
    honeyed, 271–74
    matza, 298
    Passover, 273–74
fruits, 50, 253, 255–56, 285
    chicken stuffed with, and basted with
        almorí, 117–18
fruits, dried, with bird, 136
fruta de queso fresco, 78
fruta de sartén, 78, 277
Fuente, Juana de, 289
Fuente Albilla, Juana de, 178
funerals, 75
    and food, 71, 83

Galicia, 192
garbanzos. See chickpeas
García, Elena, 244
García, Isabel, recipes of, 62–63
García, Juana, 38
García, María, 101
    recipes of, 239–41
García, María and Martín, 134
    recipes of, 135–36
garlic snacks, 281
garnishes, 150
Gaspar, George, 207
Girona, 192
goat, 187–208
Gomes, Violante, 293
Gomes Navarro, Gabriel, 285
Gómez, Ana, 178
Gómez, Antonio, 299
Gómez, Rivkah, 299
Gómez, Yaakov, 299–300
Gómez, Yosef, 299

Góngora, Luis de, 163
González, Beatriz and Isabel, 52
González, Fernán, 52
González, Isabel, recipes of, 53, 86
González, Juana, 89, 244
González, María, 30
    recipes of, 102
González, María (Chillón), 87
González, María (Teva), 87, 246
González, María (Villarreal), 50, 64–65,
    77–78, 87, 246
    recipes of, 66, 79–81, 247
González, Mayor, 38, 89, 113, 193, 199–200,
    244
    recipes of, 39, 90, 115–18, 198, 245
González Escribano, Fernán, 219
Goodman of Paris, Le Ménagier de Paris, 8, 104,
    210, 211
goose, 137
    roasted, 138–39
    stew, 142–43
Graçiana and Grauiel (tavern keepers),
    213–14
Granada (Gabriel) family, 285
Granado, Diego, *Libro del arte de cocina,* 6, 10,
    29, 56, 57, 61, 65, 97, 100, 109, 174,
    189, 210, 264, 266
Greek Sephardis, 224
green (color), 149–50
greens, 33, 34
Guadalupe (Spain), 11
Guadalupe Inquisition, 219
Guernica, Fernando de, 195
Gutiérrez, Juan, 159

Haggadot, 300
halachah, 3
Halevi, Judah, 1
halvah *(halwa'),* 264, 265
hamín, 149
haminado. See eggs
Hanukah, 270
haravehuelas, 229
haroset, 300, 301
Hasdai ibn Shaprut, 1
Hazai, Judah, 232
herbals, 7
herbs, 14, 34–36
Hernández Gómez, Domingo, 299
Herrera, Gabriel Alonso de, *Agricultura
    general,* 9
Herrera, Marina de, 50
holiday foods, 5, 284–301
homosexuality, Inquisition and, 144
honey, 253
    with chickpeas and cilantro, 62
    with chickpeas and pomegranates, 63
honeyed pastries, 266
huevos haminados, 75, 76

satiric, 46, 119, 140–41, 163, 164, 223

polvo de duque ("duke's powder"), 34, 160

pomegranates, 61
    with chickpeas and honey, 63

porging. *See* koshering

pork
    Jewish prohibitions regarding, 163–64
    stew, with beef and lamb, 172–73

Portuguese colonies, 225–26

Portuguese cookbook, 10, 77, 258

Portuguese Inquisition, 225

Portuguese Jews, 171

postre, 252

potatoes, 11

Pratica della mercatura, La, 127

proverbs, 28–29, 70, 163, 209, 223, 255, 256,
    277

Provinces, 192

Purim, 3, 75

Puxmija, Clara de, recipes of, 180–84

queso assadero, 78

Quevedo, Francisco de, 163, 223

quince, 255

quince paste, 257

Quipuz fast (Pardoning Fast), 41

radishes
    and lettuce salad, 31
    and stuffed chicken crop, 120

Ramírez, Blanca, 155
    recipes of, 156, 176–77

Ramos, Isabel, 144, 169

Recife Jewish community, 225–26

recipe sources, 6–12. *See also* Inquisition testi-
    monies of Judaizing

Reconquest War, 192

red (color), 150

rice flour, 17, 248

Rivera, Catalina de, 293

Rivera, Isabel de, 163

Rivera, Margarita de, 270

Roden, *Book of Jewish Food,* 137

Rodrigues, Beatriz, 243

Rodríguez, Ana, 254

Rodríguez, Francisca (Cecilia Rodríguez
    Cardoso), 299

Rodríguez, Isabel, 103, 266
    recipes of, 107

Rodríguez, Teresa, 119

Rodríguez, Ysabel, 171

rollilos, 295

Román, 119

Roman cuisine, 5, 6, 29, 150, 174

rosemary, bird stewed with, and capers, 135

Rosh Hashanah, 287

rosquillas, 266–69, 270

Ruiz, Juan, *Libro de buen amor (The Book of
    Good Love),* 83, 108

Ruiz, María, 189

rye, 248

Sabbath, 3, 5, 75

Sabbath stew, 18, 40, 146–151
    Toledo style, 158
    of tripe, 167–68

Sacchi di Piadena, Bartolomeo de, *De honesta
    voluptate,* 9

saffron, 150

Sahagún, 188

salads, 27–69
    lettuce and radish, 31

Salcedo, Juan de, 195

salsa blanca (white sauce), 197

salsa de pago, 34

salsa fina, 23, 34, 35

salt, 15

Sánchez, María, 32, 213
    recipes of, 33

Sánchez Exarch, Juan, 40–41
    recipes of, 42

Sánchez Serrano, Catalina, 219

Santángel family, 261

Santillana, Marqués de. *See* López de Men-
    doza, Iñigo

"Saracen Sauce" (*Sawse Sarzyne*), 141, 150

sardines
    and fish casserole, 86
    fried and stuffed, 102

sausage, 209–21
    Almazán, 215–16
    egg and liver, 220–21
    lamb, 218

sciatic nerve, and slaughtering, 147–48

seders, 3, 284

Sent Soví. *See Libre de sent soví*

Sephardic Jews, 1
    Greek, 224
    and the Inquisition, 3–5
    Levantine, 211
    modern cuisine, 10

Sephardic Sisterhood, Temple Tifereth Israel
    (Los Angeles), cookbook of, 78

Seville, 103

Shulhan Arukh, 242

Sierra, Juan de la, 52

Simuel, Rabbi, 285

skillet-fried sweets, 278

slaughtering customs, 4–5, 15, 147, 159–60

snacks, 252–83

"sops" (bread), 243

Soria, Hernando de, 229
    recipes of, 230–31

Sorian Tribunal, 232

Spanish Inquisition, 2
    and Sephardic cuisine, 3–5

spices, 14, 34–36, 160
    matza with, 291–92